Models of Influence in Psychotherapy

Models of Influence in Psychotherapy

Patrick Pentony

THE FREE PRESS
A Division of Macmillan Publishing Co., Inc.
NEW YORK

Collier Macmillan Publishers
LONDON

The Free Press
A Division of Macmillan Publishing Co., Inc.
866 Third Avenue, New York, N.Y. 10022

Collier Macmillan Canada, Ltd.

Library of Congress Catalog Card Number: 81-66604

Printed in the United States of America

printing number

1 2 3 4 5 6 7 8 9 10

Library of Congress Cataloging in Publication Data

Pentony, P.
  Models of influence in psychotherapy.

  Bibliography: p.
  Includes index.
  1. Psychotherapy. 2. Influence (Psychology) I. Title.
[DNLM: 1. Models, Psychological. 2. Psychotherapy—
Methods. WM 420 P419m]
  RC480.5.P437   616.89'14   81-66604
  ISBN 0-02-924950-3   AACR2

To my wife Kathleen

CONTENTS

Acknowledgments

THIS BOOK OWES MUCH to the many writers whose creative contributions it attempts to integrate. In particular, the works of Anthony Barton, Gregory Bateson, Jefferson Fish, Jerome Frank, Jay Haley, Vladimir Lefebvre, Magoroh Maruyama, Carl Rogers, Edgar Schein, Richard Walton, Paul Watzlawick, and Paul Wender have provided material and inspiration. While my debt to these and other writers cited in the text is gratefully acknowledged, responsibility for any errors or omissions in the interpretation and use of their ideas rests with the author.

Introduction

THROUGHOUT THIS BOOK the term "psychotherapy" will be used in a very broad sense to cover all forms of helping people experiencing difficulties, through essentially communicational and, for the most part, conversational methods. It will thus be taken to cover behavior therapy, group therapy, family therapy, and milieu therapy as well as the more traditional dynamically oriented insight therapies.

Frank (1972) has aptly described the current situation in the theory and practice of psychotherapy as bewildering. Consensus on any aspect of factors covered by the term is conspicuously lacking. It has become difficult to agree on the referent of the term, for, to use a metaphor, psychotherapy has broken its banks and inundated the whole realm of interpersonal communication and influence with its swirling currents. As a consequence, attempts at definition and conceptualization of the domain are constantly being outflanked by new developments and trends.

The course which the domain—if it is still possible to use that term—of psychotherapy has taken over the past seventy years becomes apparent if we consider the nature of the changes which have taken place in regard to who receives psychotherapy, who provides psychotherapy, and what form the therapy takes.

In Freud's time psychotherapy was directed toward the alleviation of a limited number of neurotic conditions, particularly hysteria and, to a lesser extent, obsessive and compulsive conditions. Later it was extended to psychotic conditions and to various forms of deviant and antisocial behavior including addictions and forms of delinquency and crime, to the point where almost any behavioral condition which constitutes a threat to the well-being of the individual or members of his community is likely to be defined as illness and treated by psychotherapy. At the same time there has been a spreading in the direction of its application to everyday problems of social existence for individuals from infancy to senescence. Indeed it has, in more recent times, come to be sought increasingly by persons who, though coping quite effectively with the demands of their situation, see in psychotherapy a means of enhancing their level of functioning and gaining a greater measure of personal fulfillment. The prevalence of the YAVIS (young, attractive, verbal, intelligent, successful) syndrome among patients of therapists in private practice is testimony to the widespread nature of the view that psychotherapy can raise the level of an already adequate existence. In short, psychotherapy, from being a procedure designed to alleviate a small number of distressing conditions, has come to be regarded as a means of improving the quality of the individual's life irrespective of the current level of functioning.

The proliferation in numbers and variety, with regard to professional affiliation, experience, and training, of those providing psychotherapy matches the broadening in scope of the nature of the recipients. Initially the medical profession provided all "official" psychotherapy. Currently, however, a large and ever-growing body of people with increasingly diverse qualifications is recognized as offering psychotherapy. These include the members not only of such professional groups as medical practitioners, psychologists, and social workers but also of the clerical, legal, and educational professions. They also include probation or correction workers within the penal system and nurses within the various hospitals and health services. Increasingly in recent years there has been recourse to the use of "lay" therapists who may or may not have received some specialized training for the role. The advent of the "indigenous" therapist, whose main claim to utility is based on his nonprofessional status and membership in the group to be treated, probably constitutes the most extreme development along these lines. The employment of whole families as the treatment agent for particularly problematic children is one of the more interesting modern innovations, while the numerous self-help groups add variety to the scene. The only conclusion to be drawn from the trend over the years is that the defining features of the therapist have become progressively indistinct and blurred with the passage of time.

There has also been a remarkable broadening and diversification of procedure and theory. Starting from a limited repertoire which included hypnosis and free association, the array of techniques has multiplied to the point where the modern practitioner has literally hundreds of techniques and combinations of techniques to which he can resort. This proliferation has taken many forms along a number of dimensions, which include:

1. The number of persons involved in the procedure and their roles. The dyadic therapist-patient relationship has been extended to include various forms of group treatment.
2. The frequency and duration of treatment, which may range from a few contacts over a period of weeks to almost daily contacts over three or more years.
3. The situation, which is no longer confined to the hospital or consulting room, but may include institutional settings ranging from corrective establishments to universities.
4. The procedures employed. These cover a bewildering spectrum ranging from a sensitive attentiveness to the patient's thoughts and feelings to the use of burlesque and ridicule.
5. The conceptual frameworks which purport to explain or justify the procedures. There are literally scores of theories which have little in common in terms of the concepts invoked and the aspects of behavior that are regarded as relevant.

Not only is there little consensus on the practice and theory of psychological therapy, but even agreement on research efforts which might resolve the differences seems remote. It is therefore difficult to predict how long this situation will endure. The hope is that out of the intense activity, which at least indicates considerable vigor in the area, some integrative concepts will develop and bring order to it. In this regard it is worth noting Kuhn's (1962) views on the development of sciences which have passed through similar inaugural stages.

THE ROLE OF "PARADIGM"

The situation described above is highly representative of what Kuhn calls the preparadigmatic stage in science. His description of theory regarding the nature of light before the advent of Newton's *Opticks* has a strikingly familiar ring to anyone surveying the present scene in psychology and more particularly in psychotherapy:

> No period between remote antiquity and the end of the seventeenth century exhibited a single generally accepted view about the nature of light. Instead there were a number of competing schools and sub-schools, most of

them espousing one variant or another of Epicurean, Aristotelian, or Platonic theory. One group took light to be particles emanating from material bodies; for another it was a modification of the medium that intervened between the body and the eye; still another explained light in terms of an interaction of the medium with an emanation from the eye; and there were other combinations and modifications besides. Each of the corresponding schools derived strength from its relation to some particular metaphysic, and each emphasized, as paradigmatic observations, the particular cluster of optical phenomena that its own theory could do most to explain. Other observations were dealt with by *ad hoc* elaborations, or they remained as outstanding problems for further research [pp. 12–13].

It is not that the exponents of the different versions were poor observers or irrational thinkers. At least the more able among them were of equivalent caliber to their post-Newtonian counterparts. They had, in their various ways, made contributions to a body of observations, concepts, and techniques on which Newton was able to draw. Yet they had failed to build a science. As Kuhn puts it:

> Those men were scientists. Yet anyone examining a survey of physical optics before Newton may well conclude that, though the field's practitioners were scientists, the net result of their activity was something less than science. Being able to take no common body of belief for granted, each writer on physical optics felt forced to build his field anew from its foundations. In doing so, his choice of supporting observation and experiment was relatively free, for there was no standard set of methods or of phenomena that every optical writer felt forced to employ and explain. Under these circumstances, the dialogue of the resulting books was often directed as much to the members of other schools as it was to nature [p. 13].

The difference, Kuhn tells us, between the pre-Newtonian study of light and that of the post-Newtonian era was the advent of Newton's paradigm, which, by attracting a sufficiently large and enduring group of adherents away from competing modes of scientific activity, served implicitly, for a time, to define the legitimate problems and methods of this research field for succeeding generations of investigators.

Paradigms are "accepted examples of actual scientific practice—examples which include law, theory, application, and instrumentation together—[which] provide models from which spring particular coherent traditions of scientific research," (p. 10). Among the paradigms Kuhn lists are Newton's theory of light, Lavoisier's chemistry, and Copernician astronomy. The range of a paradigm may be very broad, as in Newtonian dynamics, or relatively narrow, as in Maxwell's mathematicization of the electromagnetic field.

The essential feature of the paradigm is that it constitutes an accepted common framework within which scientists doing "normal [i.e., postparadigmatic] science" work. Such scientists are no longer free to hew their own paths. Once the paradigm is established, they are committed to a uniform set of rules and standards for scientific practice.

Since it is quite clear from Kuhn's description of the preparadigmatic stage that all of psychology is still at that level, and since the discipline cannot become fully a science until it has moved into the paradigmatic stage, the question arises as to how it is going to cross the divide.

Apart from making it clear that the task is an arduous one, Kuhn does have some thoughts on the matter. He is strongly opposed to a strictly inductive empirical approach based on the view that if enough observational data are gathered, the underlying principles will emerge. He sees theory as being essential and the paradigmatic stage as being achieved when a theory is more successful than its competitors "in solving a few problems that the group of practitioners has come to recognize as acute" (p. 23).

The weakness of the inductive approach is that "in the absence of a paradigm or some candidate for paradigm, all of the facts that could possibly pertain to the development of a given science are likely to seem equally relevant. As a result, early fact-gathering is a far more nearly random activity than the one that subsequent scientific development makes familiar" (p. 15). And subsequently Kuhn tells us, "We often hear that they [the laws] are found by examining measurements undertaken for their own sake and without theoretical commitment. But history offers no support for so excessively Baconian a method. Boyle's experiments were not conceivable (and if conceived would have received another interpretation or none at all) until air was recognized as an elastic fluid to which all the elaborate concepts of hydrostatics could be applied" (p. 28).

While historians of science are not noted for their unanimity on the principles emerging from the exercise of their craft and there are some who think that Kuhn may have overstated his case, we are sufficiently persuaded of the force of his thesis to contemplate the question of how psychology, and more particularly psychotherapy, will achieve paradigmatic status. Two issues, in particular, which arise concern the sort of approach that is most likely to be effective in arriving at a paradigm and the features that are likely to characterize a paradigm.

In regard to the first of these, it has already been indicated that theory is called for. But we already have great variety and complexity of theory in psychology. It might well be argued, for example, that psychoanalysis is top-heavy with theory. What is called for seems to involve a special kind of theorizing. "Breakthroughs" in science seem to come from a way of thinking that penetrates into theory, reveals something of the assumptions that are involved in it, and in doing so opens alternative ways of contemplating the phenomena—ways which at first glance seem strange and unreal but which, when their implications are grasped, seem obvious.

Since first reading *Naven* some forty years ago, we have been impressed by the capacity of Gregory Bateson (1936, 1972) in this regard. Bateson, who is one of the truly innovative thinkers of our time, favors what he calls a pincers movement in science. By this he means an integration of the inductive and deductive approaches. But in respect of the deductive aspect, he is no advocate of speculative leaps in the dark, but rather favors a disciplined application of ideas, drawn if necessary from remote sources, which have standing in the body of established or accepted "knowledge." It is along the lines he has followed that, in our view, the best prospects lie.

It also seems highly probable that the emerging paradigm will be characterized by a certain simplicity, elegance, and obviousness once it is arrived at. It is unlikely that it will be seen immediately to explain all phenomena which occupy competing orientations, and it is unlikely to find immediate acceptance. One of its distinctive features will be that in principle it will be in accord with the prevailing paradigms in the established sciences. This does not mean that it will involve a reduction of psychological phenomena to physical or organic processes, but it does mean that its laws will be compatible with the laws that prevail in such fields. It will, in effect, be in accord with Szent-Gyoergyi's conviction that "as scientists we cannot believe that the laws of the universe should lose their validity at the surface of our skin. Life must actually have been created by these laws" (1974, p. 13).

As with all theoretical contributions, the object of this book is to contribute to the movement of psychotherapy along the road toward a paradigmatic state. The domain will be viewed from the perspective of how influence is exerted on the recipient of treatment, and alternative models of such influence will be outlined and discussed. In the later chapters, something of a Batesonian pincers movement will be attempted, based on some modern ideas concerning epistemologies currently found in the ongoing scientific enterprise.

PART I
Psychological Forms of Therapy as the Exertion of Social Influence

CHAPTER 1
The Models Outlined

PSYCHOTHERAPY IS A PLANNED ACTIVITY, carried out by one or more persons in interaction with one or more others, with a view to bringing about lasting changes in attitudes and behaviors that will result in greater satisfaction in living and fulfillment of potentialities for the person (or persons) undergoing change. It is to be distinguished from chance encounters which may produce similar results. In principle, therefore, it is an attempt to exert influence on the behavior of another.

While the various practitioners of psychotherapy would accept that they are trying to effect change in the way the client or patient conducts his or her life, they would not necessarily agree on how the process should be conceptualized. In accepting that they are exerting influence, they would disagree on what was meant by that statement. It is our objective here and in what follows to consider this question of influence in the context of psychotherapy.

Therapists, for the most part, do not accept that any effect they may have on the well-being of their clients is due simply to the fact that they have influence over them. Typically therapists believe that the influence they exert is effective because, by using it, they are able to correct the errors in the client's way of life and put him or her on the right track. Each has developed a theory, or as some would call it, a mythology, about the nature of disturbed or maladjusted behavior, including its origins and the way in which it can be corrected. As was indicated in the Introduction, since the turn of the century, and more particularly over the last thirty years, there has been a proliferation of forms of therapeutic intervention, each with its distinctive theory. It is hardly surprising therefore that in recent years there has been an increasing tendency to propose more general models or conceptions of the nature of therapy which will incorporate the essential features of what is effective in the different systems. This quest for parsimony has been conducted largely by looking at what therapists actually do rather than by accepting their own versions of what occurs in the therapeutic interaction.

In starting from the position that therapy consists of the exertion of influence, we have sought to determine how such influence can be conceptualized. If we have a perspective on how interpersonal influence operates—and in this respect our concern is with the way it functions in producing change—we may have a better understanding of the way in which the different systems of psychotherapy play their part. Toward this end, it is suggested that three different models of influence can be distinguished. These have been labeled respectively (1) the placebo model, (2) the resocialization model, and (3) the contextual model.

The Placebo Model

The placebo model derives from the observation in medical research that if the patient is administered an inert substance in the belief that it is a potent medication which will relieve his pain or remove his symptom, there is a high probability that his pain will be reduced or his symptom alleviated. The magnitude of the effect appears to be proportional to the strength of the belief of the recipient in the potency of the substance used. This in turn depends upon a number of factors, including the belief of the physician in the potency of the drug he thinks he is administering. Evans (1974) notes that, in double-blind studies, the effectiveness of the placebo compared with a standard dose of analgesic is a constant. If the physician believes he is administering a strong analgesic such as morphine, the efficiency of the placebo is .56 compared to a standard dose of morphine. If he thinks he is administering the weak analgesic codeine, the efficiency is .54 (average of ten studies) of the administration of a standard dose of codeine; and similarly, with the intermediate-strength Darvon the efficiency index is .56. Presumably the conviction of the physician is communicated to the patient. Evans goes on to summarize some other characteristics of placebo analgesia:

> (a) Placebo medication tends to be more effective in relieving severe pain, although its effectiveness may decrease with continued treatment. . . . (b) The "pharmacological" properties of the placebo closely mimic the pharmacolog-

ical properties of an active agent with which it is being compared. For example, the dose-response and time-effect curves are similar, and the side effects of the placebo and active drug have not been distinguishable in most studies. (c) The effects of placebo and other active medications tend to interact, and may be additive. . . . (d) As with most active drugs, higher medication dosages are clinically more effective. For example, two placebo capsules typically produce a substantially stronger clinical effect than one capsule. (e) A placebo injection is usually more effective than oral administration. (f) The placebo effect is substantially more potent if given under double-blind conditions than if it is given non-blind. (g) It is also more potent if patients are told a powerfully effective drug has been given, compared to being told an experimental drug with unknown effects has been given. (h) The placebo effect is stronger with physicians who are more likely to give medications than with physicians who tend to use medication as a last resort [1974, pp. 294-295].

This summary is in line with observations under other less controlled conditions. It has been known that inert medications will heal bleeding stomach ulcers (Frank, 1973) and that the effects are related to the conditions under which the placebo has been administered such as the status of the person administering it, the context in which it is administered, the quality of the doctor-patient relationship, and the expectations of the patient. It would seem beyond question that powerful curative effects can be produced by drug-giving rituals involving nonspecific variables of belief and trust in the doctor-patient relationship.

In psychotherapy, the placebo model of influence refers to belief on the part of the patient or client that he is receiving potent treatment which is effective in producing change in his attitudes and behavior, rather than the specific variables which the particular therapeutic system postulates as the curative factors. In other words, it is the belief that psychoanalysis or behavior therapy is a potent change process that causes the individual to modify his view of himself and to change his behavior, rather than the exploration of the unconscious or the desensitization of anxiety.

This model has attracted a considerable following over recent years. Frank (1972, 1973, 1974) may be regarded as one of its leading advocates. In his terms the healing ritual is important only in that it provides a vehicle by which influence can be established and the healing message delivered. Gillis (1974, 1979) has proposed a similar position and outlined some ways in which the client's belief system can be manipulated. Torrey (1972) has noted similarities between the healing strategies of psychotherapists and of witchdoctors in preliterate societies. The thesis is essentially that the important consideration is that the client acquire the conviction that his problem has been solved, his condition alleviated, or the forces which were impeding his progress removed. There are many ways of achieving this, ranging from religious conversion to aversive conditioning.

Other writers have put forth views that are similar in their emphasis on the use of social influence to cause the individual to view his situation differently and hence to behave differently with subsequent different consequences as compared with the pretherapy situation. Goldstein, Heller, and Sechrest (1968), Strong (1968), and Strong and Mattross (1973) are a few examples of such a position.

The case for an influence model of therapy based on the placebo analog is founded on:

1. The fact that the different forms of therapy appear to be about equally effective. This tends to eliminate the specific components of the therapeutic system as the causal factor in change. Since all systems share in the placebo effect, it constitutes a plausible explanation of any change achieved.

2. The fact that there is among therapists a high degree of agreement as to what constitutes healthy living and what they want clients to believe about themselves. Thus all tend to convey the message by direct and indirect means that the client is not a helpless victim of circumstances but has the freedom to choose even if that freedom is limited, and he can take the initiative in changing his situation, exercise some control over his destiny, and have a better life. Since these messages, if assimilated and acted upon, can be expected to result in a more positive approach to life, it is to be expected that therapists who can be convincing will have an enhancing effect on the lives of their clients.

3. The nonspecific suggestion effects of such procedures as systematic desensitization. In its modern form this method, as developed by Wolpe (1958), had three essential components consisting of (a) training in muscular relaxation, (b) the construction of anxiety-arousing stimulus hierarchies based on a detailed case history of the subject, and (c) the actual desensitization process, in which the subject is presented—usually in imagination—with the anxiety-arousing stimuli in progressive steps, from the least anxiety-arousing to the most anxiety-arousing situation, while maintaining a state of relaxation.

This approach had a certain elegance and logic. From a scientific point of view,it had the particular merit that it was formulated in such a way that it lent itself to systematic study by carefully controlled research. It was possible to isolate each of the components and determine whether its presence was essential to successful outcome. Yates (1975), after reviewing the large body of research carried out toward this end, tells us:

> The original technique of systematic desensitization was precisely, if complexly, specified. Over the years, however, each and every one of the components of systematic desensitization have been shown to be neither necessary nor sufficient—like the cheshire cat left with only its smile, systematic desensitization seems to work, but there seem to be no component parts that cannot be removed, and the technique will then fail or be significantly reduced in its efficiency [pp. 162–163].

The fact that systematic desensitization "works" while none of its component parts seem essential is the type of evidence which leads those therapists who favor the placebo model to argue that it is the persuasive quality of healing rituals rather than their specific ingredients that produces the beneficial effects. The systematic-desensitization procedure, because of its plausible nature, is a favored healing ritual for therapists such as Fish (1973) who propose a placebo model.

On the basis of what has been outlined above, therapy can be formulated in some such terms as the following: The client seeks help because he is, to a greater or lesser degree, demoralized. He finds himself unable to break out of a situation which is distressing or unfulfilling or in which his behavior is self-defeating. He is depressed and anxious. The future holds little hope. His troubles stem, not from the way the world is structured, but from the way he views it and his place in it. The therapist's task is to convey to him a new perspective of the world which will give events a new and more rewarding significance for him. The therapist does this by becoming a sufficiently authoritative source to be able to convey a new way of viewing events that yields more rewarding outcomes. Because he now has more confidence and more hope for the future, the client engages more actively and more purposefully in the process of living.

It would follow from this that the therapist's strategy should be to establish a "plausibility structure," to use Berger and Luckman's (1966) term, in which the therapist's message would carry conviction to the client. A variety of principles derived from studies of persuasion in the social psychology literature might be employed for the purpose of establishing the therapist's position and increasing the plausibility of his messages.

The basic principles of such an approach are detailed by Fish (1973), who argues for the self-conscious application of the placebo effect as a mode of therapy. His systematic account provides guidelines for the practitioner and details the steps in the procedure. His orientation and its implications are discussed in detail in Chapter 4.

A strong case can be made for the placebo model. There is ample evidence from both laboratory investigations and field studies, as well as observations of the practice of therapy, to support it. It is possible to describe the various systems of psychotherapy in terms that will allow for a placebo effect. If we look at the more mystic movements in religion and at some of the border areas of psychotherapy, we can only be impressed by the susceptibility of the human being to social influence. Yet as a complete or sufficient account of what happens in psychotherapy, the placebo model is hardly satisfying.

The reservations which it evokes hinge on the resistance of clients to change. Freud drew attention to the phenomenon of resistance over eighty years ago, and even though current approaches may be somewhat more subtle, it seems questionable whether a treatment procedure based on suggestion alone will be universally applicable. A critical issue seems to be the nature of the change to be induced and how palatable it is for the client. The placebo model would seem to be most appropriate for clients who are disposed to accept the therapist's message. Such clients typically have relatively specific problems, often involving low self-esteem, lack of self-confidence, and anxiety. Their disabilities range from physical symptoms to inability to assert themselves in social contexts. Their life goals are relatively realistic and attainable once they gain confidence in themselves.

But not all cases which come to the attention of therapists fall into such a category. There are some whose problem is an inability to come to terms with some aspect of themselves or their situation that is unpalatable. It may be a matter of accepting an unwelcome change in career or family life; it may be the surrender of unrealistic, but highly prized, aspirations; it may be a recognition that a life ambition will never be achieved. In such cases it is often far from easy to set up a persuasive situation that will move an individual to accept the unacceptable. At the very least, the resolution of such situations calls for a more complex model of influence. Such a model has been proposed by Schein (1973a). Following Berger and Luckman (1966), who have outlined a position which, though stated in more abstract terms, has much in common with that of Schein, we will call it a resocialization model.

The Resocialization Model

The resocialization model is a three-stage model. Like Frank, Schein has been interested in change as this has been effected in a variety of settings —in religious conversion, in coercive persuasion, in psychotherapy, and in encounter groups as well as in a wide range of less dramatic socialization processes. He has sought to develop a general model which will be applicable to any change occurring through interpersonal exchange, whether it is the result of a chance contact or a planned intervention. Taking a neutral stance, he avoids terms with evaluative implications such as "growth" or "learning." He uses the terms "change agent" and "change target" to refer to the participants in the many forms of change situation, and the terms "behaviors" and "attitudes" to refer to that which is changed, the former being overt acts and the latter covert responses ranging from beliefs to feelings.

Schein's model is arguably the most comprehensive approach to the analysis of behavioral change in the literature. It is surprising that it has received such limited attention from psychotherapists. In view of this lack of attention and because we are proposing to develop some of the implications of this model for an understanding of some forms of therapy, it is necessary to outline, in more detail than would otherwise be the case, the relevant features of his analysis.

Perhaps the most notable feature of Schein's approach is that it encompasses the complete cycle of change from one relatively stable pattern of attitudes and behaviors to another relatively stable pattern. This may be the reason why therapists have tended to overlook the relevance of his work. Much of his emphasis is on the chronologically earlier phases of the change cycle, which may well have preceded the therapist's entry into the relationship. The therapist is likely to encounter the client at a stage when the latter is in some degree disorganized or demoralized by earlier change events induced by other parties who may be included under the broad term "change agent." He therefore tends to see his role in healing terms.

The model has two levels. At a general level, Schein envisages the broad process of change as a sequence which he breaks into three stages: (1) a demolition stage, in which the pattern of behaviors and attitudes which the individual has acquired through earlier life experiences is disrupted and made fluid; (2) a transitional stage, in which new behaviors and attitudes are acquired from available sources of information and experience; and (3) a restabilizing stage, in which the new behaviors and attitudes are rendered relatively permanent and become an integral part of the individual's life. At a more concrete or specific level, he proposes a number of mechanisms each of which plays a part at one of the stages.

A. THE DEMOLITION STAGE

Probably the most neglected aspect in the theory of psychotherapy is the problem of having to unlearn old patterns before new ones can be acquired. Changes of this sort are likely to be resisted because there is considerable investment in attitude structures which have provided guides for behavior and the commitment of resources in planning and decision making. The more radical the change, the greater the resistance is likely to be, and since psychotherapy is concerned with radical change, considerable resistance can be expected at this first stage. For the required dissolution to take place, three mechanisms must be called into play. Schein lists these as:

a) Lack of confirmation or disconfirmation
b) Induction of guilt-anxiety
c) Creation of psychological safety by reduction of threat or removal of barriers [1973a, p. 242].

Lack of Confirmation or Disconfirmation. The individual must be confronted with the evidence that his definition of himself and the situation is not viable. It must be impressed upon him that while he holds his present attitudes and engages in his current behaviors, he will be unable to achieve the satisfactions and fulfillments he seeks or avoid the noxious events that he experiences. In other words, it must be demonstrated to him that if he wants to succeed, he must change his attitudes and behaviors.

There are a great many types of situations in which such messages are transmitted. When a young man enters a military academy, he is likely to learn that some of his civilian life orientations will have to change if he is to function effectively in his new environment. Indeed any change in a person's life situation, such as starting school, commencing work, getting married, or becoming a parent, is likely to require some reorientation in attitudes and behaviors. Whether these will require radical change will depend on the situation. Most disconfirmation which precipitates change comes in the ordinary course of living from those in the immediate social environment. Schein classifies change situations in accordance with whether the change is institutionalized or not, and whether it is planned or not planned. In institutionalized change, disconfirmation takes place through routinized procedures involving the enforcement of rules. The individual is punished for the infringement of norms. Institutions which are devoted to providing change—reform or rehabilitation units, military training establishments, religious novitiates—have traditionally employed a systematic regimen of disconfirmation calculated to disrupt the preexisting identity of the change target. The best modern examples of institutional disconfirmation are probably the coercive persuasion or political indoctrination programs employed by some Marxist regimes. The disconfirmation tends to be impersonal though it may take on a personal tone through the way in which it is implemented by different members of the institutional staff. In planned but uninstitutionalized change, the change agent, whether he is a salesman, a seducer, a consultant, or a therapist (the list is not exhaustive), faces a task of a more personal nature in that his disconfirming role involves a more personal confrontation with the change target. Since this is the area of change which is of most interest here, it can be elaborated upon slightly.

The therapist would face an impossibly difficult task if the full burden of disconfirmation fell on him. In practice the function of change agent in the realm of psychotherapy appears to be divided among a number of participants who may not be aware of each other. By the time the client has reached the therapist, he has in all probability received many disconfirming messages from those with whom he is in contact. This is likely to be particularly the case with the client who seeks help voluntarily. He can be assumed to be someone who has been unsuccess-ful in his social relationships or work activities or both.

Induction of Guilt-Anxiety. An individual may respond to messages which invalidate his definition of himself or his situation by ignoring them, by depreciating the source, or by rejecting them. He may regard himself as being the victim of fate or as being unfairly discriminated against. In all such cases it is unlikely that his attitudes or behaviors will change or even that he will see any need for change.

For the invalidating messages to have impact, it is necessary that the individual respond to them by feeling some inadequacy or failure on his part. Schein thinks such feelings may arise from a sense of failing to live up to one's own ideals, from letting down someone whom one respects, or from a failure to honor an acknowledged commitment.

The manipulation of guilt was seen by Schein et al. (1961) to be a significant feature of the coercive persuasion methods used by Chinese interrogators against American and European civilian prisoners, a group of "students, doctors, businessmen, and missionaries . . . who were arrested after the outbreak of the Korean War and imprisoned for periods of three to five years." The authors point out that there were a number of different bases on which the interrogator could assign guilt to the prisoner and a further number of predispositions on the part of the prisoner which made him vulnerable to the experience of guilt. Thus a prisoner would be judged guilty for having incorrect attitudes to the party or government or for being of the wrong social origin, and he would be prone to feel guilty for such things as having had too comfort-able a life without earning it or for deceiving the interrogator. There were, in other words, multiple bases on which the prisoner might be judged guilty or at fault, and on his part the prisoner was vulnerable to the experience of guilt in terms of a number of predispositions. The interrogator could, and no doubt did, switch context on the prisoner as it suited him in order to put the latter in the wrong.

While indicating the vulnerability of the individual to the induction of guilt and anxiety, Schein does not specify the conditions which favor such induction. It can be suggested here that favorable conditions in-clude:

1. A position of power on the part of the change agent such that he can define the relationship and the matters which will be consid-ered within it
2. Apparent consensus between change agent and change target concerning fundamental values or beliefs underlying the interac-tion

It is not possible to make an individual feel guilty if he refuses to accept the premises of the disconfirmer. This has been demonstrated by radical activists who refused to acknowledge the authority of the judge or the premises of the social-political system under which they were being tried. The induction of guilt requires that the inducer be seen not only in a position of power but also in one of righteousness. He needs to have legitimate power. The disconfirmer who relies on simple physical force typically forfeits legitimacy. This is probably the reason why, in the case of the civilian prisoners interrogated by the Chinese, the most effective procedures were those which, superficially at least, were relatively benign and in which the prisoner was treated as if he were a sick and erring person who needed to be helped to health and enlightenment.

In the case of therapy, society legitimizes the therapist as a benign helper, and those other persons who are likely to contribute to the induction of guilt and anxiety—teachers, examiners, employers, and peers—are typically cast in roles which give their messages credence.

Creation of Psychological Safety by Reduction of Threat or Removal of Barriers. The third mechanism is postulated on the basis that the change target has some motivation to change, or to make concessions, but is caught in a conflict which prevents him from doing so. Schein proposes, "Either the change is inherently anxiety provoking because it brings with it the unknown, or else it is perceived by the person to have consequences which he is unwilling or unable to bear" (p. 245). He suggests that in such a situation the change agent may (1) reassure the change target, (2) help him to bear the anxiety, or (3) show that the outcome will be more positive than anticipated.

The three mechanisms of the demolition stage may be combined in an integrated attempt to produce attitudinal and behavioral change as occurs in "brainwashing" or coercive persuasion programs. More typically, perhaps, they occur somewhat haphazardly in the daily round of existence with the relevant roles dispersed to a greater or lesser degree. Different forms of psychotherapy focus more on one mechanism than the others. Confrontive forms of therapy are oriented more toward disconfirming or invalidating the client's stance. Supportive and accepting forms make their contribution in the reduction of threat and the removal of barriers. Some forms of therapy (e.g., behavior therapy) tend to ignore the demolition stage, while for the more dynamic systems deriving from psychoanalysis it is very relevant. Angyal (1965) has been particularly forthright in putting forth the view that the first step in achieving a cure is to establish the complete inadequacy of the patient's current mode of living. He tells us that the typical patient, in seeking help, does not appreciate the extent of the demands that will be made on him. "Only in the process of therapy does it gradually dawn on him that much more is involved than he had bargained for. One might say that the patient wants to learn how to sin without being punished" (1965, p. 222).

Angyal goes on to point out that the patient does not want to undergo the radical change that will be necessary, but only wants to learn how to make his current methods work more effectively.

> The neurotic places all his reliance in the complex methods he has developed for dealing with the problems of life even if they have failed hundreds of times. His failures do not convince him that he is on the wrong track; he clings to the belief that his methods need only to be improved, or that they would work if only the situation would change, or if other people would change [p. 223].

It is the task of the therapist to develop a situation such that the patient will come to recognize and acknowledge the inadequacy of his current mode of life. This is likely to cause a collapse or dissolution of the conceptual scheme whereby the patient guides his life. It is likely to produce a state of despair.

> It is the therapist's job to show and to emphasize, in the face of the patient's evasions, the hopelessness and futility of his way of life. He will do it gently at first, with a light touch, later more forcefully, but constantly gauging how much the patient can stand at the time. He must also take care not to throw out the wheat with the chaff. The healthy nucleus present even in the most destructive manifestations of neurosis must be protected, not damaged by rough handling. . . . Much persistence and ingenuity are needed to use every opportunity to the best advantage. Only when every avenue of escape has been sealed off is the patient forced to admit defeat and to give up hope that his neurotic ways may succeed.
>
> Important as the therapist's role is in preparing this event, he is powerless to bring it about. The established pattern of neurotic living will not yield to detached thinking, generalizations, and explanations; only experiences of shattering power can effectively combat it. The neurotic structure melts in the fire of an intensive and persuasive emotional experience. At the core of this experience there is always profound despair. The patient's hopes of succeeding in the ways with which he is familiar have been shattered. He sees the utter futility in his accustomed mode of life and does not know any longer which way to turn. He feels hopeless, utterly ignorant of life and of how to conduct it. Seeing no future ahead of him, he hardly cares whether he lives or dies. The work of demolition culminates in the bankruptcy of the neurosis, which the patient experiences as his own total bankruptcy [p. 224–225].

Schein, like Angyal, sees the demolition, or unfreezing, stage as critically important. He thinks that it has been a neglected area of study, particularly in the social psychological literature dealing with attitude change. Without it, the effort put into selling and persuading will be ineffective. However, he points out that in view of their nature, it is necessary to strike some optimum balance in the application of the three mechanisms involved. As he puts it somewhat wryly, "It is the achievement of this balance which makes the job of change agent so difficult and, at the same time, so creative" (p. 245).

Angyal would seem to agree with him on this. The integration of such apparently conflicting activities as disconfirmation and the creation of psychological safety raises some difficulties, which will concern us in Chapter 2. \

THE TRANSITIONAL STAGE

When the target is unfrozen, he is ripe for change. Once his existing structure of attitudes and behaviors has been dissolved, the individual is in a state of disorganization. He must acquire a new structure of attitudes and behaviors and reorient himself to the world in which he lives. This, of course, does not mean that he will necessarily acquire the beliefs and values of the wider society. The entrant to prison life may undergo his change experiences at the hands of his fellow prisoners rather than at the hands of the official agents of society—the prison staff—and change may therefore be in the direction of the criminal subculture.

Whoever may be the relevant change agents, the unfrozen individual is open to messages from them which will provide him with a new basis for dealing with the continuing exigencies of life. His resistance has gone. His old premises have failed him, but he cannot function without premises, and the task now facing him is to acquire a new way of understanding his situation which will constitute a valid basis for making decisions and taking action. Hence he will look to his environment as a source of information toward this end.

In Schein's terms, the task now is to achieve a cognitive redefinition of his situation. "This process involves (1) *new definitions* of terms in the semantic sense, (2) *a broadening of perceptions* or expanded consciousness which changes the frame of reference from which objects are judged, and/or (3) *new standards of evaluation and judgment*" (p. 250; emphasis in original). It is not necessary that these events take place at the level of conscious reasoning. The subject need not be aware of how his judgments have changed.

Schein makes the interesting point that while reinforcement theory is relevant at the stage of unfreezing (or demolition) and again becomes relevant at the stage of refreezing, it is not taken to be relevant at the transitional stage. Here the appropriate models are drawn from cognitive processes. This accords with the view that the different systems of theory and practice in psychotherapy have relevance for different parts of the total change process.

Given that the target is seeking information, the question arises as to the source from which he will get it. Schein approaches this in terms of two extreme positions on a continuum. At one extreme we have the situation where information is acquired through a single source, and it is the source which is salient rather than the content. He calls this *identification*. At the other extreme, information is gathered from multiple sources and it is the content that is salient rather than the source. He calls this *scanning*.

Identification. The process of identification is divided into two types, which are labeled defensive and positive respectively.

Defensive identification occurs in situations in which the target is essentially a prisoner. He has little power relative to the change agent, who typically occupies a formal position of institutional authority. The target is required to change and feels threatened, helpless, and fearful. In terms of the psychological processes involved, the agent is the primary source of unfreezing; the target is oriented toward the power position of the agent, lacks empathy with him as a person, and imitates only limited portions of his behavior. The outcomes are that the new behaviors are of a ritualized, stilted, and restricted nature, but are likely to meet the requirements of the influencing institution.

Positive identification occurs in situations where the target is free to come and go and experiences a sense of autonomy and freedom of choice. His relationship with the change agent is one of trust and faith. In terms of the psychological processes involved, the agent is usually not the source of unfreezing and is chosen by the target on the basis of trust. The target values the agent as a person, has empathy with him, is aware of his richness and complexity, and tends to assimilate what he learns from him. The resulting new behavior is typically spontaneous, differentiated, and enabling of further growth, but while it is personally more meaningful, it may be less acceptable to the influencing institution.

Defensive identification corresponds to what psychoanalysts call identification with the aggressor. It might also be noted that Kelman (1958), whose analysis of the mechanisms of attitude change influenced Schein's formulation, considered that identification continued to be a determinant of the attitudes of the individual only so long as his relationship with the identification figure remained salient. Schein sees the maintenance of the changed attitudes, in somewhat different terms, as the consequence of continued reinforcement.

Scanning. In contrast to identification, with its strong emotional relationship between the target and the agent, scanning has an impersonal quality. It involves noting and making use of information from any source. Thus information may be gleaned from personal contacts with others or from the various forms of mass media. The scanner is primarily concerned with utility and is receptive to any information insofar as it is useful to him in dealing with his problems.

Schein takes as examples of the three ways of acquiring

information—the two types of identification and scanning—possible responses by a member of a therapy group.

> Let us assume that each member of the group is unfrozen with respect to some areas of himself and is seeking information which will permit him to redefine his situation so as to reach a more comfortable equilibrium. An example of *defensive identification* would be the case of the group member who, because of his great fear of the authority of the therapist or staff member in the group, attempts to change by mimicking and imitating what he perceives to be the staff member's behavior and attitudes. An example of *positive identification* would be the case of the group member who establishes a close emotional relationship with another group member or the staff member, and attempts to view his own problems from the perspective of this other person. An example of *scanning* would be the case of the group member who looks to any source in the group for reactions which bear upon the particular problem he perceives, and attempts to integrate *all* the reactions he obtains [pp. 254–255; emphasis in original].

It seems that both identification and scanning are likely to be present in any change process, but that either identification in one of its forms or scanning will predominate. Looking at the various forms of psychotherapy, it would seem that the psychodynamic procedures—with their long and intimate contact between agent and target, in which intense emotions are generated—will favor identification processes. On the other hand, forms of therapy which involve less personal interaction, briefer contacts, and more problem-solving orientations can be expected to favor a scanning procedure.

THE REFREEZING STAGE

It is a common observation that people who have undergone marked change in attitudes and behavior in a variety of settings—religious conversion, political indoctrination, and psychotherapy—have subsequently reverted to their former patterns of behavior. In order to prevent this occurring, Schein considers the operation of two mechanisms to be required: (1) the integration of the new response pattern into the wider "personality" pattern, and (2) the integration of the new responses into significant ongoing relationships through reconfirmation.

1. It is possible, particularly in cases of change through identification, for a person to acquire attitudes and adopt behaviors which are not congenial to him and do not accord with other aspects of his behavior. Such a person will not be at peace with himself until some integration can be effected, possibly through discussion and some reorganization of both old and new patterns.

2. It will be apparent that if the new structure of attitudes and behaviors is not acceptable in the social context which the target inhabits

after the change has been effected, then the change will not endure. The new behaviors will be invalidated. This is a particular problem where the target is taken away from his home situation to be changed in a hospital, a rehabilitation unit, or a human relations training center. On his return, if his new behavior pattern is not reinforced, he is likely to revert to his old ways. Most of the subjects of political indoctrination, though converted to a new perspective at the time of their release from prison, reverted to their former attitudes after a short period back in the home environment.

Religious organizations recognize the importance of maintaining their adherents in a community which reinforces the desired behaviors. Crusades may change the outlooks of individuals temporarily, but unless those who are "saved" are integrated into a continuing community of the faithful, the effects wear off.

It will be noted that some systems of therapy provide their clients not only with a basis of change, but with a philosophy of life and a reference group that may go on to provide long-lasting support. Thus psychoanalysis does not merely help the patient to understand the nature and origin of his symptoms and help him to gain control over them, but also provides him with a theory of human nature. If such a patient not only undergoes analysis but also becomes involved in practice in one of the "helping" professions and maintains close contact with colleagues who share a psychoanalytic orientation, the beliefs and practices he acquired through his analysis will be maintained.

It is apparent that the refreezing or stabilizing of the acquired change constitutes an important practical problem for the change agent. From a theoretical point of view, it is only necessary to note that what is in question is whether the new attitudes and behaviors will be "reinforced." Behavior change is not a once-and-for-all process, but rather a matter of an ongoing accommodation to the social environment.

CONCLUDING COMMENTS ON THE RESOCIALIZATION MODEL

This is clearly a much more complex model than the placebo model. It is concerned with change that involves a substantial reorientation in outlook and applies to transitions occurring in a very broad spectrum of contexts. It is a model which has particular relevance for ideological reorientation.

The Contextual Model

This model is to be distinguished from the resocialization model in that it does not conceptualize therapy in terms of learning and, more particularly, not in terms of relearning. The demolition, or unfreezing, aspect which figures so prominently in the resocialization model has no place in the contextual model. It is true that some invalidation of the client's attitudes and behaviors must have occurred to bring him into therapy, but the view taken would be that he is stuck in an unsatisfactory or blocking way in his development and that he must be freed and enabled to go along his way rather than that he has to unlearn or undo something and start again. The emphasis is on doing something now that will, through a process of amplifying feedback loops in his social context, result in progressive change toward a more fulfilling future.

The model has something in common with the placebo model, but differs in that it is based on a more complex reciprocal influence view of interaction. It holds that the actual interventions are effective, not because of some general nonspecific effect, but because they are the right interventions to trigger a specific pattern or sequence of behavior that will lead to freedom and forward movement for the particular client in his particular social network.

The difference between the placebo model and that with which we are now concerned may be clarified by using a simple illustration. Suppose a remedial teacher is assigned to a small group of children with serious reading disabilities which are diagnosed as having a functional basis. Let us further suppose that in attacking this problem, the teacher adopts a policy of trying to give each child confidence in himself as someone capable of becoming a competent reader. He may do such things as praise the child for his improvement even if the child is showing little, if any, progress. He may arrange for other significant figures to comment on how much progress a particular child, or the group as a whole, is making. He may introduce new reading materials and exploit their features in the process of building up the self-esteem, interest, and self-confidence of the members of the group. Such activities could be regarded as adopting a placebo model approach.

But the teacher might proceed otherwise. He might minimize the emphasis on reading, treating it in a rather casual low-key way. Instead of focusing on reading, he might become very involved in some activity likely to engage the interest of the children. In the guise of teaching natural history he might set up an aquarium, get some mice or other small animals, make a small garden, and the like. The children could be allowed to "help" in these activities. When the situation had been structured and the children involved, the teacher, instead of telling a child he could feed the fish or perform some other minor task, would put up little cards with the instructions. The child who could first read the notice could perform the task.

In this second case, the teacher is obviously setting out to exert influence in the direction of improving the children's reading skills, but it is of a different type from that outlined in the first case. He seeks to change the context and with it the meaning of the reading task. For this reason, this can be called a contextual approach. We can say that the task has been reframed.

In terms of practice, Milton Erickson appears to be the master of the contextual approach, while the theoretical contributions come from a number of related sources including Bateson (1972), Haley (1963, 1974, 1976), and Watzlawick et al. (1967, 1974).

An account of the model can begin with Erickson's statement in his foreword to Watzlawick et al. (1974):

> Psychotherapy is sought not primarily for enlightenment about the un-
> changeable past but because of dissatisfaction with the present and a desire to
> better the future. In what direction and how much change is needed neither
> the patient nor the therapist can know. But a change in the current situation
> is required, and once established, however small, necessitates other minor
> changes, and a snowballing effect of these minor changes leads to other more
> significant changes in accord with the patient's potentials. Whether the
> changes are evanescent, permanent, or evolve into other changes is of vital
> importance in any understanding of human behavior for the self and others.
> I have viewed much of what I have done as expediting the currents of change
> already seething within the person and the family—but currents that need
> the "unexpected," the "illogical," and the "sudden" move to lead them into
> tangible fruition [1974, p. IX].

Haley (1974) in his attempt to convey the nature of Erickson's system has this to say in his introductory statement to an account of the latter's casework:

> It is easier to say what Erickson does not do in therapy than to say what
> he does, except by offering case examples. His style of therapy is not based
> upon insight into unconscious processes, it does not involve helping people
> understand their interpersonal difficulties, he makes no transference in-
> terpretations, he does not explore a person's motivations, nor does he simply
> recondition. His theory of change is more complex; it seems to be based
> upon the interpersonal impact of the therapist outside the patient's aware-
> ness, it includes providing directives that cause changes of behavior, and it
> emphasizes communicating in metaphor [1974, p. 22].

As one reads the accounts by Erickson of his handling of patients, one gets the impression of a progressive shaping of behavior by an interaction process in which each move by the therapist and its accep-
tance by the patient results in a change in the relationship that opens the way for the next move, which will take the relationship another step. In this process what the patient is capable of doing in the relationship is progressively changing. The client who goes out the door at the end of the session is not the same as the client who came in at the beginning. No doubt, in a sense, this is true of all therapies, but in Erickson's work it takes on a new and more forceful significance because he seems to be much more alert to what he is doing and events move much more

rapidly than is typical of other therapies. As a consequence of these changes it becomes possible for the client to plan and carry through projects that would initially have been inconceivable. These are often of a highly unorthodox and somewhat eccentric nature (e.g., getting a young woman to squirt water through her teeth at a young man in whom she is interested). Their effect, however, seems to be precisely what Erickson had in mind in seeking to bring currents of change in the person to fruition.

Erickson emerges, from Haley's presentation, as a highly sensitive and skilled operator of a deviation-amplifying feedback system in which the client is nudged into activity which has a snowballing effect. In deviation-amplifying feedback systems it is the direction of the initial kick that is important.

In this model the therapist, while attending to the client's version of his situation, takes his stance outside it and operates on it. The approach is intentionally and forthrightly manipulative. But having set the system moving forward again by administering the judicious kick (or kicks), the therapist exits from the scene. In this type of therapy there is no binding of client to therapist in some shared belief system and the concept of refreezing appears to be irrelevant.

As the name suggests, in the contextual model there is a heavy emphasis on the network of relationships the individual inhabits. This ordinarily means the family of which the client is a member. Where possible, the family of the client is involved in therapy from the beginning, since it is believed that the symptomatic behavior cannot be understood without seeing the pattern of events to which it is a response. Treatment which does not take into account the family context is regarded as certain to arouse resistance from the family and, where successful, to give rise to new problems in the family likely to lead to behavior pathology in some other member. The therapeutic strategy is based on the principle that both the family and the individual member are evolving systems with interlocking life cycles. The task for the family is to create a situation for the individual, to nurture him/her to adulthood, and to release him/her to establish the next cycle. For the individual, the task is to achieve competence and independence and to find a mate, establish a home, and bring up the next generation. Symptomatic behavior is evidence of an arresting of the ongoing cycles, and the therapeutic task is to free the blockage and allow the onward movement to proceed.

The nature of the contextual approach will become apparent when it is considered in more detail. Its essential principles are that the individual's behavior cannot be understood without reference to the social context and that the therapist must bear in mind that influence is reciprocal, particularly when he enters into the interacting network of relationships.

CHAPTER 2
Two Interactional Patterns

IN THE OUTLINE of the resocialization model it was noted that there was a problem in striking a neat balance between disconfirmation or invalidation of the target's attitudes and behaviors and the provision of psychological safety. On the surface, at least, there is a sharp incompatibility between the two processes. The former involves the exercise of power over the other, while the latter involves gestures of goodwill toward, and acceptance of, him. If the matter in regard to which change is sought is of some substance, then the disconfirmation, to be effective, must involve considerable use of power, and we may assume that the psychological support required to enable the target to absorb the message would also need to be substantial.

The dilemma which confronts the change agent in this regard has been analyzed by Walton (1965). He is interested primarily in interactions between groups or organizations and, more particularly, in groups seeking social change that would enable a more equitable distribution of resources and opportunities to be achieved. The question he asks is how a group seeking social reform is to convince another group having an excessive share of resources and opportunities to surrender some of these goods. While his main concern is with groups, his analysis applies equally to interactions between individuals. The husband or wife who wants the partner to change faces a similar problem.

Walton considers that, in general, those who claim expertise in strategies for bringing about change have tended to take one or the other of two extreme positions and have somewhat ignored the possibilities of the alternative. Some experts, whom he calls the power strategists, advocate a policy of getting into a position of power and then using that power to force concessions from the other group. That is, they see change as being achieved by making clear to the other party that the old pattern of behavior is no longer acceptable or possible. The alternative approach, advocated by those whom he calls attitude change strategists, focuses on overtures of love and gestures of goodwill designed to bring about a cooperative working through of the issues. Attitude change strategists see change as being achieved by openness to the information available in the situation in the absence of threat from the other party.

Power strategists are to be found, Walton tells us, among games theorists, diplomatic strategists, and students of revolution. Attitude change strategists are to be found among members of the human relations movement, which has had its main impact in the fields of industrial management, education, and mental health and rehabilitation services. He regards it as unfortunate that there should be such a sharp cleavage between the two approaches because, like Schein, he thinks that if some balance or integration between the two approaches could be arrived at, a more effective overall strategy could be developed. Unfortunately the tendency, he notes, has been for the exponents of the different strategies to depreciate the contribution of the alternative orientation to the change process.

The difficulties which are involved in any attempt at an integration of the two strategies are shown by Walton in an analysis of their implications for overt behavior. Essentially the types of behavior which would be required to implement a power strategy are the converse of those required to implement an attitude change strategy.

Thus the two strategies diverge in:

The Treatment of Differences in Interests. In the power strategy, where each party is trying to force concessions from the other, it is to the advantage of each to overstate his objectives or requirements. This has the effect of exaggerating the magnitude of the gap between himself and the other. The effect of this is to increase the probability of the parties' convincing each other that their differences run even deeper than is in fact the case, thereby leaving less hope for conciliation than would otherwise exist.

In contrast, in the attitude change strategy it is in the interest of each to deemphasize differences so that common ground may be found and conciliation and trust developed. The risk for the participant using this strategy is that it weakens his bargaining position, since, as he would seem to have less to lose, he would be expected to yield more ground.

The Evaluation of Each Other. In the power strategy it is in the interest of each party to stereotype the other, to stress faults, to impugn motives, to question rationality, and to challenge competence. This makes it easier for each to mobilize his resources and to fortify his resolution in taking an unyielding stand on the issues that divide him from the other and in enduring the sacrifices that are entailed. The effect of this is that it blinds the participants to each other's positive qualities and results in gross unfairness in their treatment of each other.

In the attitude change strategy it is in the interest of each to recognize the other's positive qualities both as a being of goodwill and as having resources to contribute to the relationship. Such a stance renders a party open to exploitation by the other should the latter adopt a power strategy.

Dependence on Each Other. In the power strategy it is in the interests of each to increase the dependence of the other on him and to reduce his dependence on the other. So each participant seeks to convey to the other that he/she does not need him/her. In consequence both feel rejected by the other.

In the attitude change strategy it is in the interest of each to communicate his dependence on the other and the importance of the other to him. This makes for vulnerability to the other.

The Use of Ambiguity and Uncertainty. In the power strategy it is in the interests of each to conceal plans and intentions from the other. The more the opponent knows about a party's objectives and purposes, the easier it is to develop countermeasures.

In the attitude change strategy it is in the interests of each to be open and predictable, for this reduces threat and anxiety. Consequently, in this strategy the parties confide in each other, thereby rendering themselves vulnerable to each other.

The Manipulation of Threat. When pursuing power strategies, it is in the interest of the participants to maximize the threat each poses for the other. Their actions may range from withdrawal to violence. Threats carry more conviction when they are implemented in some degree or when behavior consistent with their implementation is exhibited.

The attitude change strategy, in contrast, requires communication to the other of the peacefulness of one's plans, the reduction of threat to the other, and the avoidance of any action that might injure the other.

The Management of Hostility. In the power strategy, hostility is managed so that it has maximum impact on the other. The aim is to hurt the other and to make him/her aware of one's power and willingness to hurt. This helps to convey the strength of interest in the issues at stake and to make a threat realistic.

In the attitude change strategy, hostile feelings will occur and will need to be ventilated if the issues at stake are to be explored, but this is managed so as to minimize the impact on the other person. The expression of such feelings as a communication about oneself rather than as an accusation of the other constitutes an example of such hostility management.

The Isolation or Inclusion of the Other. In the power strategy, it is to the advantage of each party to isolate the other. So the attempt will be made to form groups and coalitions with third parties that exclude the other.

The attitude change strategy, in contrast, requires the inclusion of the other in groups and organizations in which common cause is made.

The Categories Not Exhaustive. Walton's behavioral categories above, while covering a wide range of issues, should be regarded as illustrative rather than exhaustive. What is involved is essentially a polarization of behavior on any aspect of relating. An example of a further category could be the way the parties listen to each other. Within the power strategy it is in the interests of each to hear only that which is detrimental to the other's position, while in the attitude change strategy it is in the interests of each to be open to the other's messages.

Integrating the Strategies

It is apparent that the integration of the power and attitude change strategies poses very challenging problems for change agents. It would indeed seem extremely difficulty, if not impossible, for one person to implement both strategies simultaneously. Since both Schein and Walton believe some balance can be achieved, the question arises as to how this can be done.

Walton suggests one way in which the conflicting consequences can be reduced and two ways in which the strategies can be coordinated. It is suggested that there is a third way of combining the two strategies which is being employed in some modern forms of psychotherapy.

MINIMIZING THE NEGATIVE EFFECTS

The change agent, in the application of the power strategy, can avoid using provocative behavior which increases the hostility and resistance of the other without contributing to the force of the message. The aim in using the power strategy is to change the behavior of the other by threatening to deprive him of something he values—his freedom, his goods, his future prospects, or whatever. In making the threat, the agent is not merely presenting an ominous prospect to the other, but is also defining the relationship between the target and himself. Such definition can be made in terms which are humiliating to the target or in terms which preserve some dignity or "face" for him. Compliance is more likely in the latter case. Thus if a threat is conveyed publicly and couched in insulting or degrading terms, the target is likely to be left with no option other than to resist. Put in more diplomatic terms which allow some preservation of dignity for the other, the same demand may be met with compliance.

COORDINATING THE TWO STRATEGIES

Walton's proposals for coordinating the two strategies are:

1. To alternate them in time
2. To use different members of the agent system to implement the different strategies

Alternation in Time. A typical example of this occurs when a power strategy is employed to gain a position of strength, but once having attained this, the agent, instead of driving home his advantage, switches to a conciliatory policy and seeks a working through of differences in the interests of both parties. This is illustrated at the international level when the victor in war, instead of crushing the opponent, works for a long-term resolution of differences and peaceful cooperation. This possibility has also been suggested by Blau (1964) in a slightly different context. In his analysis of the exchange process he points out that the party which is in a strong position to wield power can legitimize that power by not using it. In his words:

> The dilemma of leadership can be epitomized by saying that its legitimation requires that a leader be magnanimous in the exercise of his power and in the distribution of the rewards that accrue from his leadership, but such magnanimity means that he must first mobilize his power and husband the group's resources, that is, act in ways that are the opposite of magnanimous. Once a man has attained much power, however, he can easily make demands that appear only moderate in view of his strength and capacity to supply benefits. In other words, extensive power facilitates obtaining legitimating approval for it. . . .
>
> Power must be mobilized before it can be legitimated, because the processes involved in mobilizing it are not compatible with those involved in legitimating it. The dilemma of leadership is resolved by devoting different time periods to coping with its two horns, so to speak. This parallels the conclusion of Bales and Strodtbeck that the dilemma of group problem solving posed by the need for a cognitive orientation to the task and the need for supportive orientation that reduces tentions, which are incompatible, is resolved by devoting different time phases to meeting these two needs [1964, p. 204].

The Use of Different Members of the Agent System to Implement the Different Strategies. Where there is more than one member in the change agent system, it is possible for the strategies to be implemented simultaneously but by different members. Walton suggests that in international affairs the power strategy of a nation might be implemented by the formal diplomatic representatives while the attitude change strategy is being implemented informally by trade, cultural, sporting, or scientific interactions. In an area somewhat closer to the issues with which this book is concerned, it would seem to be common in group therapy or human encounter groups for one or more members of the group to engage in a power strategy with the individual who is the target of change for the moment, while other members of the group employ an attitude change strategy. What typically occurs is that several members confront the target with an aspect of his behavior that they find unacceptable, and when he is showing signs of stress under the continuing pressure, one of the more charismatic members of the group will convey an expression of emotional support by some gesture—usually nonverbal—such as reaching over to hold a hand. This is usually effective in precipitating a break in the target's "defenses." A good example is provided in the film *Human Encounter* (a film produced by the Western Behavioral Sciences Institute covering twelve sessions—the relevant incident occurs in the twelfth session) when Karen, who has been under heavy pressure from the group, which she has resisted with some skill, dissolves in tears after Jack reaches over to take her hand. Such events appear to occur frequently in at least some types of group therapy and human encounter groups. The ethics of such a combination of the two strategies no doubt depends upon the circumstances in which it occurs. A group of friends exerting mutual influence on each other in informal social interaction would seem to function most effectively when the members can express their objections to aspects of each other's behavior knowing that the target of their comments enjoys emotional support in the group. Also members who enjoy such support are likely to be less "defensive" and more responsive to the others' complaint than would be the case if such support were lacking. A somewhat less attractive situation occurs in interrogation contexts where one interrogator takes a harsh or brutal line while a second, alternating with him, plays a supportive role. Our immediate concern, however, is with understanding the mechanisms rather than with moral questions concerning their application.

A THIRD WAY OF COORDINATING THE STRATEGIES

It is suggested that a third way of coordinating the two strategies is offered by the use of humor. This is an aspect of change-inducing behavior which has received only limited attention from psychotherapists.

Humor has long been recognized as a device for restoring a "realistic" perspective in situations where matters are being seen out of proportion. The institution of the court jester in the middle ages seems to have served, at least to some degree, the function of keeping the monarch in touch with reality. Humor is an effective way of deflating the pompous or revealing the ridiculous in extravagant claims or assertions, and of undercutting the sense of catastrophe to which people are prone in times of adversity.

The significant feature of humor is its capacity to demolish another person's, or group's, position without necessarily causing resentment and resistance. It has the remarkable quality of being able to obtain the other's assent to an attack on his position. When a person laughs involuntarily at a joke against the stance he is taking, he accepts the other's position, and this makes it virtually impossible for him to continue with his stance. And it is difficult not to laugh, for humor has surprise value and catches the victim off guard. It takes him unawares and reveals to him something of the ridiculous nature of his position. In doing so, it sets a distance between him and the definition of the situation he is projecting, thereby revealing it to him in a new light. It takes him outside the context within which he has been operating and gives him a view of it from another level. This, as Watzlawick et al. (1974) point out, seems to constitute a very important element in the change process.

Modern psychotherapists appear to be making considerable use of humor. Examples are provided by Farrelly and Brandsma (1974) and Erickson (Haley, 1974).

The Relation Between Power Position and Strategy Choice

To this point, Walton's position has been presented. A theme on which he touches lightly in passing but which has relevance for the thesis being developed can now be considered.

Walton comments that there is evidence to suggest that the power strategy tends to be employed by the party in the weaker position and the attitude change strategy by the party in the stronger position. He notes that Russia's stance was most belligerent during the decade following the end of the Second World War, when its strategic position was weak. As Russia's strength built up, its attitude became more conciliatory.

This point that the relative power positions of the participants are a significant factor in determining the stance taken deserves consideration. We have already noted that the respective corps of experts in the two strategies are to be found in different areas of activity. The power exponents are to be found among students of revolution, games theorists, and diplomatic strategists. These are situations in which they are aligned with either the weaker or deprived party seeking a new social or political order or with organizations already committed to competitive power games. The attitude change strategists, on the other hand, are found in the fields of industrial management, education, mental health, and penal reform, where they are working in association with the institutionalized power structure.

This pattern is no mere coincidence. It is a consequence of the way interpersonal influence operates. The attitude change strategy requires, for its implementation, that the person using it occupy a position of relative power or security. As Blau states, once he is in such a position, he can legitimize his power by not using it—or by not using it excessively. That is, he can have it accepted or recognized by the other party to the interaction. In using the term "power," it is necessary to be clear that it is not being restricted to those situations where some form of force is employed. A person is in a position of power relative to another when he can determine whether that other does or does not get something he wants. That something may be recognition, assistance in the performance of a task, help in acquiring information or a skill, material resources, membership in a group, or any one of a great variety of objectives.

The essential difference between the person in a strong power position and the person in a weak position is that the former has much to give and the latter little. Thus an unskilled worker gets relatively little recognition in terms of his work status. If a senior executive stops to speak with such a worker and shows an interest in what he is doing, the worker is likely to feel rewarded. The paradigm of such situations is the visit of royalty or a prominent government dignitary to the work place. A similar interest on the part of the worker in the activities of the manager or of a private citizen in the activities of government dignitaries, is unlikely to be warmly welcomed. If an irate worker explodes in an angry outburst toward a manager, the most appropriate response by the manager will probably be to encourage him to air his grievance and try to understand his problem. A similar response by an office boy on the receiving end of an irate outburst from a manager is unlikely to be quite so appropriate.

This brings the discussion to an issue that has relevance for the theory and practice of psychotherapy. It is to be noted that those who are functioning in such roles as that of therapist in individual therapy, or as leader or facilitator in group therapy or encounter groups, show a remarkable ability to listen to very hostile attacks on them, by their clients or group members, with patience and understanding. They show no evidence of resentment, but rather concern themselves with receiving the message the other is conveying and the feelings which inform it.

Such lack of defensiveness and openness to critical messages from others raise an interesting question. How is it that group leaders particularly, but to a lesser extent individual therapists, can accept aggressive attacks which, if encountered by the ordinary citizen in his ordinary round of existence, would provoke very angry responses?

There are two possible answers to this question. The first is that this is a function of the personal attributes of the therapist or group leader. The second is that it is a function of the situation—that is, of the way the relationship between client and therapist, or group members and leader, is defined.

The therapist may adopt either a strategic or a reactive stance. In the former, he treats the client's behavior objectively as data which reveal the nature of the condition to be treated. In the latter, he responds to the client's behavior subjectively in terms of what it requires of him. This allows the client to control the course of the interaction. In the extreme case, the client places responsibility for the outcome of the therapy on the therapist. The skilled therapist does not allow himself to be placed in this position. Typically, he adopts a strategic stance in which he defines the context of the interaction as one in which it is the behavior of the client that is under scrutiny. The difference between the strategic stance with its watching, probing, reflecting, and testing elements and the reactive stance which characterizes ordinary social interaction is of considerable significance both practically and theoretically. As will emerge later in our discussion, it involves some fundamental principles of communication.

The view that the therapist's response to the client is a function of his personal attributes is well embedded in the thinking of dynamically oriented therapists—that is, of therapists whose views of human behavior and interpersonal relationships have been derived either directly or indirectly from the thinking of Freud. To respond with anger and hostility to verbal abuse from the client would be seen as evidence of defensiveness on the part of the therapist stemming from his repressed conflicts. Or, from a client-centered point of view, he would be seen as not being "open to his experience," because he is burdened with excessive "conditions of worth"—conditions he feels he must meet if he is to regard himself as a person of worth or value. For the therapist who was not able to respond with the appropriate detachment in the psychoanalytic case or the empathy and warmth in the client-centered case, the solution would be seen in terms of working through his defenses with another therapist. Training analysis or therapy for the therapist is seen as the appropriate way of helping him to deal with his irrational or defensive behavior.

The dynamic therapists are not alone in subscribing to a personal attributes explanation for such phenomena. Ellis (1962) would take a similar position except that he would regard an angry response from the therapist or group leader as being the result of an inability to think straight. In Ellis's terms, if the therapist or leader is attacked, he should be able to say to himself something like the following: "Either what this person is saying is true or it is not. If it is true, then I ought to thank him for bringing it to my attention. If it is not true, then he has a hole in his head and I should feel sorry for him. But there is no reason why I should get upset and angry about it."

All of this amounts to a claim that therapists are people who have been able to transcend the human weaknesses to which flesh is heir. They have grown to a more mature state in which they are less subject to the emotional reactions which are the lot of ordinary individuals. By having therapy themselves or by being analyzed, they are freed of either the "conditions of worth" or the unresolved conflicts that cause defensiveness.

Now if this were an adequate explanation, it would be expected that such people—therapists and group facilitators or leaders—would be able to show similar nondefensive behavior in all their interpersonal relationships. There would be, in principle, no reason why a person who was more mature and more open to experience should be selective regarding the situations in which he exhibited these qualities. However, all the evidence suggests that in their daily interactions with their fellow men—whether these are colleagues, superiors, subordinates, friends, or family members—therapists as a group are remarkably similar to other people in their behavior. They get upset when things do not go their way, they can be remarkably deaf to information they do not want to hear, they quarrel and wrangle with others, often over apparent trivia, they dispute among themselves, often in a heated manner, they break up their marriages, commit suicide, and do all the thousand and one things that the ordinary person does. It is not suggested that their record in these matters is any worse than that of their nontherapist friends. It is merely claimed that, when such variables as socioeconomic status are taken into account, there is nothing to suggest that it is any better.

It would seem that the ability of therapists and group leaders to function in the "mature" and nondefensive manner they exhibit in therapeutic contexts is not to be accounted for in terms of personal attributes. This leaves the alternative that it can be accounted for in terms of the way they define the situation. In such a case it is necessary to consider how such a definition is arrived at and what is the nature of power in the therapist-client relationship.

In approaching this issue, it is possible to consider the nature of the relationship at three levels. At the most general level there is the relationship between the role of the therapist and that of the client as this would apply to all therapists and all clients. At a somewhat less general level there is the relationship as this is conceptualized or defined within particular systems of therapy. For instance, the relationship between a Freudian analyst and his patient is conceptualized in very different terms from that between a Jungian analyst and his patient. Finally we might think of the relationship in terms of the relatively concrete and particularized transactions between a particular therapist and a particular client. Even within the same school or system of therapy there are differences in the interaction patterns between therapists and their clients. Fiedler (1950) was one of the first to document this.

For the present, the discussion will be confined to the first or most general level. The therapist will be considered as functioning in the role of healer, though it is appreciated that he may also be seen as teacher, adviser, trainer, or counselor. Therapists, for the most part, locate themselves within a healing framework, and society broadly accepts that definition.

Society has always accorded the healer a position of status and power. In the primitive village and urban metropolis alike, his services are in high demand, and within his recognized area of competence his directives are followed by all irrespective of their stations in life. The individual who refuses to accept and conform to the ministrations of the healer is regarded as misguided and may be subjected to considerable social pressure to submit to the treatment. This pressure may even take the form of compulsion, as happens when persons who have been diagnosed as being mentally ill are committed to institutions.

THERAPY WITH INVOLUNTARY PATIENTS

Psychotherapy, in common with other forms of treatment designed to reduce suffering and promote physical and mental well-being, is ordinarily provided for those who voluntarily seek it and are motivated to benefit from it. There are, however, circumstances in which it is provided for unwilling or involuntary patients. In such cases the recipient is deemed to be incompetent to make decisions in respect of his own welfare. The position of the therapist who treats an unwilling and resistant patient is a very different one, in terms of the nature of the relationship, from that of the therapist treating a person who has voluntarily sought help. The therapist who treats the involuntary patient usually works in an organizational setting in which he has a relatively clearly defined role and status. The patient typically responds to that role or status, at least initially, rather than to the individual occupying it.

Superficially, the therapist in an organizational setting would seem to occupy a position of very considerable power relative to the patient. He is likely to be in a position to determine, directly or indirectly, the regimen of treatment that will be applied in each case, and he may be able to affect the degree of freedom the patient enjoys or the special privileges that may be allowed. Since the patient is dependent on the organization for the satisfaction of even his most elementary needs and the therapist occupies a position of power in the organization, the latter is well situated to enforce outward compliance by the former.

In psychotherapy, however, the aim is not outward compliance, but an inward change in attitude which will sustain long-term behavioral change. This requires the implementation of the attitude change strategy. In this respect, the therapist is in a good position to make the overtures of friendship and conciliation which are required. He does not have to worry lest the patient take advantage of such advances. The patient, in this respect, is largely impotent. Should the patient reject the advances or assume a hostile stance, this can be attributed to his state of mind rather than to any shortcomings on the therapist's part.

Nevertheless, despite his apparent advantages, it is by no means easy for the therapist in an organizational setting to develop a mutually trusting relationship with the patient. Insofar as the therapist is identified with the organization and the patient views the organization as opposed to his interests, the patient is in no position to make concessions or render himself vulnerable to the therapist. Consequently, the therapist in an institutional setting in which the patient is present in an involuntary capacity is likely to find it very difficult to convert a position appropriate for the implementation of a power strategy into an effective attitude change relationship. His difficulties are likely to be even greater if he has administrative commitments which must take precedence over personal relationships.

The problem, then, for the therapist in the organizational setting who occupies a position of power is to gain the patient's acceptance and to personalize it. Otherwise his impact on the patient is likely to be limited to obtaining overt compliance in accordance with the rules of the institution.

THERAPY WITH VOLUNTARY CLIENTS

The client who seeks help because he is to a greater or lesser degree demoralized and does not know how to cope with his problems constitutes the more typical case and has been the subject of most of the literature in the field of psychotherapy. Whether such a person is "treated" in an institutional setting or in private practice, the interaction lends itself more readily to a flexible use of both power and attitude change strategies.

In seeking help, the client places himself at a marked disadvantage in any subsequent power struggle with the therapist. It can be said that he:

1. Admits to his incapacity to manage his situation unaided
2. Invites the therapist to intervene in the management of his life
3. Defers to the expertise of the therapist as to how his problems are to be approached
4. Commits himself to cooperation with the therapist in working on his problems

It may be that the client will deny having made any such commitments. It will, however, be quickly borne in upon him that only by terminating therapy can he shed them. The help he seeks is available on the therapist's terms, and insofar as it is important for him to have such help, he must accept such terms. He cannot, as does the involuntary client, refuse to be involved.

The therapist, on his part, will be careful not to throw away the power which is thus granted to him. If we assume for the moment that the client is in difficulties because he is pursuing interpersonal strategies that are inappropriate, then it is to be assumed that he will continue to employ them in his interaction with the therapist. It does not matter, for the present, whether we regard these strategies as being learned habits or as involving misconceptions of the self. What is important is that they must not be allowed to foul up the relationship between client and therapist as they have fouled up other relationships. This means that the therapist must be able to counter them while at the same time developing a cooperative working relationship with the client on the latter's problems. Such a task requires a complex combination of the power and attitude change strategies. Unless the therapist can be comfortable—that is, secure—he cannot be expected to expose himself in the relationship. To be secure, he must be able to nullify those irritating or anxiety-creating behaviors of clients which have alienated their associates.

Psychotherapists do not dwell upon this aspect of their work, but in subtle ways they have incorporated power strategies into their practices. What happens when a naive therapist ignores this aspect has been nicely documented by Rogers (1942) in his early attempt to demystify the practice of psychotherapy. He gives an instance of a teacher who undertook the role of counselor and offered help to an intelligent freshman, twenty-one years of age, who was missing class and doing poor work. An appointment was made for an interview, but the student did not keep it. When the counselor subsequently drew his attention to this, the student asked if he might come in at once. The counselor agreed, and the student talked for three hours but again missed class. Later, when returning some books, he again sat down and talked about his problems of procrastination and the like. When asked what he was going to do about them, he replied that that was the counselor's job, that he must have helped other people, and that he would enjoy seeing someone get out of a mess. When the counselor demurred, the student agreed the counselor did not have to bother, but he had hoped the counselor meant it when he said he was there to help whenever help was needed.

Rogers points out the obvious defects in the counselor's procedure and comments that it was not surprising that the student again came in and wanted the counselor to act as his secretary, taking down his thoughts for the paper that was due the following day, or at least listen to him while he explained his ideas. Rogers concludes:

> The student now feels he is in complete command of the situation. It is no longer in any sense therapeutic. It has merely become a new arena in which he may put into effect his customary patterns. If suitable limits had been set, it could have become a situation in which he would have endeavoured to follow out his usual patterns and would have been helped to become conscious of them, but would not have succeeded in either his dependence or his domination [1942, p. 100].

Rogers is taking this counselor to task for allowing himself to become involved in an ordinary reactive interpersonal relationship with the client instead of taking a strategic stance. His point is that the therapist must ensure that he, and not the client, defines the nature of the relationship and thereby determines the sort of behaviors that are to be exchanged.

CHAPTER 3
Ideological Change or Problem Solving

IN THE FIRST CHAPTER we considered three perspectives on the nature of influence as this is exerted in the practice of psychotherapy. In the second we looked at two sharply contrasting strategies employed in the production of change, one involving a competitive or adversary relationship requiring the exercise of power and the other a cooperative relationship based on a mutuality or community of interest. In the present chapter we will begin to consider some general aspects of the different systems of therapy currently being practiced.

As was noted in the Introduction, the modern practitioner has a great variety of therapeutic systems from which to choose. At least superficially, the different systems can be said to advocate modes of therapeutic intervention which do not merely differ from each other, but appear to be diametrically opposed. The situation gives an impression of chaos, and it is not surprising that Frank has described it as bewildering.

An obvious first step in the search for order in a complex and apparently chaotic situation is to seek common elements in the available observations and to group together such phenomena as exhibit common properties. This calls for the formulation of a set of categories into which the data—in our case the different systems of therapy—can be classified.

There are many ways of doing this, depending upon the particular orientation and objectives of the person drawing up the classification system.

Our approach to this task will be to begin by making a distinction between those systems of therapy which focus on changing the person and those which focus on solving the problem. It is recognized that these two procedures are not independent or mutually exclusive. When changes are effected in the organization of the person—that is, in the set of beliefs and assumptions, whether conscious or unconscious, which govern his actions—then the nature of the problem changes, and it may even cease to exist. On the other hand, the resolution of a problem leads to changes in the person's perception of himself and his resources, with probable consequent changes in his belief systems. In other words, in dealing with some behaviors, we may be dealing, not with isolated independent events, but with system processes in which change occurring anywhere in the system can be expected to result in either change-amplifying or change-reducing events elsewhere in the system.

Nevertheless, it is clear that in some systems of therapy the emphasis is very strongly on changing the person - that is, on changing his habitual or organized structure of beliefs or attitudes concerning himself and the universe he inhabits. These approaches virtually ignore the particular concrete problem which brought the individual into therapy. Such a problem is typically referred to as a symptom and is assumed to arise from the faulty world view which the individual has acquired in the course of his socialization. The symptom, it is argued, will disappear or will be capably dealt with by the client as the world view is corrected. Further, from this standpoint, if attention is focused on the problem - or symptom - and it is eradicated without correcting the underlying psychic structure which gave rise to it, then a new symptom will emerge to take its place.

Psychodynamic therapists would no doubt question this as a description of their endeavors. They would probably want to tell us that they enlarge awareness, resolve internal conflicts, enable the individual to become more open to his experience, or promote the development of the archetypal self. These phrases, however, are metaphors. It is not clear what they mean. What we do know is that the client, if he persists with the therapy, emerges at the end with a somewhat different description of himself and his world from that with which he entered it.

At the other extreme are to be found systems of therapy which focus on the problem. Instead of trying to reorganize the client's conceptual framework, these approaches aim at helping him to define his goal (or goals) in specific terms and then to achieve it. It is assumed in such systems that the client is unable to achieve his goals without help because he lacks certain skills or information, because he has acquired certain habits which handicap him in his efforts, or because he inhabits a network of relationships which maintains his inappropriate ways of dealing with his problems or working toward his goals. In other words, they see his problems in specific and remediable terms. In consequence they see no reason why, on the resolution of the presenting problem, the individual should experience a new symptom, and they maintain that, in fact, when the particular problem is ameliorated or the specific goal is achieved, there is no evidence of symptom substitution. On the contrary, it is claimed that the usual outcome is a process of change amplification in the direction of increased resourcefulness in problem solving and goal achievement on the part of the client.

There is thus a sharp divergence between these two stances on the nature of psychotherapy. These differences are relevant to the different models of influence outlined in Chapter 1. Those processes involved in the implementation of strategies designed to change the person—or, perhaps more correctly, his system of beliefs and attitudes—constitute a good fit for the resocialization model, while those which are operative in the problem-solving approach accord rather with the placebo and contextual models. We will refer to the former goal as ideological change, though we recognize that the term implies a rationality going beyond the structure of beliefs and attitudes we have in mind.

The two approaches can now be considered in more detail:

Ideological Change Systems

Included under this heading are such systems as the psychoanalytic school originating with Freud and its many associated and derivative forms of depth therapy including the approaches of Jung and Adler; the person-centered approach of Rogers; gestalt therapy; the various forms of therapy embraced by the term "existentialism"; systems of Eastern thought such as Zen Buddhism, yoga, and transcendental meditation; and indeed all those systems which profess to have found and which seek to impart the secret of the good way to live. The distinguishing feature is the tendency to broaden the specific problem or treat it as a manifestation of a faulty orientation to life which calls for a reorientation in outlook and style of living.

These systems have in common the following features:

1. There is a body of theory or belief concerning the nature of man, the relation of the individual to society, the nature of psychopathology including its origins and the means whereby it can be alleviated, and the nature of the good life and how it can be fostered.

2. Each proponent of such a system sees the relevance of his own particular orientation as extending well beyond the alleviation of the

distress of the patients or clients who seek aid. The fields of education, rehabilitation, management, family relationships, and social order are some of the areas in which such proponents' insights are seen to have an application.

3. Clients treated within such systems undergo a relatively intense and frequently emotional learning experience in which they come to live out aspects of the ideology as active participants in co-constituted realities.

4. The criteria of improvement or benefit tend to be couched in the language of the particular system and to relate more to the degree to which the client has come to assimilate, and live in accordance with, the tenets of the particular orientation than in terms of the degree to which the initial presenting problem has been resolved.

There would seem to be parallels between such systems and religious and political ideologies which also claim to have the secret of the good life and the good society. Some of the therapeutic systems currently enjoying a vogue have derived their inspiration from sources which traditionally have been regarded as forms of religion.

Such similarities to religious systems raise problems for anyone attempting to establish criteria whereby the relative merits of the different forms of therapy can be established. The problems of determining the validity of different religious systems need no emphasis here. Psychotherapy seems to have moved in a similar direction to religion with its trend toward the equipotentiality of the different orientations. The statement that one religion is as good as another has taken on a new content. But as long as the therapeutic outcome is assessed in terms of the particular values of the practitioner, we cannot expect to arrive at a commonly accepted yardstick.

The view that the resocialization model constitutes a relatively good fit for such systems as those listed, but not necessarily for other systems of therapy, rests on the following grounds:

1. The requirements for ideological change
2. Descriptions of the change process occurring in such contexts as religious conversion and political indoctrination
3. Accounts of psychotherapy as practiced in some of the better-known systems listed above

The first two grounds will be discussed here, while the third will be considered in the next three chapters.

THE REQUIREMENTS FOR IDEOLOGICAL CHANGE

The distinctive feature of the resocialization model is its emphasis on unfreezing. This has been a neglected area in discussions of change not only in psychotherapy but also in social psychology in the treatment of attitude change. Schein's position is essentially that since it is not possible to subscribe to conflicting perspectives simultaneously, it is necessary to demolish one before another can take shape.

A person' belief system or ideology constitutes the foundation on which he orients himself in the particular domain to which it applies. It defines for him the nature of reality. While it is essentially a theory he holds concerning some aspects of himself and of the world he inhabits, it is not usually experienced as a hypothesis to be lightly held. Rather, it is, ordinarily, for him a description of how things "really" are in the area in question, in an absolute and fundamental sense, and it constitutes the basis on which he makes decisions and commits himself to action.

It is a feature of theories (or of ideologies) that they do not allow inconsistencies either between their internal components or between the theory and accepted "facts." When such inconsistencies arise, the theory can only be maintained either by keeping the conflicting elements separate and thus avoiding recognition of the inconsistency or by depreciating the "facts" as irrelevant or unreliable data, depending upon where the inconsistency resides.

That the individual has a strong personal commitment to his theory or ideology covering any issue need hardly be stressed. Even some so-called "objective" scientists show a strong emotional attachment to their theories and have, on occasion, not been beyond falsifying the data in order to maintain them. Without seeking to provide an exhaustive explanation, we suggest that such attachment can be attributed to one or more of at least three factors: (1) Invalidating evidence for a theory is frequently presented in an interpersonal setting in a climate of competition, and to accept it and abandon the theory would be to concede defeat with consequent loss of standing and influence, and of future credibility when related issues arise. (2) Theories to which a person is attached are not simply remote abstractions unrelated to the person's daily existence. They define the nature of the world in which he must live and act, and hence they constitute the basis on which he commits his resources of time, effort, material goods, and prestige. To admit being in error is to lose what has been committed. There are, therefore, good reasons for clinging to one's position so long as it has a possibility of yet proving viable. Since completely conclusive invalidating evidence is rare outside the laboratory, it is usually possible to sustain such hope. (3) Perhaps the most important consideration is the lack of an adequate alternative. A theory gives order to the domain to which it is applicable. In the absence of a theory the domain is chaotic. Since the individual cannot function in a state of chaos, he requires a theory in order to be able to make decisions and embark on a course of action. The alternative is paralysis or random behavior. In such circumstances a theory that has any validity is better than no theory at all. Since a radical change in orientation requires the dissolution of the old pattern with the security that it offered, it is understandable that the individual will resist the threat of chaos and loss of control that radical change requires.

From what has been said, it will be apparent that changing the ideology—or, as others might put it, the assumptive system or mythology—which an individual lives by is a major undertaking. It can be expected to encounter strong resistance from the individual concerned and to involve substantial emotional elements in the transition process.

It is well established that the systems of treatment which belong in the ideological change category are characterized by deeply moving experiences, associated resistance, and reports of internal struggle. This is not the case with those other systems of therapy which are oriented toward solving problems rather than changing people.

RELIGIOUS CONVERSION AND POLITICAL INDOCTRINATION OR THOUGHT REFORM

Religious Conversion. Frank (1973, pp. 79–85) discussed the similarity between aspects of religious conversion and psychotherapeutic change as this occurs in therapy of the psychodynamic type. He points out that much of psychotherapy is concerned with broad philosophical issues related to the goals and purposes of human existence and that successful outcome ordinarily involves the acquisition by the client of a more positive outlook. In this respect there are clear similarities with religious conversion.

Within the systems we are considering, psychotherapy is characterized by intense emotional experiences. This is true of such different orientations as the relatively mild client-centered method, the emotional process of Janov's (1970) "primal" therapy, and the systematic regression process of psychoanalysis. The "release of feeling" in which the patient undergoes distress, confusion, and turmoil is frequently the prelude to the state of "cure" in which there is serenity, openness, and a sense of being part of some larger whole. Very similar features are to be found in religious conversion, where, prior to the transformation into the new state of grace, the individual is confused and troubled and experiences a sense of estrangement from others. It is the "dark night of the soul." The person is torn by guilt, resentment, and despair. There is an overwhelming need for identification with and surrender to some benevolent order or being. In yeilding to it, the individual experiences a sense of affinity with the infinite and with it a sense of tranquility and inner harmony.

Such experiences are well documented. The best-known account is that of James (1936). Kelman (1969) has provided a rather broader perspective in which he discusses both religious experiences and psychotherapy. His focus is on *Kairos,* a term taken from the name of a Greek god who personified opportunity. For Kelman, *Kairos* constitutes a critical moment of opportunity for change. He defines it as "an event in the life of the individual, prepared for by many smaller such events in which the effective agents, as therapists, may be life and/or one or more specific persons. Intrinsic to such events and as a consequence of them will emerge experiences of a spiritual dimension. This means that all dimensions of being participate, and to such extents that new orientations will be experienced with a new clarity, toward living and dying, and toward the cosmos, of which we are an aspect" (p. 61). He sees Kairos as a culminating moment in a sequence of events of a minor nature leading to a state in which a relatively small intervention may have quite profound effects either immediately or over a period of time. Thus he describes a case of a young schizophrenic patient who had been receiving treatment from psychiatrists and psychologists over a period of years without apparent effect, but who, getting the same advice once more, heeded it and became a useful, productive, and fulfilled person. Commenting on this, Kelman says:

> Although Kielholz had given this patient the same advice as others, the structure of the situation in which he had done so was different in many regards. Each time he received it, his existential situation was different by virtue of his having lived a certain length of time, and what was going on in him contributing to the process we call schizophrenia also was changing. The same advice had the momentum of a number of others having given it [p. 63].

Kelman's point is that change of a quite radical nature, whether it occurs through religious conversion, a moving encounter with another person, or the outcome of psychotherapy, and whether, as is commonly the case, it is an intensely emotional experience or not, occurs at a critical point when the individual is ready for it and the right intervention is made. He points out that the literature of religion is rich in the discussion of this moment.

Religious conversion usually results from contact with a spiritual leader. The most obvious cases are provided by the evangelistic work of men like John Wesley or Billy Graham, each using the methods appropriate to his period. At a less obvious level is the work performed by the disciples who, in dedicated service, convey to the potential convert that they care enough about his material and spiritual well-being to be deeply concerned as to whether he is saved or not.

Once the conversion is effected, there remains the question of maintaining it. Within the religious context this is achieved by integrating the convert into the local congregation and involving him in the regular and frequent religious services it conducts. Berger and Luckman (1966) stress the importance of the ongoing interaction with a group of the faithful in the maintenance of the newly acquired beliefs. Frank (1973, p. 83 footnote) draws attention to the tendency for many therapy systems to make provision for the posttherapy maintenance of the attitudes, beliefs, and behaviors acquired in therapy. All such efforts are in keeping with Schein's emphasis on the importance of refreezing.

A further aspect in which parallels between religious conversion and psychotherapy are to be found relates to the population that is most responsive to such activities. Adolescents are particularly susceptible to religious conversion just as they are particularly responsive to psychotherapy. Theirs is an age in which conflicts associated with biological change, continuing dependence on others, environmental demands, and problems of identity are prominent. Other characteristics of the person susceptible to conversion are low self-esteem and somewhat marginal identification with the established culture patterns. These are also features which characterize the candidate for therapy.

There are thus marked similarities between religious conversion and psychotherapeutic change as this is found in systems of therapy which are concerned more with attitude change than direct problem-solving techinques. The former constitute a relatively good fit for the resocialization model. It would seem that in both religious conversion and psychotherapy the main unfreezing mechanisms that are operative are the induction of guilt and anxiety and the provision of psychological support, with considerably less emphasis on disconfirmation. Presumably those who are of most interest to both the religious group and to therapists are substantially disconfirmed in their interactions with the environment outside the therapy or religious setting.

Political Indoctrination. The use of coercive methods for ideological indoctrination by the regimes of Russia and China has given psychotherapists of psychodynamic persuasion cause for thought. There would seem to be even more reason for concern now than was the case twenty years ago. Frank (1973) was probably the first among practitioners of psychotherapy to make a firm case for the resemblance between thought reform methods and the techniques of psychotherapy. It would seem as if that resemblance is closer today than it was at the time of the initial publication. In his more recent strictures on the activities of humanistic psychologists, Farson (1978), in commenting on the model the leader provides for the participants in some "human potential" programs, says of the participants that "they learn what the leader thinks is alright to do to ensure that the participant achieves the goals of the program. So when we have programs, as we now do increasingly, that demonstrate that it is acceptable, even necessary, to demean, incarcerate, abuse, exhaust, humiliate, and terrorize the participants 'for their own good,' *that* is what the participants learn" (p. 18). Similar comments have been made byKoch (1971).

A major difference between thought reform and psychotherapy is that there is a very much wider gulf initially between the belief system of the reformer and his target than there is between that of therapist and client. The latter are usually in general accord on broad social and political issues, and it is only in respect of the more personal aspects of living that differences are likely to be relevant. Consequently, in terms of the resocialization model, there is less initial unfreezing to be carried out and hence the lesser emphasis on disconfirmation that was noted above. Indeed it seems to have been the problems posed by the task of unfreezing, to the stage necessary to bring about the sought-for reorientation, in thought reform procedures that alerted Schein to the important role played by unfreezing in attitude change processes.

A detailed discussion of the similarities and differences between the practices of thought reform and psychotherapy is beyond the scope of this book. Clearly the similarities between the two are greater in proportion as the therapist is an agent for established authority and the client is present in an involuntary capacity. Our concern, however, is not with the ethical issues, which are clearly important, but with the technique that is involved in the change-producing process.

In this regard, the way the relationship was defined in thought reform is to be noted. The aim of the program was to win the prisoner over to the communist cause. The attitude taken—in the case of the Chinese, which is the position we will consider here—was that he was guilty of crime against the Chinese people, but a distinction was made between the crime and the person committing it. The latter was deemed to be suffering from a diseased condition in that he had a false consciousness. The objective was the eradication of the disease and the restoration of the person in the tradition of hating the sin but loving the sinner. The procedure used to achieve this included the following features. Schein (1973b) tells us the prisoner

> . . . was usually not told of the charges against him, yet it was made clear to him that he was considered to be guilty from the moment of arrest on. Once arrested he was expected to come to understand the following version of his predicament: he was in prison because the government considered him a criminal; his crime was obvious to everyone but to him; his first task was to understand the nature of the crime and in this task the authorities and fellow prisoners would do all they could to help him; through analysis of his past behavior he would be shown and would discover how the ultimate consequences of his actions had been harmful to the Chinese people. Once he saw his guilt, he was expected to confess, repent, and reform the undesirable thoughts, attitudes, feelings, and actions which had led to his crimes in the first place [p. 290].

On the other hand,

> From the prisoner's point of view his arrest was unjustified, the accusations of guilt in the initial confrontation with judge or interrogator ridiculous, and the statements about leniency to those who confess meaningless. Only as the full force of the prison regimen made itself felt on him did he come to be able to appreciate, intellectually and emotionally what was wanted of him [p. 290].

There will be a somewhat familiar note about that last sentence for the person who has read the quotations from Angyal in the opening chapter.

The process of exploration which the prisoner is required to undertake has two main features: (1) a detailed review of his past life, which takes the form of a very personal autobiography to be presented to, and discussed with, his interrogator, and (2) a continuing interaction with a small group of cell mates whose function is to "help" him to find the truth about himself.

1. *Life review.* The review of the individual's life with the interrogator has something of the quality of a series of interviews with an analytically oriented or client-centered therapist. Its most distinctive feature, which it shares with such systems, is that the initiative as to what will be presented or discussed is left with the prisoner. The interrogator merely comments on what is produced and expresses satisfaction or dissatisfaction with it in whole or in part as it suits him. We call this the audience-performer strategy, and it will be discussed in Chapter 5 in examining certain features of psychoanalysis and client-centered therapy. We may note the following features:

a. If the interrogator were to make specific charges, he would be confronting the prisoner with something which the latter would know to be true or false and which he would acknowledge or deny as seemed appropriate, but no change would be effected in his perception of himself and his place in the universe. The whole procedure would be factual, and factual interchanges serve little purpose in the reorienting processes of either psychodynamic therapy or thought reform.

b. By making specific charges, he would be limiting the range of possible sources of guilt with which the prisoner would have to deal. This would simplify the prisoner's defense task. By not doing so, he leaves open a wide range of behavior in respect of which the prisoner may feel guilty and anxious.

c. If he were to make specific charges, it would be the interrogator who would be sweating at the task of trying to make some progress and produce some change. The onus would be on him to get some action, and the prisoner would be able to sit back and counter his moves. As it is, the reverse is very much the case.

d. In this procedure it is important that the interrogator be in no hurry and that the prisoner be undergoing an ordeal which will continue as long as he is unable to produce a satisfactory statement.

In all these respects the parallel with psychotherapy is close. In psychotherapy the therapist is typically comfortable and under no great pressure to hurry things along, while the client is under considerable pressure to achieve progress as he hopes for a better life, pays his fees, undergoes the inconvenience of attending his sessions, and places himself in the dependent role. As Haley (1963) has expressed it, therapy is a process in which the client is subjected to an ordeal in a benevolent context such that the ordeal will continue until therapeutic change occurs. The position of the prisoner in thought reform is precisely parallel with such a predicament.

Anyone placed in such a situation and subjected to long-continued interaction in which pleasing the audience—the therapist or the interrogator—assumes a high value will inevitably find his thinking shaped toward what he discerns to be desired by the audience. Even factual data, let alone attitudes or beliefs, are not immune to such bending. Frank (1973) tells us:

> The cumulative effects of the influencing procedure in thought reform might be sufficiently intense to cause prisoners to confess sincerely to "crimes" that they could not possibly have committed. One, for example, described in circumstantial detail and with full conviction how he had tried to attract the attention of an official representative of his country who passed by the door of his cell, only to discover that no such person had been anywhere near his prison at the time [p. 100].

Frank relates such fabrication to Freud's early experiences with his patients, who "confabulated infantile memories—in itself strong evidence for the influencing power of his techniques" (1973, p. 174). Similar points regarding the fallibility of memory have been made by others on a more general level. May (see May et al., 1959), in noting that memory is not a reproduction of past events, tells us, "Alfred Adler used to point out that memory was a creative process, that we remember what has significance for our 'style of life' and that the whole 'form' of memory is therefore a mirror of the individual's style of life. What an individual seeks to *become* determines what he remembers of his *has been*. In this sense the future determines the past" (p. 69).

Berger and Luckman (1966), in their discussion of the sociology of knowledge, have some interesting comments on radical change in the individual's perception of reality—a process which they call an alternation as it means the individual moves from one "reality" to another—in which they spell out the requirements for such events (pp. 146–148). They point out that any such alternation must not only include a reinterpretation of the past *in toto* but also cover in detail particular events. They state that it would be most convenient if such events could be completely forgotten, but this is extremely difficult if only because there are others around who remember them. They tell us:

> Since it is relatively easier to invent things that never happened than to forget those that actually did, the individual may fabricate and insert events whenever they are needed to harmonize the remembered with the reinterpreted past. Since it is the new reality rather than the old that now appears dominatingly plausible to him, he may be perfectly "sincere" in such a procedure—subjectively he is not telling lies about the past but bringing it in line with *the* truth that, necessarily, embraces both present and past [p. 147].

There would seem to be a similarity between psychotherapy and thought reform in the encouragement given to the client or prisoner to "explore" his biography. Essentially they are asking him to reconstruct it. It might be noted in passing that the criticism by more directive therapists that a focus on the past is misguided, since the past is no longer relevant, misses the essential point of what the psychodynamicists are in fact doing.

2. *The use of groups.* Both psychotherapy and thought reform make extensive use of groups. There is a lack of systematic theory which will account for the effects produced by groups, but the *reason* why groups are employed can be given in three words: *Groups are powerful.* It is the power of groups to bring about reorientations in attitudes and behavior that constitutes their appeal to thought reformers and psychotherapists alike.

The power of the group over its individual members is directly proportional to the degree of dependence of each individual on the other members in their roles as members of the group. The degree of dependence can be manipulated in many ways. Forming an isolated "culture island" setting where the group constitutes the total social context is more conducive to the creation of dependence than forming it in an urban setting where the participants break off to attend to work chores and go home to their families at night. This was realized by Lewin and the other innovators of the "training groups" movement. Dependence can also be promoted by making the individual rely on the other members of the group for the satisfaction of his most basic biological needs (e.g., by tying his hands behind his back). Various rules which emphasize the "differentness" of the group situation from other social contexts also enhance its power, since the individual member is prohibited from utilizing his developed social skills.

It is beyond the scope of this treatment to develop an explanation for the power of groups, but two points can be made:

a. As mechanisms for integrating the power and attitude change strategies discussed by Walton, groups are particularly well equipped. It is relatively easy to develop a situation in which the majority of the group denounces some aspect of the individual's behavior. Typically in such attacks his maneuvers in defending himself against one assailant leave him open to attack from another position. The individual can resist such pressure by mobilizing his resources against it. However, at a point where he is hard pressed and experiencing stress, one member is likely to make a gesture of psychological support such as reaching over and holding a hand. This undercuts the defense, which is based on hostility and opposition to the attack. Such events are run-of-the-mill occurrences in therapeutic groups. They are less typical of thought reform in that interaction is of a more drastic type in which there is continual harassment of both a mental and a physical nature that wears down the prisoner's morale. Nevertheless, it is his identification with his fellow prisoners that is most salient in effecting change. As Schein puts it:

> ... even more difficult for the prisoner was his increasing recognition that his cellmates really took the lenient policy of the government seriously and were making a genuine attempt to reform themselves. As the cellmates came to be seen as real people rather than merely agents of the prison authorities, the prisoner felt increasingly guilty for his hostility toward them and increasingly committed to trying to understand their point of view. Because his own beliefs, values, and attitudes had been undermined, and because he found himself in an insoluble situation, he became increasingly disposed to trying to find a solution through forming relationships with others who seemed to have found a solution. As his identification with one or more cellmates grew, he came increasingly to understand the basic premises underlying "the people's standpoint," and how he might be perceived to be guilty from this standpoint [1973b, pp. 292–293].

b. Both psychotherapy and thought reform make use of groups which allow for the utilization of the person in transition as a positive identification model. Schein 1973a, discussing this point, says:

> A few comments must be made on the role of the "person in transition," because this type of person is potentially the most powerful model of all. The person in transition still belongs to the peer group, but his movement out of the group implies that he is embracing some values other than those of the group. If the group trusts him enough, and if it seems clear that these new values are being rewarded by the organization and are rewarding to the transitional person, it is possible that the entire group will change with him in the direction of these new values [p. 258].

Schein goes on to quote some instances of the use of such a model, among which he includes the practice of the Chinese thought reformers: "Prisoners who were already partly reeducated were assigned to the same cell as the lone newcomer to the prison and proved to be powerful agents of influence" (p. 258). Anyone who is familiar with therapy groups and human encounter groups will be aware of a similar pattern.

Those members who have committed themselves to the new orientation are very active in drawing others with them. As Rogers (1970) tells us:

> As time goes on the group finds it unbearable that any member should live behind a mask or front. The polite words, the intellectual understanding of each other and of relationships, the smooth coin of tact and cover-up—amply satisfactory for interactions outside—are just not good enough. The expression of self by some members of the group has made it very clear that a deeper and more basic encounter is *possible*, and the group appears to strive intuitively and unconsciously, toward this goal. Gently at times, almost savagely at others, the group *demands* that the individual be himself, that his current feelings not be hidden, that he remove the mask of ordinary social intercourse [pp. 27-28].

This brings us to the question of the motivations of therapists and thought reformers. Frank (1973) suggests there is a complementary relationship between the prisoner and the interrogator:

> The interrogator's zeal is enhanced by his wish to believe in the genuineness of the patient's confession. According to his ideology, the prisoner would not have been arrested if he had not been guilty. Therefore, the prisoner's admission tends to confirm and support the interrogator's world view. It also helps him justify to himself the suffering he had inflicted on the prisoner. . . . Thus both prisoner and interrogator may collaborate in erecting a shared delusional system, each confirming the other in the false belief [p. 88].

What Frank is suggesting is that a process of co-constitution of reality occurs through the interaction of interrogator and prisoner. It is proposed to argue later that such co-constitution of reality is a common feature of systems of psychotherapy. For the moment we can merely note that a successful outcome of therapy within each psychodynamic system is typically taken as presumptive evidence for the validity of the theoretical basis of the system.

We can close this discussion of what we have called ideological change systems with the conclusion that they bear a strong resemblance to other forms of ideological change such as religious conversion and thought reform in terms of the technology of change employed. Such technology conforms to the resocialization model.

Problem-solving Systems

Whereas the class of change-producing therapies we have been discussing above tend to diffuse the problem which brought the individual into treatment—whether that problem is a fear of particular situations or a sex problem or an incapacity to work—and to aim at a reorganization of the individual's approach to the world, there is another group of therapies which try to sharpen the problem and state it in quite specific terms of what must happen before it can be regarded as being solved. For instance, if an individual seeks help because he is unable to get his work finished, he would be required to specify the precise nature and quantity of work in a given time that he would regard as a satisfactory level of accomplishment. The therapeutic task then becomes the achievement by the individual of the goal so set.

Watzlawick et al. (1974) have provided a good statement of this approach in their four-step procedure, which involves:

1) a clear definition of the problem in concrete terms;
2) an investigation of the solutions attempted so far;
3) a clear definition of the concrete change to be achieved;
4) the formulation and implementation of a plan to produce this change [p. 110].

These four steps are all regarded as critical by the type of therapist we have in mind—a type that seems to be becoming more common. The four steps may be elaborated slightly before considering the systems that follow them.

A clear definition of the problem is necessary in order to be sure that it is a problem and that it is such as to admit of a solution. Should it turn out to be a pseudo problem, the completion of this step will dissolve it. Should it not admit of a solution (e.g., one cannot prevent aging or resurrect departed loved ones), then it will be clear that the situation must be borne. If the problem is stated in as clear and concrete terms as possible, the way is cleared for the search for a solution.

The investigation of the solutions attempted so far is necessary in order to know what not to do. It may reveal precisely where the problem lies. Within a framework of reciprocal causation the attempts at solving problems are often the means whereby they are maintained. For example, the dependent person, who is unhappy because others do not care for him, in stepping up his efforts to obtain such care, typically alienates his associates; and the efforts of parents to get their children to behave often have the effect of accentuating the misbehavior. Whether such effects are seen in terms of reinforcement theory or in terms of feedback loops, an examination of the previous efforts at solution is likely to be suggestive of the course to be followed.

The definition of a clear goal to be achieved is a distinctive feature of such systems and distinguishes them from the person-oriented systems in which the goals are extremely vague and broad. Goals such as wanting to be happier or to be more fulfilled are regarded as meaningless. The client is asked to specify what would have to happen for him to be happier or be more fulfilled, and this becomes the target. Also a time limit is often set for its achievement.

The formulation and implementation of a plan to produce the particular change is then worked out and put in terms that utilize the client's way of conceptualizing reality. No attempt is made to change the client's philosophy of life or concept of the nature of the universe or of his own functioning. Rather, the attempt is to engage with him in an attack on the problem utilizing, in the process, his formulation of it.

The most clear-cut examples of therapeutic approaches which employ this approach are to be found in the various forms of behavior therapy and in the more recent problem-solving therapy which derives its inspiration mainly from the "uncommon therapy" of Milton Erickson (Haley 1974, 1976; Watzlawick et al., 1974). There are some notable differences between the behavior therapists and the latter group in that behavior therapy belongs within a linear influence model and what Maruyama calls a "hierarchical and non-reciprocal causal epistemology" (1977), while the Ericksonians belong within a systems model and a reciprocal causal epistemology. In terms of what we have been considering in this chapter, they share common ground in their focus on problem solving rather than on changing the person.

In contrast to attempts to change the person that aim at helping him to achieve self-fulfillment, the problem-oriented approach takes a more mundane view. We will consider first the contextual, or Ericksonian, position. From its perspective, problems are endemic in social existence. They are inevitable in the way an individual, a family, and a community develop over time. To quote Haley:

> Symptoms appear when there is a dislocation or interruption in the unfolding life cycle of a family or other natural group. The symptom is a signal that a family has difficulty in getting past a stage in the life cycle. For example, an anxiety attack in a mother when she gives birth to a child is an expression of the difficulty of that family in achieving the child-rearing stage of development. While focussing sharply on symptoms, Erickson's therapeutic strategy has as its larger goal the resolution of the problems of the family to get the life cycle moving again [1973 pp. 24-25].

In other words, the task of the therapist is to intervene when an impasse occurs in order to get the life process moving on its way again and to do this with a minimum of disruption and disorganization of that ongoing process. The type of intervention employed to find a way past the blockage is tailored to the individual case. In reading the case examples, one has an impression of the need for a keen intuitive sense of the inner life of the family group and its members to guide this intervention. To quote Haley again:

> Although with some people Erickson will go out of his way to use shocking words, with others he is equally careful to say something in such a way that the patient only realizes later what he has said. Or he will be extremely cautious with someone who is frightened about discussing something un-

mentionable. He believes that what is to be done must fit the particular person who comes in and does not attempt to fit all patients into a similar therapeutic mold [1973, p. 140].

The distinguishing feature of the placebo model and those forms of therapy which are seen as conforming to it, in contrast to the contextual model, is the nonreciprocal causal logic on which the former model is based. Influence or causation is seen to flow in one direction. All forms of behavior therapy, with the notable exception of biofeedback, are seen to fall into this category, as are such procedures as those of Ellis (1962), whose approach is essentially problem-oriented. Biofeedback requires as a basis for its explanation a systems-oriented reciprocal causal epistemology.

A good example of therapy which fits the placebo model is systematic desensitization. Numerous other methods which involve a direct attack on the symptom, but in which the effective agent appears to be the mobilization of social influence in a healing ritual, have been developed. Typically such procedures are relatively elaborate, are plausible, and convey an impression of scientific methodology and technology. They include remedial programs for addiction to smoking, to alcohol, and to drugs as well as for a range of deviant behaviors. Some alcoholic remedial programs include such features as training the alcoholic to discriminate a particular level of alcohol in his blood content, then requiring him to continue drinking with painful electric shocks being administered during the extended drinking; another program consisted of getting alcoholics to role-play alcoholic behavior in a mock-up bar, filming it, and then requiring the patient to watch the films of the scene while receiving electric shocks. These illustrations are offered as examples from a wide-ranging technology of healing rituals, many of which have a high degree of plausibility and in which some of the components of treatment may well have remedial effects quite distinct from the social influence impact.

A feature which distinguishes placebo therapy from contextually based therapy is that, in the former, the client is presented with a plausible account of the particular procedure employed. This description, which is tailored to the client's beliefs, includes a rationale and an indication of the expected effects, thereby providing him with a route map to recovery. This is an important part of the communication of the placebo. In the contextual model explanations are avoided.

It must be stressed that in their focus on the problem the two approaches have much in common, and this common ground seems likely to expand as the narrower and more rigid versions of the behavior modification approach lose their hold. Both approaches are characterized by a concern for a precise statement of the problem and a precise goal for therapy, together with the formulation of a plan for achieving the goal. They both tailor the treatment to the particular case after a careful diagnostic study of the variables which seem to be relevant. In these respects they stand together.

CONCLUDING NOTE

The aim in this discussion has been to arrive at a basis for categorizing systems of therapy—or at least of defining a continuum along which they might be located. It is suggested that one useful way to do this is to distinguish between those systems which focus on changing the person, which we call ideological change systems, and those which aim at removing a block in the individual's path, which we call problem-solving systems.

It is not claimed that the processes are independent. A change in the person's ideology will change his perspective and hence what he will regard as a problem, while overcoming an impasse will result in changes in the individual's perception of himself and of this world. However, the stance taken by the therapist does seem to affect the way therapy is conducted and the type of experience the client goes through.

PART II
Systems of Therapy That Illustrate the Models

CHAPTER 4
The Placebo Model

IN THIS SURVEY of models of therapy, the aim is to outline the general nature of each model and then to consider a system of therapy which conforms to the model. In the case of the placebo model, there are some difficulties in that the placebo effect is seen as entering into all systems of therapy just as it does into all forms of physical treatment of illness. Confidence in the efficacy of the procedure and belief in the competence of the person administering it contribute to a favorable outcome. At the same time, it would seem hazardous to claim that any particular system owes whatever success it achieves entirely to the ubiquitous nonspecific placebo effect. It would be difficult to convince any therapist that the specific and distinctive elements of his treatment procedure do not make a useful contribution to the therapeutic outcome.

Fish (1973), however, has proposed a strategy of therapy that is designed to maximize the placebo effect in the cause of the patient's welfare. While he is not concerned with arguing that psychotherapy can be reduced completely to placebo effects, he does regard such effects as sufficiently potent to warrant careful study so that they can be utilized to the full. He presents a strong case for designing therapy around such effects. This introduces, as a major aim, the task of making the treatment provided for any individual plausible and convincing to him in the light of his particular belief system.

55

Before considering Fish's position, some brief comments may be made about faith healing, which has had a long past but a short history. Faith healing seems to be as old as Homo sapiens and may have predated his advent, but it is only in very recent times that it has been investigated in any systematic way. Its occurrence is ubiquitous. The most sophisticated urban dweller is as susceptible to its effects as the most primitive tribesman, providing that the healing ritual accords with his particular world view.

Among modern writers on the practice of psychotherapy, Janet (1925) seems to have been the first to give serious attention to faith healing. However, it has been only in the last few decades, with the advent of rigorous drug-testing programs, that serious attempts have been made to study its effects. In such studies the faith-healing component—the placebo effect—was initially seen as a nuisance factor in demonstrating the efficacy of the drug being investigated. It was noise in the system. The aim of the studies was to try to assess its effects so that allowance could be made for them in determining the "real" effects of the pharmacological agent under investigation. Subsequently, however, there developed an increasing interest in the placebo effect as an important phenomenon in its own right.

As was pointed out earlier, the placebo effect is substantial and is consistently related to the belief of the physician administering a drug regarding its potency. The administering agent communicates to the recipient his expectations as to its likely effects, and such communications cause the latter to have appropriate experiences of relief of his symptoms.

It is hardly surprising, therefore, that some observers of the current scene in psychotherapy, in which almost every form of intervention appears to have its share of therapeutic success, are wont to account for such success in terms of the placebo effect. Since it can be assumed that psychotherapists and their clients have faith in the efficacy of the procedures being used, the placebo effect constitutes the most parsimonious explanation that would account for the apparently equal success achieved by each of the diverse collection of therapies practiced.

As was noted earlier, Frank (1973) was perhaps the first to state in forcible terms the case for viewing psychotherapy as essentially a form of persuasion in which the important consideration was to be convincing. His survey of healing and change processes spreads across a wide spectrum of human interaction from the use of modern medication to miracles at Lourdes, and from the rituals of primitive magic to the coercive persuasion techniques of the Chinese Marxists. A significant feature of his position has been his adherence to the medical model of healing while presenting a case that favors an orientation which views psychotherapy as the application of social psychology in the cause of interpersonal influence.

Since Frank's initial publication, numerous statements of a supportive nature have appeared in journals or in book form. Two particularly forthright views have been put forward. Gillis (1979) has outlined a case for a social influence perspective on therapy in which he indicates a range of tactics, derived from research in social psychology, that are available to the practitioner. Fish (1973) develops a case for a self-conscious application of the placebo effect in which he spells out systematically the steps to be taken in its implementation. We can regard his version as a formal statement of placebo therapy.

THE STRATEGY OF PLACEBO THERAPY

Fish starts from the principle that psychotherapy consists of using "one powerful set of the patient's beliefs (his faith) to change another set of his beliefs (*his problems*)" (1973, p. 16). These latter typically comprise a set of irrational and unrealistic beliefs the client holds about himself and his resources or the situations with which he has to deal. They typically involve feelings of helplessness, inadequacy, and lack of worth. Though he is afflicted by them, the client is ordinarily aware that his reactions to his world are unreasonable. As Fish puts it, people do not go to therapists to get rid of their fear of swimming in crocodile-infested waters, but they may do so to be freed of a fear of cats.

The faith that is to be used to bring about change in symptoms is the belief in the potency of the therapeutic intervention. This means that the treatment procedure—the healing ritual—must be tailored to the world view of the client. A voodoo rite is not likely to be an effective treatment for an urban business executive who is losing confidence in himself.

This necessity for a good fit between the client's view of reality and the form the placebo takes makes it essential that the therapist inform himself as to the former's pattern of attitudes and values. This means that an orderly approach must be made, involving some careful initial exploration with the client, of the nature of the presenting problem and the client's expectations regarding therapy. Fish sets out the therapeutic model in a three-stage sequence beginning with an exploratory phase that culminates in the formulation of the placebo. This is followed by the healing ritual stage, and in the final phase are the measures taken for the maintenance of the "cure."

The main task in the exploratory stage is to obtain as much specific and relevant information about the client as possible, while at the same time maintaining a comfortable relationship with him. The therapist seeks factual information. He wants to know in detailed terms what the client does or has done, who the relevant people in his life are, what they say to him or do in relation to him, and what he says or does in relation to them. The interest is in information about actions rather than feelings.

Fish maintains that, while anything approaching an aggressive interrogation is to be avoided, careful fact gathering is essential for planning the second stage of treatment and has the effect of creating a favorable impression on the client, who will appreciate the thorough and scientific approach that is involved.

While gathering factual data about the client, the therapist is also assessing the degree to which the client is susceptible to influence. The less susceptible the client to suggestion, the more elaborate and carefully designed the healing ritual will have to be in order to carry conviction. The basic orientation of the therapist is conveyed in Fish's words:

> ... probably the most distinctive aspect of the therapist-patient relationship in placebo therapy is the therapist's attitude during the interview. This attitude involves great sensitivity to the impact of his words on his patients - especially the impact on their interpretations of the healing process. For example, a therapist should be able to judge whether, if he should say, "I can help you," his patient would view him as a savior or a fool. Once a therapist acquires this skill, he finds that the rest of the therapy becomes much easier. Although outwardly his interviews may seem relatively unchanged, a therapist working in this way says things for the effect they will have rather than for his belief that they are true. Thus, instead of speaking empathically because he believes that empathy cures, he does so because he sees that such statements add to his credibility in his patient's eyes. Furthermore, once his patient feels understood, the therapist can on occasion take the liberty of distorting his empathy for a therapeutic reason. Instead of saying, "You feel worthless because she left you," he might say, "I sense a reluctance on your part to admit that you also feel relieved that she's gone." Of course, such distortions must be used sparingly and must bear directly on the goals of therapy. From a social influence viewpoint, however, such distortions (as well as truly empathic statements) should be judged in terms of their therapeutic effect rather than in terms of their truth [1973, pp. 31–32].

As the therapist comes to understand the nature of the client's problems, a contract is entered into. By contract is meant a clear understanding between therapist and client as to what the goal of therapy is to be. In this regard, the object is to set clear-cut goals that are capable of attainment. Fish would insist on the client's presenting clearly defined problems. If, in the course of the exploration process, it becomes apparent that the client cannot present a clear-cut problem on which to work, then it would be assumed that in fact there is no problem and hence no need for therapy. If the client proposes some vague goal such as wanting to be more fulfilled or more productive, he would be asked to indicate in specific terms what would have to happen for such a situation to be achieved. Then that could, if it were attainable, become a goal to work toward. In this matter of setting specific targets for therapy, the directive therapists of both the placebo and contextual models differ sharply from the ideologically oriented group.

Once the contract has been entered into—that is, once the client and therapist have arrived at a goal to be worked for and matters such as fees and schedules of meetings have been arranged—the therapist explains the treatment strategy that will be employed. In Fish's terms, he formulates and communicates the most important placebo. The way is then open for the implementation of the healing ritual.

While the foregoing account represents the way the initial stage of treatment is seen to take shape, in practice the therapist usually begins, at an early stage in the interaction with the client, to devise a healing ritual that has a good chance of being effective. With that in mind, he proceeds to develop a strategy for communicating it to the client in a way that will be convincing in the light of the latter's beliefs and problems. Much of the initial interaction, therefore, while outwardly concerned with getting information from the client, is directed at orienting him toward viewing his situation in terms such that the proposed treatment will appear realistic and appropriate. So, while from the patient's point of view the treatment appears to emerge logically out of an examination of his situation, from the therapist's point of view the order is reversed, with the treatment procedure having priority in time. In Fish's words, "Thus, the therapeutic strategy appears to the patient to grow out of the goals set in the therapeutic contract, but the goals are selected because the therapist already has a good idea of how to go about reaching them" (p. 41).

The Healing Ritual

When the contract has been made and the treatment strategy has been explained to the client, the therapist proceeds to implement the healing ritual.

There are many kinds of healing rituals. Indeed, for Fish all current therapeutic practices would fall into this category, but for obvious reasons he is interested in those which are relatively easy to employ and rapid in their effect. Some have validity in the same sense that some pharmacological preparations have validity. From the point of view of the placebo model, the validity of a given ritual is relevant only insofar as it increases the client's faith. The critical question is how persuasive the ritual is for the client.

Rituals are persuasive, irrespective of their validity, to the degree to which they are either intrinsically believable or are intriguing and impressive. A ritual which is clearly related to the therapeutic goal is more likely to be believable than one which is not, and, for the many patients who view therapy as a form of magic, intriguing, impressive, and mysterious rituals are likely to carry conviction.

Behavior therapy is a rich source of healing rituals. It consists essentially of a body of techniques which, for the most part, have "face" validity. They deal with the symptomatic behavior directly and offer the prospect of quick results. Systematic desensitization, operant and aversive conditioning, and implosive therapy in their various forms and combinations provide considerable scope. Other strategies include such paradoxical procedures as prescribing the symptom. Hypnosis and self-hypnosis are further techniques in the armament of the well-furnished placebo therapist.

These rituals typically involve the patient's engaging in a course of action which leads to a "cure." Thus a man with the problem of squandering his paycheck each payday by buying drinks for everyone at a series of bars on his way home was required to list the bars in sequence, the number of rounds he ordered for others at each bar, and the number and kind of drinks he had at each bar. He was then instructed to follow the list exactly on the next payday. As might be expected, the man went home without completing the list, since there was no longer any fun in his spree.

The problem in setting such paradoxical tasks for the patient lies in providing plausible and convincing explanations as to why the client should perform them. In a case such as that just described, a therapist might tell the client that in order to help him, it was necessary to have more information about exactly what he felt at critical stages on his binge and therefore he wanted him to make notes on his feelings before he ordered each drink.

The most common type of ritual described by Fish employs the little-by-little principle. This can be applied to a wide range of problems varying from difficulties in relationships with others to coping with the physical environment. One form of it occurs in systematic desensitization of anxiety or phobias. Other forms involve assisting a highly disorganized person to gain control of his life by getting him to list all the tasks he has to perform, to put them in order of difficulty, and then to start by handling the simplest and easiest ones. The confidence and self-esteem that come from even minimal achievement and the approval it brings enable progressively more difficult tasks to be attempted and accomplished as the person moves up the hierarchical order. This amplification of confidence and achievement, consequent upon the feedback from success, figures prominently in Fish's presentation.

An important feature of the healing ritual is the emphasis on self-cure. It is essential that the client be encouraged to perceive his improvement as being accomplished by his own efforts. This enhances his faith in himself and in his capacity to cope with his situation. At an early stage in therapy he is encouraged to see his efforts and their outcome as progress and improvement, and at a later stage to see them as constituting cure. This shift is accomplished by drawing attention to the contract and pointing out that the goal has been accomplished. It is possible at this stage that the client may want to work on some new goal, and if so, a new contract may be embarked upon. If not, the client is ready for the third stage of the placebo strategy, which involves the maintenance of the gains that have been made.

Maintaining the "Cure"

Fish describes in the following terms the therapeutic process as he views it:

> A person entering therapy is often entangled in a vicious circle of self-aggravating problems. For example, his low self-esteem may make him feel incapable of accomplishing anything, and this feeling may in turn lead him to try less hard to meet life's daily challenges. His diminished efforts naturally lead to failures, and his experience of failure tends to decrease further his already low self-esteem. Placebo therapy attempts to break this circle. The new behavior and beliefs which arise from the healing ritual lead to an upsurge of hope, which in turn promotes the sequence of zeal, success, and increased self-esteem. The strategy of the therapy stage, which aims at creating a self-perpetuating virtuous circle, involves the following: helping the patient to develop new behavior and beliefs, strengthening the new behavior and beliefs, strengthening the patient's ability to cope with challenges to his new behavior and beliefs, and getting the patient to act in a manner ensuring that others will respond positively to his new behavior and beliefs [1973, pp. 56–57].

The new behavior will persist if it leads to positive consequences, and it is the task of the therapist to ensure that the new behavior is such that it will have this effect. Therapy is concerned with helping the individual to become an effectively functioning member of society who will be rewarded by society for his contributions to it.

Two ways in which Fish considers that the therapist can be of help to his clients as the latter move out of therapy are the following:

1. He can provide them with a basis for explaining the change in their behavior to their friends and associates
2. He can prepare them for the occasional setbacks and difficulties they will encounter in their posttherapy life

In regard to the first point, Fish draws attention to the often overlooked fact that when a person begins to behave in a noticeably different manner, people who know him well are uncertain how to respond to him. Since it is important that they respond positively to the new behavior, efforts should be made to ensure that they do so. The most likely way to do this is to provide them with an explanation to account for the change. Such an explanation must convey that the change is real and not simply superficial role playing, and it must be tailored to the belief systems of those to whom it is given. For those who believe in therapy the explanation can be couched in terms of having received therapy. For others "he might attribute his new behavior to the salutary effects of a vacation, a raise, the discovery of new meaning in his marriage, or an uplifting sermon in church" (p. 63). In other words, the client is encouraged to take note of the belief systems of others and apply a little placebo work of his own.

In regard to the second point, the therapist in the closing stages of treatment can convey a number of messages to the effect that (1) the client will inevitably have some difficulties in the course of life's "ups and downs," but these are in the natural order of things; (2) although he is unlikely ever to have to do so, he can always return to see the therapist should new problems arise; (3) he has some self-mastery techniques now which he can bring into play when any problems arise.

On this basis the patient is launched into a life without therapy, hopefully with faith in himself and his capacity to cope with life's vicissitudes.

An Evaluation of Placebo Therapy

In attempting to assess the contribution of placebo therapy, the point must first be made that in terms of what the therapist does in his interaction with the client, there is little to distinguish this approach from other therapeutic systems. The healing rituals are largely those found in behavior therapy, but Fish is prepared to use a ritual from any source provided that it seems appropriate for the particular case and promises relatively quick results. It is not in the practical techniques he employs that his system is distinctive, but in the way he conceptualizes the "healing" process.

Taking his stance on the grounds that psychopathology derives from erroneous beliefs—or, as Raimy (1975) would call them, misunderstandings—about the self and its situation, Fish sees therapy as a project in belief modification. In this activity, some of the client's beliefs are mobilized in the cause of modifying others. This, for him, is the core of therapy. It is on this basis that the various systems of psychotherapy achieve their success. However, as he goes on to point out, the practitioners of the different systems are taken in by their own explanations and are essentially true believers.

We might note here, in passing, that within Fish's framework there are practical advantages in this. The firm belief of the therapist in the truth of his system contributes to the impact of his message to the client. When a client-centered therapist says that one must have confidence in the growth potential of the client in order to release it, he is recognizing, albeit in a somewhat indirect way, the potency of transmitted conviction. Clearly there are fewer problems in transmitting a conviction to which one subscribes than one which one does not hold. This is a problem for Fish, which will be discussed below.

Nevertheless, Fish takes the position that therapists would be much freer in their work and have a much broader armament of interventive procedures if they were less narrowly committed to the validity of their theoretical formulations. Thus the exponent of systematic desensitization who accounts for its success in terms of the principle of reciprocal inhibition limits himself to applying it to people for whom such a view of treatment is acceptable. Since it is necessary to give the client some explanation for the treatment procedure that is to be used in order to enlist his cooperation, a true-believing systematic desensitizer will present the client with its complex and scientific-sounding rationale. This will be very effective if the client happens to be one who is favorably impressed by scientific-sounding ways of handling human problems, but it will be counterproductive if he should view such approaches as mechanistic, manipulative, and dehumanizing. Fish would want to use the strategy which is basic to this procedure in a flexible way with the explanation for its use tailored to the world view of the client. So to a client who gave the impression that he would be turned off by an explanation couched in behavior modification terms, he gave the following explanation:

> "I think I know a way that would enable you to deal with your fear fairly rapidly, but it would involve your experiencing some hypnoticlike phenomena. Would you be willing to consider such a possibility? [Naturally, he agreed.] The approach I have in mind involves your learning to achieve a semihypnotic state of relaxation. Once you were in this state, I would help you little by little to experience your fear, confront it, and eventually overcome it. By lowering your conscious defenses, the state of relaxation would enable you to experience your feelings more fully and in this way overcome your fear by becoming totally aware of it" [1973, pp. 97–98].

PROBLEMATIC ISSUES

Three questions confront the person who would adopt the placebo approach to psychotherapy:

1. Is it ethical to mislead the client in regard to the therapeutic strategy?
2. Will the therapist be convincing when he is not a true believer in the ritual he is carrying through?

3. If placebo therapy becomes general and clients become aware of its nature, will they lose faith in the healing rituals and hence render these ineffective?

It is not proposed to consider the ethical issues here. The purpose of this book is to explore the nature of influence in psychotherapy and its implementation. This is an area which raises many difficult ethical issues going far beyond the question of misleading the client regarding the therapeutic strategy. It is beyond the scope of our objectives to deal with such issues. The interested reader is referred to Fish for a justification of his position.

The other two questions, however, are directly relevant. They are empirical questions, but there are obvious difficulties in carrying out the investigations that will resolve them. We must content ourselves here with some theoretical comments. It will be recalled that in the case of pharmacological studies using placebos, it was the belief of the administering physician, conveyed in some way in the process of giving the medication, in the potency of the medication that was the determining factor. It might therefore be expected that if the therapist has little faith in the healing ritual per se, this will convey itself to the client, with consequent impairment of the healing effect. With regard to the third question of the effect on clients, or potential clients, of the perception of therapy as the utilization of the placebo effect, it is difficult to see how this could have any consequence other than that of undermining the potency of the treatment.

Fish handles the second question—the issue of the therapist's belief—by arguing that the placebo therapist has faith in the power of faith. Effective faith healing, he tells us, is a process which takes place between two believers, and hence "a therapist who believes in placebo principles need never be guilty of being a con artist. He not only realizes that the placebo communication must be in his patient's best interest but also believes that the patient's faith, not his own brilliance, is responsible for the cure. Such a therapist need not worry that he will communicate the smile of one-upmanship" (1973, p. 21).

He handles the third question—the issue of the client's belief—by asking the client to approach therapy with faith in its efficacy. An objective attitude toward therapy can only prevent faith from doing its work. Psychotherapy should not be regarded as a rational process. Patients go to therapists "only after all attempts at rational persuasion or reasonable advice have failed" (p. 20). Such attempts have failed because the patient's problem is irrational and requires an irrational solution. The faith in therapy which is required of the patient is no more irrational than the belief which constitutes the problem to be treated.

Something of Fish's position is revealed in the following advice to therapists:

A therapist's first responsibility is his patient's welfare. Thus, when he says something to his patient because of the effect that it will have rather than because of its truth (that is, the therapist makes a placebo communication), he is acting in the highest therapeutic tradition. To be professionally responsible, such actions must not be self-aggrandizing. If the therapist uses the therapeutic situation as an opportunity to demonstrate his omnipotence, he is likely to distort the normal therapeutic contract—"I'll try to help you to cure yourself." "I'll try to be cured."—into something like the following. "I'm so much smarter than you that I can con you into being cured." "I'll try to be cured, . . . but you can't con me into anything." Such an approach would not prove therapeutic because the appropriate response to a con artist is a refusal to be conned. Moreover, not only is such an affirmation of the therapist's brilliance irrelevant to the patient's welfare, but the competition disrupts the harmonious work toward a mutually agreeable goal [p. 21].

In response to the foregoing arguments of Fish, two points can be made:

1. To the extent that the healing ritual is considered to have some validity, there would seem to be no case to answer.
2. To the extent that the client is asked to have faith in a method of therapy on the ground that his faith, and not the specific properties of the healing ritual, is the healing agent, he is posed with an untenable paradox.

If the ritual has validity, even though this may amount to no more than the validity in the "commonsense" methods current in the culture, then the position is no different from that of the use of any effective healing agent. Behavior therapy consists for the most part of a collection of training principles and procedures which are part of the common stock of conventional wisdom in the community and which ought to be, but usually are not, utilized sensitively and thoughtfully by those responsible for influencing the development of others. The healing rituals which Fish has in mind seem to be drawn largely from this and related sources. The fact that these procedures are packaged more impressively in terms of the client's world view in order to intensify their impact on the client can hardly be regarded as a cause for concern.

We would go further and maintain that the more irrational the belief that constitutes the symptomatic behavior, the more legitimate it becomes to utilize procedures which rely on faith rather than on the specific properties of the procedure. The following example reported by Fish can be used to illustrate the point:

One day the police received a telephone call from a frightened woman who asked for someone to come to "get them to stop shooting those rays at me." An officer was despatched, and, when he arrived, the woman repeated her complaint. "Are you grounded?" the policeman asked her. The woman seemed puzzled and said that she was not. The officer explained that, once she was grounded, the rays could not hurt her. He asked where the rays were coming from, and the woman pointed to a window. He then took some wire he had brought with him, attached it to one side of the window, strung it around the apartment, and attached it to the other side of the window. As he left, he assured her that she was well grounded and that the rays would not bother her anymore. Nothing further was heard from the woman until she called again several years later. She explained that she had recently moved and that they were shooting the rays at her again. She asked whether the police would send over that nice officer to ground her once more. This inspired bit of placebo therapy calmed a frightened woman and saved her from months or years of a far more wretched and degrading existence [pp. 148–149].

Clearly such a procedure would be inappropriate both practically and ethically if there was a realistic basis for the woman's fears. Also, in the very complex area of interpersonal relationships, attempts to provide simplistic and absolutist formulas for conduct have no place.

On the point that the client should be asked to approach the treatment with faith in its efficacy even though he may be aware that the treatment is based primarily on the placebo principle, the issue of paradox in communication arises. The traditional religious injunction "Have faith and you will be made whole," like the command "Be spontaneous," poses a paradox for the recipient. As phrased by Fish in his "Note to patients" (pp. 19–21), the patient is advised to enter therapy with an irrational belief in its effectiveness. That is, he is asked to make a rational choice to be irrational. So we have the paradox that if the client behaves irrationally, he is behaving rationally—that is, in his own best interests. And if he behaves rationally—that is, approaches therapy in an objective rational manner—he is behaving irrationally, or against his own best interests.

Consequently, insofar as he is proposing that a client will benefit from therapy while knowing that its effects will depend not upon its intrinsic potency, but upon his (the client's) belief in its potency, Fish is less than convincing. It would seem necessary that the client have faith in the efficacy of the treatment as such. This is quite a different matter from having faith in his faith in its efficacy.

The logical problems that arise through reflexive processes, touched upon above, recur and are discussed in later chapters of this book.

CHAPTER 5

The Resocialization Model: Two Ideological Systems

THE TWO SYSTEMS of psychotherapy which will be discussed as representative of the resocialization model are those of Sigmund Freud and Carl Rogers. There are a number of reasons for selecting these as exemplifying the characteristics of the broad spectrum of psychodynamic formulations which have been proposed over the last three-quarters of a century.

Freud's system is included because it has priority in time, has had a profound impact on the intellectual world, and constitutes a coherent and internally consistent body of theory and practice. It occupies a preeminent position in the field of psychodynamic systems and constitutes a standard and reference point against which other systems have defined their stances. Furthermore, standing as it does at the beginning of the era of these versions of the human situation, it provides a basis on which to assess the nature and degree of any change in this domain.

While Rogers's system is not so elaborately developed as that of Freud and its impact outside the area of psychotherapy and education has been limited, it has been very influential within those fields. He and his students can claim to have played a major part in demystifying the practice of psychotherapy and opening it up as an area for systematic investigation. Furthermore, he states a theoretical position which is clearly identifiable and which has interesting features both in common with, and in contrast to, those of Freud. Just as Freud stands at the opening of the era, so Rogers's person-centered orientation can be seen as the last of the major formulations within the field. By including it, it is possible to note some trends which are related to the passage of time.

There is much common ground between Freud and Rogers. Both were concerned with that ubiquitous issue of the relation between the individual and society, which, broadly stated, is the problem of reconciling the biological impulses of the human organism with the maintenance of an orderly society. Though, in general outline, they come down on opposite sides of the fence in their conclusions as to whether society or the individual must take precedence, their differences are not as great as might appear from a superficial reading. To understand the relation between Freud and Rogers, it is necessary to consider them against the background of their times.

THE HISTORIC SETTINGS

It might be said that Freud's orientation to life was formed in a stable society. He was into middle age at the turn of the century, well before the upheavals that ravaged Europe and shattered the old order of Western society. Rogers came to maturity in a more turbulent and changing era, and his work has continued over a period of ever-accelerating change. Consequently, one difference between them is that the world the individual inhabits has become more fluid and requires greater fluidity in response patterns.

That, however, is only half the story. While superficially stable, the world Freud knew was already being shaken to its foundations, and sensitive intellectual minds of the time were aware of the fact. The second half of the nineteenth century saw the publication of *Origin of Species* and *Das Kapital,* and Nietzsche was proclaiming the death of God. The solid institutions which provided guidelines for living were under threat. In particular, traditional religious positions were becoming less defensible on intellectual grounds. In consequence, the informed mind could no longer look outward with confidence for answers to the problems of conscience which beset it. It is understandable that Freud should look elsewhere for such answers, and it is hardly surprising, in the light of his training and the background of his time, that he should seek them in the human capacity for rational thought.

There are obvious advantages, in times of change, in centering the source of decision making with the individual. When institutions are crumbling, the individual who relies upon them for guidance must of necessity find himself confused and at a loss. But the centering of decision making within the individual calls for a heightened self-awareness, which, of course, has been the aim of Freud and others who followed him.

But the state of society in Freud's time was different from what has prevailed during Rogers's life. Society was still outwardly stable at the end of the nineteenth century. The individual still accepted without question that he had to live within it and conform to its dictates. The prevailing view of biological nature was that of an unenlightened self-seeking essence that would destroy the hard-won and necessary order which society imposed upon it. Civilization was seen as a veneer over irascible forces always ready to erupt. Freud's own fascination with rationality, which for him constituted "the god within," inevitably alienated him from the impulsive biological imperatives of animal nature.

Nevertheless, the whole strategy of his treatment was directed toward finding leeway for the expression and satisfaction of the biological imperatives within the social restrictions which he saw as both inevitable and desirable. This leeway, or extended bounds for freedom of expression of the impulse life, was to be achieved by enlarging awareness, which would both extend the scope for achieving gratification of the primitive urges and, at the same time, put the individual in his own hands. Freedom and control, in the sense of self-control, were two sides of the one coin and the name of that coin was awareness.

In contrast to the apparently stable social order of Freud's era, the world Rogers knows has been one of turbulence, change, and fluidity. This rate of change seems to be increasing as the years advance. In such a world, the centering on self has become even more important as the most hallowed institutions dissolve. Quick-footedness is called for to remain erect when the ground beneath heaves and rolls in unpredictable ways. Long-term commitments and involvements that will restrict freedom of movement are to be avoided.

Clearly such a state of affairs calls for an increased centering on self. The individual must rely ever-increasingly on the god within him and find strength and resourcefulness in his own roots. It becomes axiomatic that this is the basis of healthy living. The essence of Rogers's message is that the strength and resourcefulness are there. All that they want is the opportunity to unfold and reveal themselves. The social institutions merely restrict and impede the flowering of the natural inbuilt potential. Conforming to the edicts of society no longer has the value it had for Freud. In any case, society now speaks with many voices and its edicts are anything but clear. The individual has become the measure of all things. His task is to attune himself to his organismic experiential processes, which constitute the only reliable guide available. The aim must be to live in accord with the inner dictates of his being.

While the Rogerian system places great value on independence, autonomy, and reliance on the inner world of feeling as the ground on which to take a stand, there is also a heavy endorsement of activities which appear to involve quite pronounced dependence of the individual on the temporary encounter group as a form of corporate body. These groups have no purpose other than fostering an interpersonal intimacy and sense of communion. There are no long-term commitments or entanglements. It is hard to avoid the conclusion that the somewhat feverish search for belongingness in such instant and evanescent groups is an attempt to compensate for the lack of common ground and shared activity consequent upon the disruption of institutional structures and organizations. Insofar as the client-centered orientation is identified with such group activities, it would seem as if on the one hand it seeks to strengthen the individual's capacity to function alone and on the other to provide him with moments of community in the essentially contentless activity of transitory groups. In other words, it attempts to meet the human needs of the age.

To summarize, it is suggested that in the Freudian period changes which called into question the foundations of the established ideology that defined ethical behavior called for a reformulation which would be more intellectually defensible yet still consonant with the social order. Freud's solution was an ideology which favored internalized control through the enlargement of a rational awareness. This gave the individual more leeway between the necessary but restricting rules of the social order and the inherently given biological imperatives. Awareness could not bring about complete gratification of the individual's wishes, but it could enable him to make the best compromise. Rogers, in contrast, living in an age when the external order was in decay, when the rules could no longer be relied upon and were likely to change in the middle of the play, internalized the rule making. The individual was urged to consult his own organismic processes when making his decisions. It might be said that in Freud's time the problems were those of an elite, and in Rogers's time they are those of a mass society.

For both Freud and Rogers, flexibility has a high priority. The aim is not simply to change an individual so that he adheres to one position rather than to another, but to change his ability to change. A higher order of change is sought, one involving a more radical process. Change is intimately related to awareness. In the realm of mental events, it is that which is novel and changing that is in awareness, while the routine and recurrent proceed outside it. Consequently, both Freud and Rogers are concerned with fostering an awareness of intrapersonal processes. Awareness and ability to change mean freedom and independence. Both Freud and Rogers seek to increase the freedom of the individual and to make him more independent of those forces which they see as controlling his behavior. For Freud, this is to be achieved by a reflexive awareness watching the self in action, catching it out in its irrational involvements and redirecting its action patterns. For Rogers, it is to be won by a tuning in to bodily sensed meanings following the principle that the organism as a whole is wiser than is a socialized awareness.

STRATEGIC ISSUES

The goal of ideological change is not easily won. In terms of Schein's account, radical change in attitudes and behavior calls for an unfreezing process in which the individual goes through a stage of disorganization. Unless he enters therapy already in a disorganized or "unfrozen" state—in which case the therapist's task will be simplified—the mechanisms of the unfreezing stage must be brought into play. Since most persons entering therapy have not become "unfrozen," though they may have moved some distance toward this condition as a consequence of receiving disconfirming or invalidating feedback on their behavior from their associates in the home, work, or recreational arenas, it will be necessary to implement one or more of the three mechanisms of disconfirmation, induction of guilt and anxiety, and provision of psychological support.

The client-centered method, with its emphasis on a warm, empathic relationship, is particularly appropriate for the provision of psychological support. If the client is being hard pressed in his environment and is under considerable strain in maintaining a stand against the pressure, such support from the therapist may be all that is required to precipitate the collapse of his "defenses" and the completion of the unfreezing stage. A person who has been desperately maintaining a stance against a threatening and hostile social context becomes extremely vulnerable when he meets warmth and understanding. It would seem that such a relationship opens him to the full impact of the disconfirming messages he has been receiving. As regards the psychoanalytic mode of interaction, while it is in principle one of detached neutrality toward the patient and his behavior, in practice it seems to be infused with courtesy, respect, friendliness, and consideration which also constitute support.

The other two mechanisms are more problematic. The psychoanalytic procedure, as will be clear when we consider its detailed implementation, has more resources for the employment of disconfirmation and the induction of guilt and anxiety than has the client-centered approach. The latter is weak in these areas and seems to require that the disconfirmation be provided by some third parties. It is probably for this reason that client-centered therapists show considerable interest in the use of groups. As was apparent from Schein's analysis of coercive persuasion procedures, groups are powerful sources of disconfirmation and reorientation. Their use will be discussed below.

It was argued earlier that the implementation of the attitude change strategy which incorporates the mechanisms of psychological support and positive identification requires for systematic implementation that the operator occupy a position of power relative to the target. The operator will not be able to remain warm and empathic if the target attacks and hurts him at either a physical or symbolic level, or succeeds in making him angry or hostile. The definition of the relationship typically involves the prohibition of physical violence and leaves in the hands of the therapist control over questions of time, duration, and place of meeting. Such steps have the effect of disarming the client. Nevertheless, the long-continued close interaction between therapist and client is fraught with possibilities of the client's bringing into play the strategies by which he has manipulated others in the past and either alienated them or forced them into unproductive power struggles. The therapist requires a systematic procedure that will maintain his relative power position.

In this regard both the psychoanalyst and the client-centered therapist employ the same basic strategy though they differ somewhat in the way they implement it. This is the strategy of establishing and maintaining for themselves the role of audience to the client as performer. In the case of the analyst this is achieved by treating all behavior of the patient as data for interpretation, while in the case of the client-centered therapist the client's behavior is considered only in terms of the feelings that are being expressed and these are reflected back to him. Both procedures are effective in maintaining the patient or client in the performer role with the therapist as the audience that comments on the behavior.

One way of viewing human interaction is to see it in dramaturgical terms. Goffman (1959) has developed and elaborated such a perspective in great detail. Our interest is in only a limited aspect of such a perspective—the relative power positions of the audience and the performer. The audience occupies the position of power. It is in principle one up on the performer. Insofar as it has the right to comment on the performance, it is the judge.

It is necessary to make clear that by audience is meant the person or persons before whom a performance is staged and to whom it is addressed. It is possible for a performance to occur in the presence of others but not be staged for their benefit or addressed to them. Such individuals are treated as nonpersons. Their reactions do not matter. For all practical purposes they are no more than part of the scenery. Slaves, household servants, and children have in different times and places been in such a category, and of course the stronger an individual's position of power, the more indifferent he can be to the reactions of many of those who may witness his performances. An audience, then, is the person or persons for whose benefit the performance is staged and who have the right to comment on it.

In social intercourse between equals the roles of performer and audience alternate. Each has the right to treat the other's behavior as a performance on which to comment. In asymmetrical relationships this is no longer the case. The superior may comment on the performance of a subordinate, but the subordinate may not comment on the performance of the superior. The office boy who comments to the manager on the way the latter performs some function is likely to be put in his place very sharply.

The one-up situation of the audience is to be understood in terms of communication as the means of interpersonal control. A performance constitutes a communication. A comment on the performance is a communication about a communication. That is, it is a metacommunication and thus of a higher logical order than the communication on which it is a comment. The person who metacommunicates defines the relationship. If a metacommunication is allowed to stand, it accords to the person making it the position of power in the relationship.

As we noted in Chapter 3 in discussing thought reform methods used on political prisoners, the prisoner is not charged with specific crimes. If the interrogators were to take that stance, they would be placed in the position of having to make a case against the prisoner. They would be placed in the performer role. This is avoided by placing the onus of discovering his crimes on the prisoner, who is required to review his life and present it in autobiographical form, showing due insight into the nature of his guilt, for the perusal and comment of the interrogator. The latter is thus placed in the position of judge or evaluator of the prisoner's productions and progress toward the new consciousness.

But Freud predated the Chinese Marxists by more than half a century. In developing the technique of free association and combining with it the principle that all behavior was appropriate material for analysis and interpretation, he assigned the patient to the performer role for the duration of the analysis. What this involved will become apparent when the implementation of the psychoanalytic strategy is discussed in more detail.

The client-centered therapist achieves the same effect by the process of treating the client's behavior in terms of the feelings that are sensed in it and conveying these back to the client. All productions of the client, however intended, can be treated in this way. This treatment of each statement by the client as data about the underlying reality of the speaker's feelings, rather than in terms of its truth or falsity, places the therapist in a powerful position. Should the client ask a question or make a complaint or endeavor to challenge the therapist on some point, the latter treats the matter not in terms of what it requires of, or says about, the therapist, but in terms of what it reveals about the client.

As was suggested above, the point at issue can be rephrased in terms of Whitehead and Russell's (1910) theory of logical types, to which Bateson (1972) and others who worked with him, or were influenced by him, at Palo Alto (Haley, 1963; Watzlawick et al., 1967, 1974) have drawn attention. Both the interpretive response and the reflection of feeling response are of a higher logical order than the statements that they purport to be a response to. They are statements about (meta) such statements. Instead of constituting a response within the same frame, they serve to reframe the patient's or client's statement. When the analyst interprets or the client-centered therapist says, "What I hear you saying is . . .," he is taking a stand outside the frame of discourse of the other's statements and reframing them.

THE USE OF GROUPS

Although Freud himself was considerably less than enthusiastic about groups of any kind, regarding them as reducing the general level of rationality to that of the least rational member, group therapy has come to be a feature of the psychoanalytic approach. The introduction of group programs into analytic treatment was a relatively gradual process. Psychoanalytic theory did not predict that groups would constitute an effective way of conducting therapy. Groups were used initially because they seemed to offer a more economical form of treatment, even if they provided a somewhat inferior quality of therapy. It came as something of a surprise that group therapy had some distinctive advantages of its own to offer. The particular nature of the group contribution has remained somewhat vague despite a large body of literature devoted to it. There is a dearth of established theory covering the operations of groups. However, group therapy and its turbulent relative the encounter group have been very widely used over the last three decades.

Client-centered therapy was becoming established as a system of therapy in the late 1940s at a time when the group approach in both therapy and human relations work was beginning to gather momentum. The new system was quick to join in the movement as one of its main avenues of application. Indeed the group medium seemed to be a particularly suitable channel for the use of the client-centered method.

Without attempting to go into theories of group processes, it can be stated that groups have a great capacity for constituting their own realities. This is particularly the case if the group can insulate itself from its social environment. It is relatively easy for a "stranger" group—that is, a group of people who are meeting together for the first time—to come to hold the views and values of a competent leader, particularly if the members were attracted to his teaching in the first instance. Once a group—or the major part of it—adopts an ideology, then it becomes extremely difficult for an individual member to make a stand against that ideology. An emotionally committed group will not allow an individual to maintain an independent stance no matter how willing he may be to allow the remaining members to hold their particular views. A group of true believers cannot tolerate an unbeliever in their midst, for his scepticism threatens their own convictions and his conversion strengthens their faith.

The point has already been made that the use of groups allows for Walton's power and attitude change strategies to be brought to bear simultaneously on the individual. This seems to be of particular relevance for client-centered therapists. The weakness of client-centered therapy as a change-producing strategy is that the therapist is precluded from confronting and invalidating the client's behavior in any forceful way. Consequently, the therapist must rely on other agents to provide the disconfirmation. Someone else must provide the confrontation. In the group this service can be provided by one or more members. Usually the therapist or group leader does not participate in such confrontations, but typically he encourages their occurrence by "picking up" any feelings of resentment, anger, or hostility that one member may intimate with respect to another.

This enables us to account for the discrepancy between the client-centered theory that the ideal social climate for "growth" in the individual is one marked by the absence of threat, and the practice of client-centered group leaders and facilitators of promoting a climate of tension and strain in the interaction between group members.

Although the psychoanalytic orientation is better placed than the client-centered system in respect of the confrontation and invalidation of the patient's behavior, groups provide it also with a useful technology for unfreezing and changing the target.

It is now time to consider the distinctive features of each system.

Psychoanalytic Therapy

Psychoanalysis embodies the doctrine and practice of Freud. Freud's doctrine was that rationality is the means whereby man comes to terms with and exerts control over his biological nature. The goal of life is to approximate as closely as possible to the truly rational. "Where id was, there shall ego be." The task of analysis is to enlighten the patient in respect of this truth, to help him to apply his reason to the understanding of his predicament, and to provide him with a basis for living his life as a rational man.

Such a project implies a teaching role, and psychoanalysis is a long and intense teaching or training exercise. As such, it requires for its successful outcome that the analyst be accorded the authority of a teacher by the patient, that there be something to impart, and that the patient be able and willing to learn.

In the practice of psychoanalysis the analyst's authority or power is granted to him by the patient because the former is seen as being able to provide what the latter wants—a way to a less troubled and more fulfilling existence. The patient comes as the seeker of help and is therefore ready to accept the terms of treatment set down by the analyst, usually without questioning them. Should he refuse to accept the terms, the analyst will refuse to embark on the treatment.

The analyst wants the patient to attend to him and to learn from him over a long period of treatment. He therefore has to ensure that he will be able to maintain his influence in the relationship throughout. To be sure of this, he requires a general strategy and a practical means for implementing it. It is part of the genius of Freud, who had more than a passing interest in military ideas, that he developed a remarkably efficient system for conducting such a teaching campaign.

The basic strategy and implementing it. Freud seems to have been the first to use systematically the audience-performer strategy. No doubt others have employed it as a transitory tactic, but Freud built his system on it. Others, notably Rogers, have developed their own versions of it. The essential features of this strategy have already been outlined. The mode of its implementation can now be considered.

To put the basic audience-performer strategy into practice, it was necessary to do two things:

1. To set up an appropriate definition of the relationship
2. To develop an operational procedure for the tactical implementation of the strategy over the duration of the treatment within the limits imposed by the definition of the relationship

Barton (1974) has provided a detailed and penetrating analysis of the practice of therapy by Freudian analysts. We will follow his account. He sees Freud as having achieved the two objectives listed above primarily by the technique of free association and the interpretation of its products within a highly structured relationship.

DEFINING THE RELATIONSHIP

As a power strategist, Freud seems to have been as sensitive to the significance of physical arrangements, such as seating patterns, as any modern diplomat. In considering how he established the definition of the relationship, it is important to note such aspects as the location of the participants in relation to each other as well as the contractual undertakings regarding the behaviors to be exchanged.

Location of the Participants. In regard to the location of the participants two features of the analytic situation are worthy of attention:

1. The use of the couch
2. The asymmetry of visibility of the participants with respect to each other

1. *The use of the couch.* The use of the couch is a distinctive feature of the analytic procedure. It is an extremely useful device in structuring the complementary aspects of the patient-analyst relationship. The effects on both patient and analyst can be considered in turn:

a. *Effects on the patient.* First, the prone position is essentially a position of helplessness and dependency. The man in a prone position is effectively at the mercy of the man in the upright position and in that sense subordinate to him. Physical contests of a combat nature typically have as their objective the reduction of the opponent to the prone position. Assuming this position can be expected to induce in the patient feelings of loss of potency or control.

A second feature of the prone position is that it has a disorienting effect on the hierarchical ordering system which is a feature of human thought. High and low have a metaphorical application in terms of such matters as relative importance, urgency, and significance. When the individual is placed in a horizontal position, there is some disturbance of this sense of hierarchy. The patient's ability to "think straight" and remain "level-headed" is likely to be affected.

A third feature is the unconventional nature of the posture. Lying prone on a couch in an office, when there is no obvious reason for doing so, is a distinctly unconventional way to carry on a conversation. Insofar as the patient accepts such unconventional behavior as part of the process, he opens the way for accepting other unconventional elements. It becomes difficult for him to assert social norms or rules which he might insist on in ordinary social interaction.

Fourth, lying on a couch promotes relaxation both physically and mentally. There is a tendency for the patient to let go, to lose something of his alert vigilance and generally loosen up.

Fifth, lying down is the normal position for sleeping and hence is conducive to lapsing into reverie and fantasy. The patient tends to become comfortable, at ease, and to some extent out of touch with his environment.

All of these features are conducive to changing the patient from an alert, assertive being facing the real everyday world and coping with it in accordance with his normal repertoire of strategies and tactics, into a relatively helpless, somewhat disoriented person who has lost some of his bearings concerning what is appropriate behavior and is disposed to drift away from the immediate everyday reality.

b. *Effects on the analyst.* First, the analyst in his upright position looking over the recumbent form of the patient laid out before him like a specimen for dissection and analysis is confirmed in his authority and control in the relationship.

Second, since he retains his realistic orientation, his sense of priority and hierarchical ordering of reality, he is reinforced in his status as the person whose judgment is to be trusted. He has his feet on the ground, can look ahead, and can see things in balance and proportion.

The respective postures of patient and analyst thus underline the dependent, helpless, passive, directionless, and disoriented condition allocated to the patient, whose grasp of reality is to be loosened, and the stance of active competence, mastery, and control assigned to the analyst.

The Asymmetry of Interpersonal Visibility. The analyst sits behind the patient in a position where the latter cannot see him but he can observe the patient. This has important consequences.

1. *Consequences in respect of the patient:*

a. The fact that the analyst is not visible, when combined with the further fact that he rarely speaks, and then only in nonjudgmental and nonrevealing terms, means that the patient is deprived almost entirely of social feedback. He has no means of monitoring the effects on his audience of what he is saying or doing. He cannot tell whether his remarks are producing amusement, shock, approval, or disapproval. The subtle cues which enable the individual in ordinary social contacts to keep in touch with the social "reality" and adjust his comments on the basis of the other's reaction are missing. This dearth of feedback has something of the effect of sensory deprivation.

b. The patient is thrown back on his own imagination. Since he gets no external cues to go by, he must draw on his subjective set of expectations and beliefs. He forms fantasies about what the analyst is thinking and doing.

c. In constructing such fantasies, the only source available to him is his store of past experiences. That is to say, he must inevitably cast the analyst in terms of his perceptions of significant figures in the past. His experience of the shadowy ambiguous figure that hovers behind him thus necessarily involves a revival of earlier experiences with significant others. In other words, the invisibility of the analyst tends to maximize the transference effect.

2. *Consequences in respect of the analyst:*

a. The analyst is preserved from scrutiny by the patient. Therefore he does not have to concern himself with maintaining control over his nonverbal expression of thought or feeling, which might provide cues or directions for the patient. He can give his whole attention to the patient.

b. Because of the foregoing the analyst knows that he can safely attribute the patient's attitudes and feelings toward him to the patient's past experiences in relationship with significant figures. The patient orients to him in terms of the way he has learned to orient to parents and similar figures in the past.

As Barton makes clear, the invisibility of the analyst, his comparative silence, and the unrevealing nature of his nonjudgmental comments combine to make the truth of the interpretations of transference overwhelmingly convincing for patient and analyst alike. When the patient in his fantasy has an image of the analyst as a disapproving, rejecting, hostile, dominating figure who despises him, both he and the analyst are confronted with the discrepancy between this picture and the actuality of the emotionally detached, sensitive, skilled professional helper. In Barton's words:

> The truth and reality of the transferential interpretation is enormously convincing within the analytical setting because the patient knows that the analyst is not really the fantastic ogre-father, threat, and so on. The analyst is, after all, the analyst, a professional helper of skill, learning, and sensitivity. "This is the way you saw your father, isn't it?" asks the analyst. In analysis, the patient understands this, and the analyst will always find that this is how the patient felt toward somebody in the past [1974, p. 28].

This invisibility, taken together with the use of the couch, contributes enormously to the power position of the analyst. However, the physical location constitutes only a beginning to, or setting for, the real action, which hinges on the free-association technique.

Contractual Undertakings Regarding the Behaviors to be Exchanged. The patient normally enters analysis because he is dissatisfied with some aspect of his life and wants to improve it. Whether he is suffering from a phobia, has problems of a sexual nature, or has difficulties in interpersonal relationships, what he would most likely want from the analyst is a straightforward technical solution to his problem which would leave him comparatively untouched. However, he is probably aware that rather more will be involved, though he will be more or less unclear as to what it will be.

The initial discussions between analyst and patient, in which an agreement is entered into to embark on the analysis, serve to arrive at a contract as to the behaviors that will be exchanged. Apart from such practical matters as times and duration of appointments and payment of fees, the commitments in the contract tend to be implicit rather than explicit, and their full implications emerge only later.

The basic operating agreement is that the patient will lie on the couch and free-associate. That is, he will express all that comes into his mind no matter how trivial, embarrassing, distressing, nonsensical, or irrelevant it may seem to be. The analyst, on his part, will endeavor to understand the patient and the nature of his predicament from these free associations and convey this understanding to the patient so that the latter may come to understand himself and thereby gain control over his behavior.

The full implications of this apparently simple arrangement emerge only later as both parties become involved in the concrete details of its implementation. A brief outline of these implications can be given now, with further elaboration later as the actual process of analysis is described.

1. *Implications for the patient:*

a. In agreeing to free-associate, the patient commits himself to the role of being a source of data for analysis and interpretation. What he produces or has to say is for consideration within that frame. He generates the data which the analyst will interpret and they both will eventually come to understand.

b. This means that all the productions of the patient are appropriate data for analysis whether they comprise casual greetings or comments, deeply emotional reminiscences or arguments with the analyst. They all fall within the one frame of being material produced for examination, analysis, and interpretation. If the patient were, in effect, to say, "I want to talk off the record for a moment—I just want to give you my ideas on this point," his behavior in doing so would simply be further material for analytic interpretation.

c. It means giving up rational control. The patient, in effect, is asked to refrain from behaving as a thoughtful, responsible, self-correcting being and to function rather as a mine of material for interpretation. He is, as it were, to let material, in the form of his "fantasied" reality, "pour out of him" (Barton, 1974, p. 30) without concern as to the consequences.

d. It means abdicating the right to be, for himself, the center of intentionality, purpose, and meaning. That is, it means relinquishing the right to speak his own truth as truth and regarding his own truth rather as simply material for analysis and interpretation. In short, it means turning himself into an object to be observed.

Implications for the analyst:

a. In asking the patient to relinquish control and rationality in order to turn himself into a data source for the analysis, the analyst implicitly accepts responsibility for providing the rationality, order, and structure necessary for a purposeful enterprise. His function is complementary to that of the patient. As the latter gives up control and direction, so the analyst assumes the obligation of providing them. This gives the latter great power in the relationship. It is he who is deemed to see events in their true light and who has the vision and understanding to carry through the analytic task.

b. In requiring the patient to reveal everything that comes to mind irrespective of its aesthetic, moral, or logical significance, the analyst implicitly undertakes to suspend the ordinary social norms and to refrain from making evaluations in terms of them.

c. The analyst's neutrality toward the patient's productions goes further than refraining from imposing social values or sanctions on them. It involves an equality of regard for everything that the patient produces. That is to say, the analyst does not attend selectively to particular aspects of the patient's productions which happen to fit a favored theory or interest. Instead, the analyst maintains what Barton calls "an evenly hovering attention" capable of entertaining all ideas or images without preconceptions.

d. The analyst is committed to maintaining a cool dispassionate objectivity in which he reflects the patient back to himself realistically, firmly, and without bias. His role is that of the uninvolved professional, unemotional and imperturbable, whose rationality and reasonableness are beyond question and whose only concern is to help the patient to see himself clearly and without distortion.

There are, however, inherent difficulties in fulfillment of the contractual understandings entered into by patient and analyst which we have been considering. The patient will inevitably find that it is not possible for him to turn himself completely into an object such that his behavior is only data for analysis. This inability will manifest itself as resistance. The analyst on his part will find himself straying from the path of a strictly impersonal objectivity and taking a human interest in the patient.

Beyond this there is also inherent in the understandings a degree of paradox. The patient is to be regarded as a source of data for analysis. His perceptions, beliefs, and values have no status as a perspective on reality. They exist merely as data concerning his version of "reality," which is the object under dissection. Yet simultaneously the patient is treated as a rational being who shares something of the analyst's reality and whose learnings and insights under the analyst's tutelage have high validity. Here again is the confusion of logical levels of the type discussed by Russell and Whitehead (1910) to which attention has been drawn above. It is a confusion of levels which allows the analyst to switch context so that when the patient disagrees with the analyst, his behavior is treated within the frame of data for analysis, but when he is docile and agrees with the analyst's point, the frame no longer applies.

THE OPERATIONAL PROCEDURE

The analytic relationship is initially structured or defined by the agreement that the patient will lie on the couch and free-associate and the

analyst will sit out of sight and interpret the products of the free association. The implications of this arrangement have been outlined. The
unfolding of the relationship can now be considered.

Interpretation. The central element of the analytic intervention is the
act of interpretation. It is by interpretation that the patient will be led to
understand the basis of his behavior and provided with a means for
achieving control over it. The whole analytic strategy is oriented toward
maximizing the efficiency and impact of the interpretation process. Barton puts it well:

> By interpretation is meant any statement by the analyst which points to a
> way of understanding the actual motivations that inspire the patient's activi-
> ties.... In a preliminary interpretation the analyst may do nothing more
> than connect one behavior with another ("I notice that you smile when you
> say that")....
>
> The interpretation could also be more elaborately constructed. Noticing
> the patient's smile, the analyst might say: "You know, it's very interesting that
> whenever you say something that is a little bit nasty to anyone you smile. After
> you've been a little bit aggressive, you become *very* agreeable and nice, and I
> notice it here. I wonder if when you were with your father you discovered
> that the only way to keep him from attacking you was to become more
> sociable, amiable, in this kind of smiling, passive way."... This rather elabo-
> rate interpretation connects a whole pattern of activity in the patient's life - a
> certain kind of smiling passivity - to both a behavior in the analytic situation
> and to a relationship in his past life as well. Thus, current events in the
> session can be connected with events outside the situation, with events during
> recent years, and even with early childhood in one differentiated interpreta-
> tive construction....
>
> For the patient, the interpretative act and its incipient beginnings in such
> little connecting remarks point also to the root meaning of the analysis. To
> the degree that it rings true, makes sense, and vivifies, it is in the interpreta-
> tion that the patient discovers the fundamental point of the analysis. He
> begins to understand himself analytically and to anticipate being able to
> control the behaviors that fall under the interpretation. In a moment he sees:
> "Yes, I really do get this nice, smiling, benign attitude when I am a little
> annoyed. It really has been that way all my life, and I really did learn it first
> from my father." Seeing sense and daylight, he hopes now to be able to
> control this behavior and to have himself back in his own hands [1974, pp.
> 33-34].

But as Barton goes on to point out, it is one thing to have an intellectual insight into what one is doing and quite another to put it into
practice in the everyday reality of coping with people and events. The
patient discovers, as Freud discovered early in his practice of
psychoanalysis, that an intelligent comprehension of what is happening
can exist without the ability to change the behavior.

The interpretation provides, at an abstract level, a vista of possible applications, but does not in itself establish the close link with the concrete ongoing behavior that is necessary if there is to be a change at the level of action. The patient has not yet seen how automatic and autonomous his behavior is. He has not come to appreciate at a concrete feeling level his dread of his own aggression or his panic before someone else's anger, or to experience how helpless and dependent on the approval of others he makes himself.

For the necessary connections to be made, they have to be seen in relation to the down-to-earth daily occurrences in the patient's life. Again to quote Barton:

> For the term "passive acquiescent tendency" to be meaningful, he has to become aware of, for example, his tendency to swallow often when someone else is assertive, his failure to object when someone pushes ahead of him in line, his hesitation to ask a waiter or clerk for attention, his tendency to wait for others to start a conversation, his tendency to become anxious and sweaty instead of angry, and so on. He must see and interpret all this as "fear of aggression," "castration anxiety," or whatever. This must occur repeatedly and be seen and understood by him repeatedly [p. 35].

As the whole range of such behaviors becomes subsumed under this interpretation, a disrupting thing begins to happen. The reflexive awareness of what he is doing interferes with the performance of the act, just as reflexion on any skilled movement interferes with the smooth performance of the movement. The patient begins to catch himself in the act of being 'passively acquiescent" and has the experience of "Here I go again" in time to change his behavior. This is called the "working-through process" and may be regarded as the operationalizing of the insight in day-to-day living.

Resistance and Transference. The discussion of the role of interpretation is necessary for an understanding of the analytic procedure and its objectives. It is to be noted that we have merely touched upon it. Interpretation proceeds ever further back in the history of the patient. However, for the purposes of the analysis of influence in therapeutic systems, the more interesting features are those concerning the interactions between patient and analyst. Here are to be found the phenomena of resistance and transference.

Resistance. Resistance is said to occur when the patient blocks in the production of the stream of free association. The patient stops talking. He claims that nothing comes to mind. Resistance may also be exhibited by an inability on the part of the patient to recognize the validity of an interpretation. It will suffice to discuss resistance in the form of association blockage.

The patient has undertaken to let his thoughts and feelings pour out of him unimpeded by conscious control—that is, to treat his thoughts and feelings simply as data to be processed by the analyst, who is to be an impersonal, objective, dispassionate analyzer of data in the image of a highly complex computer.

It is the inability of the patient to play this role, particularly his inability to see the therapist as no more than an information-processing machine, that underlies the resistance.

Resistance is exhibited when the patient who has been associating freely suddenly stops and says that nothing comes to mind. According to classical psychoanalysis, the stoppage occurs because something has come to mind which conflicts with the patient's scheme of values. It would reveal him in an unacceptable light if expressed. He is protected from shame or embarrassment by his mind going blank.

Three aspects of resistance can be noted:

1. Resistance against revealing the threatening feeling or thought occurs because it conflicts with the patient's own standards, which were originally learned from his parents or other primary socializing figures and now constitute part of the framework through which he structures his world. He cannot accept the thought or feeling as being part of him. It violates his deeply ingrained sense of decency, morality, propriety, or logic.

2. Resistance against revealing the threatening feeling or thought occurs as resistance against revealing it to the analyst, who is now seen as the feared figure from whom the patient withheld such material earlier in life. This resistance against the analyst as a substitute for an earlier significant figure in the patient's life is of great significance, for it constitutes a powerful means for the analyst to make interpretations that are virtually irrefutable in the context of the analysis. It is this aspect of resistance that is critically important for the analytic process, and it will be treated at some length below.

3. While the two foregoing aspects of resistance are recognized and utilized in the analytic system, there is a third aspect which may be noted briefly in passing but which will come up again. This is a resistance to the patient role in which the patient is cast. He is required to suspend judgment and to free-associate, thereby turning himself into an object for analysis, and this he resists, often arguing with the analyst. Barton, discussing this, says:

> To relinquish the right to speak his own truth . . . is temporarily at least to give up his sense of being a person. To become nothing but a source of analytic data in need of interpretation; a poor, incomplete, amorphous, confused, determined, helpless, souce of data; an object buffeted by the winds and tides of life within, unable to steer his own course—to become all this is something which many resist. It may well be that in so resisting, the patient is not always mistaken. He may sometimes speak from a more comprehensive

vision of reality and a better grasp of the truth of human life than the analyst himself. By refusing this reduction, he may be trying radically to maintain his integrity [1974, p. 42].

In this departure from his expository role, Barton is hinting at some complexities in the task assigned the patient. As indicated earlier, these complexities are best understood in terms of the theory of logical types, which inspired the concept of the double bind (Bateson, Jackson, Haley, and Weakland, 1956). The patient is asked to suspend judgment and lose control, but to do this he has to exercise control. This is to be placed in a paradox of the same nature as that imposed by the instruction "Be spontaneous." The logical implications of this are far reaching.

Resistance and the transference experience. The patient knows, as he lies on the couch free-associating, that the analyst is a cool, objective, dispassionate analyzer of data whose task is to give him back to himself. But experientially the analyst is cast in the role of a person who looks at him or, to use Sartrean terminology, holds him in his gaze. We might say the analyst constitutes an audience for him.

As the tabooed thoughts, desires, and impulses find their way into the association stream, the patient blocks because he expects to lose the respect or arouse the dislike of the analyst. Whenever this happens, the analyst knows both that the patient is withholding something and that he is perceiving the analyst as someone other than the strictly neutral objective professional that he is. That is, the resistance is occurring because the patient is casting the analyst in the role of a significant figure from the former's past. The analyst has become the forbidding parent in the patient's fantasy.

The patient's continuing expectation of incurring the analyst's anger and hostility is the transference and constitutes the major resistance to bringing the unconscious into consciousness. The analyst's invisibility, silence, and adult position, in contrast to the visibility and childlike position of the patient, promote fantasies that recreate those parents whose disapproval led originally to his losing contact with some parts of his life. This provides the basis for helping the patient to look at rather than from the distorted stance. In Barton's words:

> As it is brought to life again, this transference ground is *the* ground on which the fundamental analytic movement must be made. The patient does not merely remember his past but recreates it in the open space into which the analyst invites him. Always in the background of the analysis is the analyst's promise to assist in unravelling this complicated web, to be a reliable guide who has travelled down these paths before and knows the way. With this trust in the background, the patient is able to amplify and relive those buried aspects of his life. Usually, though, the first movements involve a transference and a resistance to the process of remembering. Instead of

remembering, his natural tendency is to relive and repeat. Instead of remembering his tendency to fight every authority, he fights the authority of
the analyst.

The analyst must show the patient repeatedly that this is a transference
until the patient is unable to resist the authority without remembering that
this is just like his fight against his father. After a while, repeating the rebel-
lion becomes increasingly difficult. The behavior itself, of becoming impo-
tently angry in the face of authority, is now accompanied by a reflective
awareness in the form of an analytic interpretation [p. 44].

This reflexive process makes the patient's behavior an object of observation for him rather than the means whereby he lives out his wonted
axioms. In Polanyi's terms (1962, 1967), his perceptions of others and of
his world become events to attend to rather than to attend from. In this
process, spontaneous feelings of anger, hostility, and the like are cut off
and changed by this process of self-observation. As he looks at his experience and comes to analyze and interpret it in the new analytic frame,
the nature of the experience itself is changed.

In his relationship with the analyst, the emerging analytic way of
viewing his experiences brings about a subtle but marked change. He
now has some distance between him and this relationship - it too has
become something of an object to be looked at from above rather than
lived out from within. When he begins to experience some fear or anger
toward the analyst, he sees that it is just another example of an irrational
survival from the past and has nothing to do with the reality of the cool,
dispassionate, accurately understanding professional helper. As it comes
to carry conviction, this is a deeply reassuring experience. The patient
now has a handle on his situation. He has learned how to live the hour
with the analyst and, in principle, how to live all the other hours of his
life as well.

Barton points out what he calls the bifurcated—or twinned—
consciousness of both analyst and patient that constitutes an inevitable
feature of reflexive awareness. From the analyst's point of view, the
patient on entering analysis has a false consciousness. He is viewing life
from within a perspective acquired in childhood which has given him a
distorted outlook on reality. The task is to get to the roots of the distortion and help the patient to grasp its nature and thereby to gain a more
accurate awareness of the real nature of events. The true meanings of
the patient's behavior can be revealed only through the highly attuned
ear of the analyst.

The approach of the analyst to the understanding of the patient's
experiences is somewhat analogous to the approach of a physicist to an
understanding of the structure of matter. In both cases it is necessary to
move away from the immediately given. What is really happening is
inferred through the constructions of the scientist-analyst, who pene-

trates the veils of the immediately given to the hidden reality that lies beyond the commonsense vision. The consequences of this stance are outlined by Barton:

> This formal standpoint greatly emphasizes the analyst's capacity as comprehending theoretical intellect and schematizer of reality. Schematizing the patient removes the analyst from immediate observation of the here and now and reinforces his cool, surgical distance. He replaces the immediately given with the theoretically constructed. The analyst stresses finding the truth, reaching an understanding, comprehending, constructing, and reconstructing, making coherent lines of interconnections between the different aspects of the data which the patient speaks to him. He lends himself formally, by contract, so to speak, as agent-intellect, as the person who can make intelligibility live.
>
> The analyst's attitude is therefore largely determined by his characteristic style of interpretation. The basic mode of analytic interpretation not only gives a specific content to the analysis but also determines that for him, finally, everything in the analytic situation is seen in the light of "fostering-the-optimal-truth-within-the-analytic-framework." At the same time, this defines as negative everything that impedes the analytic interpretive task. If the patient's feelings interfere, this is called resistance. If the therapist's feelings interfere, this is incompetence or countertransference [1974, pp. 48–49].

The analytic task thus requires that the analyst treat the patient's behavior as having no validity in its own right, but as being relevant only for the light it throws on the fundamental reality behind the surface appearance. Truth exists in the analysis only as the truth revealed by the analytic method. Consequently, insofar as the analyst adheres fully to the principles of the analytic scheme, he would exhibit no feelings of warmth, compassion, or sorrow or other distinctly human response toward the patient.

However, the analyst is also a human being who inhabits a world of other human beings with whom he lives out an everyday existence in social interaction. This is the analyst as a unique social being with his own particular social adjustment to his situation. While the involvement of the analyst at this level on a personal-social basis of friendship with the patient would constitute technical incompetence or countertransference, nevertheless some softening of the hard and formal working relationship occurs. The analyst will, when the occasion warrants it, as in bereavement, express his sorrow or other appropriate feelings. And inevitably in their long-continued interaction there will be many occasions on which the analyst as a person with feelings and his own private existence will have an impact on the person of the patient. While, within the analytic frame, the true consciousness is that of analytic "reality," there exists side by side with it a moment-to-moment consciousness. While this second consciousness is relegated within the analytic frame to the status of epiphenomenon, it nevertheless constitutes an essential basis for the establishment and maintenance of the working relationship. The ordinary relationship with its notes of friendship, tender regard, cooperation, sincerity, care, and practical reasonableness is an essential ingredient of the analysis and the nature of the outcome, but there is no way to incorporate such elements in the formulation of the analytic scheme.

The patient on his part begins with an everyday consciousness. As the analysis proceeds, he is led to doubt it. He learns to see through what he once thought were his motives. He questions what once made sense to him and comes to look for the real reasons for his behavior. Commenting on the paradoxical process of the patient's conversion, Barton tells us, "He thus undermines his own ground of reason and sense making while presuming that he can and does make sense through the development of his budding analytic consciousness. He presupposes the power to see, comprehend, and validly understand by showing to himself, through the analytic perspective, that he does not see, comprehend or validly understand" (p. 52).

We have, then, two levels of reality, or two universes of understanding. One is the world of everyday events, while the other is the constructed world of the psychoanalytic schema. The analytic project has as its object the enlightenment of the patient in the analytic view of truth and reality so that it becomes an essential part of his way of making sense of his world. In short, it involves a radical ideological change which is closely related to, and has profound effects upon, the patient's strategy of living.

The life style that emerges is characterized by a somewhat bland mode of responding to life's challenges. Those persons who have undergone psychoanalysis tend to equate emotional behavior with irrationality and to view with suspicion any ideals held with great conviction. Strong commitment to religious, political, or social causes is likely to be regarded as an expression of personal problems. Psychoanalyzed persons with their detached, onlooking preoccupation with intrapsychic life, give an impression of being calm and controlled rather than exciting persons.

The Client-centered System

The client-centered system of psychotherapy has more the quality of a stance or orientation than of a developed system of theory and practice. Its distinguishing feature is its focus on the internal frame of reference of the client, and its most characteristic component is the reflexion of feeling response.

Because the client-centered position is relatively fluid, it is not easy to define its boundaries. Barton (1974) discusses two forms of client-centered therapy - that of the mainstream version with its emphasis on feeling and that of Curran (1952), who, from a Thomist rationalist tradition, would emphasize rather perceiving, reasoning, and judging. Another variation is provided by Truax and Carkhuff (1967), who adopt a more distinctively training orientation.

The relatively rudimentary level of theorizing allows for the development of alternative ways of formulating the effective ingredients of the therapy process, and though these have much in common, relatively subtle differences in phrasing may prove to be of considerable theoretical moment. Hart and Tomlinson (1970) give a cross section of the thinking of writers who identify themselves with this orientation, and it is apparent that there are some important differences, at least in emphasis, among the contributors. Rogers's own writing tends to be couched in language that is forceful and persuasive, rather than precise, and his views appear to have undergone some change over the years. It is therefore unlikely that any statement of the client-centered approach will satisfy all who identify themselves with it.

Since Barton has provided a lucid account which brings out the broad features of what may be called mainstream client-centered therapy, it is proposed to first outline the process in his terms and keep for subsequent comment any reservations or elaborations on his description.

THE RATIONALE

The client-centered system, like many other systems of therapy, grew out of practice. Practice preceded theory. Indeed, for many years Rogers and his students worked with little more than a set of hunches that by attending to the client and trying to understand his perception of his world, the therapist would move the client toward a more realistic appreciation of his situation, more harmonious relationships with others, and a more fulfilled life. Why such attempts to achieve a meeting of minds should have therapeutic effects remained something of a puzzle, and, during its first decade (1940–1950), a recurrent criticism of the client-centered approach was that it was a method of treatment without an explanation as to how it worked—or, to put it in less kindly terms, that its practitioners did not know what they were doing.

The emerging theory, which had taken shape by 1954 and was finally published (Rogers, 1959), is therefore to be understood as an attempt to integrate observations arrived at in the practice of therapy, rather than as a set of principles which provided the basis for the development of a method of conducting therapy. The point is made because, in a different conceptual context, a quite different explanatory system might well have evolved. The emphasis, for instance, might well have been on the inter-connectedness of client and therapist which is so obviously promoted by the receptive listening that characterizes the process, rather than on individuality and the self, which is the central feature of the theory. Rogers, like all thinkers who have a new vision, saw it from within the intellectual context in which he was embedded and, given his cultural background and the prevailing view of psychotherapy at the time, framed his explanation in terms of the individual. Once he had done so, the theory acted back on the practice and subsequent practice on the theory in a formative process.

Basic to Rogerian theory is a profound faith in a force toward growth or actualization in the individual, and, for that matter, in the universe as a whole. When the individual acts as a whole, allowing the totality of his current experiencing at all levels to enter into his decisions, plans, and actions, then he can be relied upon to function effectively, both in his own interests and in the interests of others on whom his life impinges. Problems arise when the individual functions in terms of only part of his total being by excluding some of his experiencing from awareness and from consideration in his decisions, plans, and actions. Such part functioning arises as a consequence of the socialization process, in which the individual learns that some aspects of his behavior are not accepta-ble, while harboring such behavior. The practice of psychotherapy is intended to restore the capacity of the individual to function as a total being by a nonselective valuing of all aspects of his person, thereby repairing the effects of the conditional or selective valuing to which the individual had been subjected in his earlier years.

THE THERAPY PROCESS

While client-centered therapy is much less elaborately structured than psychoanalysis, it can be approached on the same basis. The interaction can be considered in terms of (1) non-verbal and (2) verbal elements.

Nonverbal Elements. In client-centered therapy, perhaps the most distinctive feature is the intense concentration on the person of the client. In Freudian therapy, the focus is on the productions of the pa-tient as data for showing how the reality of the past relives itself in the present. In Adlerian therapy, the participants direct their attention to an analysis of the behaviors of the client as component elements pointing to the underlying life style. Similarly in other systems, there is a focusing on the client's acts or productions as pointers to some reality behind the superficial appearances. In client-centered therapy, however, it is the client as a feeling, experiencing being that is under the searchlight.

Typically, during the interaction "the therapist ... looks, listens, and otherwise attends to the client; the client characteristically looks into space or at some object in the room so as to focus on himself" (Barton, 1974, p. 186). The seating arrangements are such as to emphasize equality and to allow the participants to look, either at each other or away from each other, easily and naturally. Ordinarily, as Barton indicates, the therapist's gaze is on the client, while the latter's gaze is directed elsewhere.

Verbal Elements. In its pure form, client-centered verbal interaction consists of the client exploring his feelings with the therapist responding by verbalizing his understanding of the feelings expressed. The therapist "keeps in touch" with the client's feelings. A client-centered therapist likes to think of himself as being "right there" with the client, particularly when the latter is experiencing some very profound emotions. It is not uncommon, within this orientation, for the therapist to use the metaphor of being a companion to the client on his journey into his "depths."

Irrespective of what the client says, the therapist's response is in terms of the feelings he detects in what is said. Barton sees the essence of the client-centered message as being embodied in the three words, each deserving of its own emphasis, (1) *you*, (2) *really*, (3) *feel*.

1. *You.* As Barton points out, the client, when he enters therapy, "does not start by saying *I* with the kind of underlined emphasis that the therapist gives to the *you*. Rather, he discusses his world as it surrounds him, the externals of his life, the people and things that he experiences as troublesome. He describes the difficulties of his work or his social problems and feelings as if they belonged out there in the world. He offers, in short, a complex panorama of statements which describe his situation, other people in it, behaviors, external objects, and so on, in response to which the therapist uniformly responds *you*" (pp. 190–191).

The therapist, in other words, always brings the issue back to the client. He does this smoothly and unobtrusively but nevertheless relentlessly. Even if he does not actually use the word, his concentration on the other's feelings of necessity also conveys the *you*. There can be no sidetracking into a discussion of the content material, of what other people are doing, or of how the world is functioning. The issue is always brought back to the *you* "of *self* attitudes and feelings" (p. 191).

The *you* is the focus of the therapist's attention. "The therapist's task is an attunement to, a reflection, amplification, and expression of 'you.' He wishes to express with purity, fullness, and accuracy the 'you' of his client" (p. 190).

In time the *you* of the therapist becomes the *I* of the client. The client begins to speak of himself as a force in his situation. There is a centering on self as the locus of causation in the client's life. The client speaks increasingly of being the determiner of his own destiny. In the successful case we find the client at the end of therapy making such statements as "I don't know what I am going to do, but I do know that *I'm* going to do it."

2. *Really.* When the therapist says *you,* he is aiming at the "*real you.*" In the client-centered terminology—and pervading the broad area of humanistic psychology on which Rogers has had a major impact—there is constant use of such terms as *real, authentic,* and *genuine.* Beneath the superficial veil of social interchange, there is the realm of the *real.* Just as for the Freudian there is, beneath the patient's conscious living out of his life, the "real" reality of the past reliving itself, so for the Rogerian there is beneath the façade of social give and take of lived-out roles a true, authentic, organismically experiencing *you* whom the therapist addresses and strives to reach. Barton expresses it well:

> The therapist is always reaching for and trying to express the client's real self, or as close an approximation of this as he can. This "you" which is "real" is declared by the therapist to be fundamental in virtually his every response. In this way, together with his exquisitely concentrated attention, the therapist concretizes his theoretical lived-faith that the pathway out of the blocked or inadequate life lies in increased contact with the real self. It is obvious that this emphasis on the real adds weight, force, and power to the therapist's impact. The client, a somewhat lost, confused, not too well ordered person, has typically never met anyone with such a powerfully directed focus and lived-belief. As already indicated, the client's position as a failed person hoping to find his way also lends substance to the therapist's power. It is obvious to the client that he is in some way fragmented and at cross purposes with himself [pp. 191–192].

Thus the therapist's constant firm message that the individual's problems arise from loss of contact with the real self falls on receptive soil. It makes good sense to the client that he is out of touch with his own roots, that he does not really know himself, and hence he is responsive to the therapist's continuing concern with helping him to know his real self. Furthermore, as Barton points out, "It must also be kept in mind that the concentrated attentiveness to his person, concerns, and his feelings is an extraordinary event in the client's life, naturally increasing his sense of substantiality and reality and lending dignity to his self and his concerns" (p. 192).

3. *Feel.* The word *feel* is the hallmark of client-centered therapy. Just as the therapist constantly brings everything back to the *you* of the client, so also does he bring it to the realm of feeling. The client is not encouraged to theorize or speculate in a cognitive way. Should he do so, the therapist will respond in terms of feelings rather than in terms of the validity or adequacy of the theory. Should the client reject the response as not adequately describing what he is feeling, the therapist will try again until he has caught the flavor of what the client is trying to express.

As the therapist sees it, the client is, in greater or lesser degree, alienated from his feelings or not clearly aware of them, but he, the client, is the only available guide into their realm, and he must be trusted to judge whether the travelers are on the right path or straying from it. In other words, the client can be trusted to recognize his feelings if the therapist can put them into words. So the client speaks, and the therapist points his response at the context of feeling from which he senses the former's remarks to have come.

The ability of the therapist to articulate the vague and inchoate feelings toward which the client is groping is often a source of astonishment to the latter, who is likely to say, "That's it exactly, that's just what I was trying to say." Or he may comment, "You seem to know me better than I know myself."

Such sensitive and skillful tuning in on, and reflecting back to the client of, his feeling flow is a powerful force in convincing him that the therapist knows what he is about and in keeping him focused on his feeling self.

COMMUNITY OF FEELING.

In an attempt to spell out his perception of himself as a therapist in the actual interaction with the client during the session, Rogers (1955) has provided us with a highly subjective account of the nature of the experience:

> I launch myself into the therapeutic relationship having a hypothesis, or a faith, that my liking, my confidence, and my understanding of the other person's inner world, will lead to a significant process of becoming. I enter the relationship not as a scientist, not as a physician who can accurately diagnose and cure, but as a person, entering into a personal relationship. . . .
>
> I let myself go into the immediacy of the relationship where it is my total organism which takes over and is sensitive to the relationship, not simply my consciousness. I am not consciously responding in a planful or analytic way, but simply in an unreflective way to the other individual, my reaction being based (but not consciously) on my total organismic sensitivity to this other person. I live the relationship on this basis [pp. 267–268].

The outcome of such responding is the development of a relationship

> . . . without any type of diagnostic or analytic thinking, without any cognitive or emotional barriers to a complete "letting go" in understanding. When there is this complete unity, singleness, fullness of experiencing in the relationship, then it acquires the "out-of-this-world" quality which many therapists have remarked upon, a sort of trace-like feeling in the relationship from which both the client and I emerge at the end of the hour, as if from a deep well or tunnel [p. 268].

Rogers tells us here what the therapist is striving to be in the relationship with the client—someone so closely attuned to the feeling life of the other that he obliterates himself except to the extent that he is a reflexion of that feeling life. As the therapist does so, the client with whom he is resonating is likewise reduced. In Barton's words, what they are both living out, in their moments of community of existence, is a specialized way of being "as feeling-life, organismic-life, as a bodily life of sense feeling" (1974, p. 193). Barton goes on:

> On both sides of the therapeutic dialogue, therefore, there is an enormous emphasis on a pathic, bodily, sense-feeling life, and real communication is understood to exist at that level. Thus, the therapist, putting aside his judgments, opinions, and reactions (at least within his formal project), suffers pathically with the feelings that come from the client. "I suffer in, through, and for the other. By expressing this shared feeling-life as clearly as I can, he comes to experience his own feelings more clearly." This shared pathic involvement means that, sometimes to a lesser degree, the therapist participates at an organic bodily level in the pathos of the client's feeling-life, and to the degree that he has reduced himself to attunement to this organismic bodily life the distinction between his feelings and his client's feelings seemingly disappears [pp. 193–194].

It is not surprising, therefore, to note that the client-centered therapist tends to replace the word *you* with the word *I* spoken for and with the client. In echoing the client's sense of distrust in someone on whom he is dependent, the therapist may say with heavy emphasis, "*I* don't really trust him," rather than "*You* feel you can't trust him." That is, both client and therapist come to use the first person as if they both speak from a more fundamental unity of being that transcends their separateness. As Barton puts it:

> When, in moments of supreme empathic understanding and communion, the client-centered therapist says *I* for the client, he becomes to an enormous degree an affectively feeling, sensing, organic, bodily, resonative communion with the suffering and feeling flesh of the other. *I* may be expressed in dramatic utterance as well. The therapist may plead for the client: "Mother, mother, I need you," or "It's so damned lonely." In fact, whenever the therapist is powerfully moved by the client's affective life, he speaks the *I* or *you* ambiguously, as both he and the client are involved at the "communion-of-bodies" level [p. 194].

As Barton goes on to point out, the ability of the therapist to find the words to express the client's feeling more accurately than the client can do himself is understandable

> ... because the therapist is a specialist in this kind of empathic attunement. In the communion of bodies, the therapist feels the client's sense-feeling bodily life more clearly and intensely than the client does himself. Thus, the

client may express but the barest hint of sadness to the therapist, who amplifies it back as, "Sounds as if you're feeling pretty forlorn, is that it?" Such amplification and underlining of a mood increases the client's experience of the mood so that he can insert himself more fully into it [p. 195].

The objective of this intense effort on the part of the therapist is to reach and bring out the basic natural given but unrealized being of the client. For the therapist, the client is one who is misliving his life because he is leading it in terms of introjected cultural values rather than in terms of his own inward reality-oriented, self-regulating, information-processing system. At the core of the client there is the real organismic experiential self. The therapist's role is that of a catalytic agent, acting through an attunement to this ongoing process, whose only influence on the client is that of providing the warmly accepting environment for the unfolding of the client's pregiven real or natural self.

The therapist's presence, however, is not, and cannot be, simply the nonimposing ethereal warmth that bathes the client, as its proponents claim. In his concentrated attentiveness and attunement to the feeling life of the other, the therapist communicates not only his warmth and empathy but also the reality of, and priority in significance of, that feeling life. He does not crudely assert the reality of the feeling self, but lives it intensively in his relationship with the client. His every response bears witness to his convictions and, in total, constitutes a powerful force in transforming the client's understanding of his own being. Throughout the interaction, as Barton puts it, "the feeling-self . . . is developed, fostered, articulated, differentiated, spoken of, and spoken to" and in this way "the ideology of client-centered therapy is transmitted and made into a faith to be lived" (p. 204).

Therapist and client alike are unaware of how much they have, between them, co-constituted this organismic feeling self. To them it has a reality of being, in an absolute sense, independent of its location in time and space, of others, and of culture. They ignore the profound teaching effect of their intense interaction, just as they ignore the power position of the therapist and the extraordinary extent to which the perspective transmitted is that of the therapist. In Barton's words:

> . . . the client-centered theorist-therapist is totally enraptured within the natural attitude by the purity, depth, and intensity of the feelings emerging from within the client-over-there. He is *in principle,* by virtue of his theory, its biases, and the very enrapture of client-centeredness, unable to notice the fundamental structure of what he is doing. He can only understand himself as understanding, empathizing, or expressing the feelings that belong to the client. He cannot understand himself *in principle* as transformer, selector, emphasizer, indoctrinator of ideology, teacher of theory, convinced expressive articulator of a view of reality, life, and values or understand the actual centering of the process in that space-between shaped by client and therapist

together. In short, he is not able to make focal, thematic, and theoretical what is actually going on in the "lived-world-space" between his client and himself. . . .

The peculiarity of the specilization, then, is that on the one hand it provides a way to go, a focus to maintain, a pathway of openness between client and therapist, while at the same time it creates a fundamental structural blindness to reality for the therapist and ultimately for the client as well. That is, reality is present to both under the rubrics and style of an ideologized, narrowed, and specialized vision of such a nature that most of it must be systematically ignored. Since the reality which must be overlooked is precisely that which is lived between them, this is a serious matter [pp. 245–246].

Barton is not arguing that the client has no feeling life any more than he would argue that the past did not play a part in shaping the responses of the analyst's patient. He does not claim that Rogers and his colleagues have managed to create feelings out of thin air. People do have feeling experiences. What he argues is that there has been a selective emphasis on an aspect of the client's being which, insofar as it gives to it a priority in significance as constituting what is "really" real in the person's existence, reduces the richness and complexity of the reality of existence as this is lived at the human level.

Such a selective emphasis is not confined to the client-centered endeavor. It is an inevitable consequence of the attempt by the conscious mind to grasp and order the complexity of the given world. The attempt to explain of necessity reduces the richness of that which it attempts to explain. It means viewing the world in a specialized, narrow way whether that way be the way of the physicist, the economist, the historian, or the psychologist. When Skinner explains behavior in terms of environmental reinforcement contingencies and a psychoanalyst explains Skinner's theory in terms of the latter's defensiveness against his own inner unconscious impulses, we have such reduction carried to extreme lengths; but it is of the nature of the scientific technical endeavor that the domain of investigation must be viewed in a specialized way. The scientist, as he analyzes the phenomena and formulates his theory, is usually only very vaguely aware of the extent to which his "discovery" is a creative act. He believes that he has only found what is already there, and fails to see how much his specialized way of viewing the world structures what is "found." As Barton puts it, "Reality always speaks the language one knows best, at least when it follows one's systematic, theoretical biases. To be fascinated only by that which presents itself as an 'in-itself' is to forget the perceiving consciousness as a co-participant in the shaping of reality" (p. 248).

While psychotherapists share with all other scientists, technologists, and other specialists in this tendency to ignore the extent to which a specialized approach shapes the phenomena as perceived, their position has special features which are of the greatest significance. The physicist or chemist dealing with inert matter does not have to concern himself with the effect of his stance on the behavior of the object he is investigating. The situation for the therapist is far otherwise. He is observing and trying to understand someone who is observing and trying to understand him—someone who is noting aspects of him of which he is himself unaware. We have already seen, in the discussion of ideological change, that persons undergoing such change co-constitute reality with their interacting partner to the extent of remembering events which never occurred. That the co-constitution phenomenon is an important factor in the intense and long-continued therapeutic interaction can hardly be questioned. Yet the literature of the therapies involved is remarkably silent on any such possibility. In Barton's words:

> ... none of the orientations is able to penetrate to the significance of having an orientation or a theory of therapy. None of the languages developed within each special group is able to speak to the fact that the development of a special language *is* the cure, or at least a fundamental structure of the help. Each theorist enters into his specialization more or less blindly, living out his conviction unaware of the power of the convinced living-out. The theorist-therapist is radically unaware of the principle of co-constitution; hence, for him, the patient *is as he is.* This patient's independent being, this "being-in-itself," is understood as merely revealed, not transformed, by the theorist-therapist [pp. 244–245].

SOME RESERVATIONS AND ELABORATIONS

As was indicated in the introductory remarks on the client-centered approach, this system is a somewhat fluid one and it is difficult to formulate it in terms that will be acceptable to all its advocates. In this regard, one difficulty is that none of the exponents of this orientation impresses as speaking with a single voice on the process of therapy. In this regard Rogers is no exception.

Like Freud, Rogers has written much, and like Freud, he emphasizes different points when dealing with different contexts. Much of his writing is closely in accord with the very able description provided by Barton. Thus if we take one of his recent publications, we find him saying:

> At its best the therapist is so much inside the private world of the other that she can clarify not only the meanings of which the client is aware but even those just below the level of awareness. When she responds at such a level the client's reaction is of this sort: "Perhaps that *is* what I've been trying to say. I haven't realized it, but yes, that's how I *do* feel!" [1977, p. 11].

And a little farther on:

Over the years I have come to see more and more clearly that the process of change in the client is a reciprocal of the attitudes of the therapist.

As the client finds the therapist listening acceptantly to her feelings, she becomes able to listen acceptantly to herself—to hear and accept the anger, the fear, the tenderness, the courage that is being experienced. As the client finds the therapist prizing and valuing even the hidden and awful aspects which have been expressed, she experiences a prizing and liking of herself. As the therapist is experienced as being real, the client is able to drop façades, to more openly *be* the experiencing within.

. . . As the client is more acceptant of self, the possibility of being in command of self becomes greater and greater. The client possesses herself to a degree that has never occurred before. The sense of power is growing . . . Life is now in her hands, to be lived as an individual [pp. 11–12].

Such statements are very much in keeping with Barton's presentation. Yet at other times we find a different note being introduced. Thus when Rogers is speaking of achieving communication with people who are bitter and angry because they have experienced oppression and exploitation, he tells us:

Rage needs to be *heard*. This does not mean that it simply needs to be listened to. It needs to be accepted, taken within, and understood empathically. . . . the truth about rage is that it only dissolves when it is really heard and understood, without reservations. Afterward, the blacks or other minority members change in what seems a miraculous way, as though a weight has been lifted from their shoulders.

To achieve this kind of empathic listening the white needs to listen to his own feelings too, his feelings of anger and resentment at "unjust" accusations. At some point he too will need to express these, but the primary task is to enter empathically the minority world of hate and bitterness and resentment and to know that world as an understandable, acceptable part of reality [1977, pp. 133–134].

It seems that what Rogers is saying here is that if we would bridge the gap of hate, we will not achieve it in the role of facilitator—that is, in the role of someone who would help the other to get in touch with and express his feelings. The person who is hostile and bitter does not want to be facilitated. He wants to convince his listener that he has a case that should be heard. There is a marked difference between listening to another in order to hear what he has to say and listening to him in order to facilitate him. It is the difference between a reactive stance in which the listener responds to the other's message in terms of what it requires of him and hence is bound by it, and a strategic stance in which the communication is treated as symptomatic of an underlying condition which must be remedied. There is a recurrent ambiguity through Rogers's writings on this issue. Thus he sees the therapeutic task as the removal of "conditions of worth" in the client through unconditional valuing of him—a stance which implies that the content of the client's communication is irrelevant. Yet we also find him, as in the instance just described, advocating what appears to be a reactive stance in which the listener takes to heart very personally and seriously the other's message.

In our view, what is important in communicating with angry or bitter people is the exchange of information and the impact of the information on the listener, not the expression of feelings. It is only insofar as the speaker gets the feedback information that his message has struck home and made a difference in his listener that he can relax. Only then is the weight lifted from his shoulders. His rage has stemmed from his helplessness—from his inability to move those whom he sees as being in a position to do something about the things that distress him.

To the extent that this type of listening characterizes the client-centered position and informs its theory, Barton's account, which has been outlined above, is incomplete. There are places in Rogers's writings where it seems that this is what he has in mind. Yet it is hard to avoid the conclusion that, by and large, Barton's description holds.

CHAPTER 6
The Contextual Model

THE ESSENTIAL FEATURE of the contextual model is that it views the behavior of the individual within a systems framework and conceives of changing the individual's behavior by changing the system of interaction of which it is a component part. An example of the model in action is family therapy, but conceptually the issue extends beyond family therapy into the network of relationships which an individual inhabits.

Systems thinking is a feature of our age, and in order to view the contextual model within its setting, it is appropriate to consider some aspects of the systems approach in rather broad terms. This must lead us temporarily into issues somewhat remote from the therapeutic encounter, but hopefully will provide a structure within which the model we are considering will be more clearly outlined.

DEFINITION OF A SYSTEM

Weiss (1969), who has been a pioneer in the application of systems thinking to biological processes, defines a system as

> ... a rather circumscribed complex of relatively bounded phenomena, which, within those bounds, retains a relatively stationary pattern of struc-

ture in space or of sequential configuration in time in spite of a high degree of variability in the details of distribution and interrelations among its constituent units of lower order. Not only does the system maintain its configuration and integral operation in an essentially constant environment, but it responds to alterations of the environment by an adaptive redirection of its componental processes in such a manner as to counter the external change in the direction of optimum preservation of its systemic integrity [pp. 11–12].

In elaboration of this definition he goes on:

... the complex is a system if the variance of the features of the whole collective is significantly less than the sum of variances of its constituents. ... the basic characteristic of a system is its essential *invariance* beyond the much more variant flux and fluctuations of its elements or constituents... . the elements ... are subject to restraints of their degrees of freedom so as to yield a resultant in the direction of maintaining the optimum stability of the collective. ...

To sum up, a major aspect of a system is that while the state and pattern of the whole can be unequivocally defined as known, the detailed states and pathways of the components not only are so erratic as to defy definition, but even if a Laplacean spirit could trace them, would prove to be so unique and non-recurrent that they would be devoid of scientific interest. This is exactly the opposite of a machine, in which the structure of the product depends crucially on strictly predefined operations of the parts. In the system, the structure of the whole determines the operations of the parts; in the machine, the operation of the parts determines the outcome. Of course, even the machine owes the coordinated functional arrangement of its parts, in the last analysis, to a systems operation—the brain of its designer [pp. 12–13].

The comments by Weiss emphasize the stability or relative invariance of the organization or system as a whole in comparison with the variability of its component parts. This applies on a hierarchical basis. As he puts it:

any one of the particular complexes that show that high degree of constancy and unity that marks them as systems loses that aspect of invariance the more we concentrate our attention on smaller samples of its content. So, at each level of descent, we recognize entities comparable to relay stations sufficiently well defined to be described in their own terms (e.g., organs, cells, organelles, macromolecules; or brain functions, as expressed in concepts, thoughts, sentences, words, symbols), but whose methical behavior on that level cannot be ascribed to any fixity of regularities in the behavior of the units of next lower order; just as knowing purely the properties of those intermediary "relay" entities would not permit us to describe by sheer additive reconstruction the behavioral features of their next superordinate level in precise and specific terms [p. 15].

We can note three aspects of Weiss's description of a system:

1. Systems have a hierarchical nature, in which the "substations" are themselves systems composed in turn of similar "substations."
2. The stability of a system at any level in the hierarchy is not of the same nature as the stability of its component systems or superordinate system though each has its own particular stability.
3. The stability of a system is not an additive function of its components, but a product of their interaction or interrelationship.

These aspects may be considered in a little more detail with reference to the situation of the individual.

The Hierarchical Nature of Systems. Koestler (1964, 1969) has been particularly interested in the hierarchical structure of systems and its consequence that any system must be viewed both as a whole constituted by its subsystems and as a part helping to constitute a superordinate system. He has coined the term "holon" (from Greek "holus" meaning "whole" and "on" meaning "part") to refer to this dual aspect. As he puts it, neither wholes nor parts exist in an absolute sense in the biological or social domains, but rather "intermediary structures on a series of levels in ascending order of complexity, each of which has two faces looking in opposite directions: the face turned towards the lower levels is that of an autonomous whole, the one turned upward that of a dependent part" (1969, p. 197). Examples of holons in the case of the human hierarchy are cells, organs, individual, family, clan, tribe.

This dual aspect of being both an autonomous whole and a dependent part involves the holon in treading a line that involves both asserting its independence and autonomy and participating as a subordinate part in a superordinate system.

Stability of a System and of Its Components. The maintenance of the stability of a system in a steady state does not require stability in the behavior of its component elements. Indeed the stability of the system may depend upon variability in its components to counteract environmental changes. Thus the maintenance of stability in the ecology of a stretch of woodland, the temperature of a warm-blooded animal, or the operation of a family will typically require that as environmental changes occur, component elements of the system become active to restore the dynamic equilibrium.

System Stability a Product of Interaction of Its Components. The maintenance of a steady state in such a system as the ecology of a stretch of woodland is not to be understood by noting the separate characteristics of the various forms of animal and plant life and then summing them. It is only by noting the way these varied members of the animal and plant communities relate to, or interact with, each other that the operation of the system can be understood.

SYMPTOM AND CAUSE

Within a systems approach, what is conceived to be the symptom to be accounted for and what is conceived to be the cause which accounts for it depend upon the stance taken or the position from which the issue is viewed. If we consider a person who becomes ill and is found to be suffering from a stomach ulcer, we might regard the illness as the symptom and the ulcer as the cause. At this point we have a choice as to whether we seek an explanation in terms of social determinants or seek it in terms of physical and chemical determinants. In either case we can move further away from our initial point of departure with, at each successive step, what was previously seen as being the cause becoming the symptom and the related process at the more remote level becoming the cause. So if the physician in the case of the stomach ulcer seeks biochemical explanations, he may account for the ulcer in terms of excessive acid in the stomach. In that case the ulcer is the symptom and the acid is the cause. He may then proceed to account for the acid, in which case it becomes the symptom and that which accounts for it the cause.

However, if the person responsible for treatment is behaviorally oriented, he may see the ulcer as the result of interpersonal stress arising from an unhappy home life with a nagging bad-tempered wife, in combination with a relatively demanding work situation. In such a case the behavior of the wife might be seen as a major causal factor. Then the ulcer would be the symptom and the interpersonal stress the causal factor. But the behavior of the wife may be seen to be the outcome of a family structure which denies her any opportunity for the fulfillment of her needs and hence leaves her frustrated and embittered. Now the family organization is the cause and the interpersonal stress the symptom. But the family organization does not exist in a vacuum. It is a consequence of the wider community system or pattern of which it is a part. So the family structure becomes a symptom and the pattern of the wider order is the cause. And so we might proceed to the point where we are, through a series of steps, attributing Mr. X's ulcer to the socio-political-economic system in which he lives.

If the cause can be seen to exist at different levels in the hierarchical system, then clearly intervention to remedy the disability can be attempted at each such level. The physician might intervene at any level in the biological organic order for which the appropriate means are available. The applied social scientist, a category within which we must place our therapist, can be expected to intervene at the level in the social order at which he believes he has most likelihood of effecting change that will relieve the stress on the client. At one extreme he might contemplate trying to reorder the pattern of relationships in the immediate face-to-face group of the client's family or work situation. At the other extreme he might contemplate a revolutionary reorganization of society. In principle, either approach would fall within the framework of the contextual model we are considering. Since the client may be dead and the therapist retired (or vice versa) before the revolution is accomplished, the more usual choice is to attempt to reorder the immediate relational network. However, it is to be noted that there are psychotherapists working in underprivileged areas who question the validity of such a decision.

The contextual approach thus seeks to bring about some reorganization of the social network the patient or client inhabits, and for practical purposes this is ordinarily the group of intimates that the patient encounters regularly at a face-to-face level in his daily life. Typically, that circle of intimates will consist of a family, but it may be some other salient group.

THERAPIST BECOMES PART OF THE SYSTEM

When the therapist enters the client's world, he becomes a significant element in the latter's relationship network. As was evident in the discussion of the ideological model, a therapist and client tend to co-constitute a new reality—a process which has consequences not only for the client but also for those who are in intimate contact with him. As he takes his place as a member of the client's circle of intimates, the therapist not only enlarges that circle but also poses the issue of how it is to accommodate itself to his entry. A question that is of critical importance for the therapeutic outcome is whether he will be assimilated into the prevailing network of relationships or whether his entry will force substantial changes in that pattern of interaction.

It is possible to consider the patient-therapist dyad as a small two-person system within a larger framework. From a systems point of view this is the way individual therapy would be seen. Change so produced would be understood, not as requiring the resolution of some intra-psychic conflict in the client, but as change in his pattern of communication—that is, in the way the client goes about influencing others.

Ordinarily, systems-oriented therapists are unwilling to confine their intervention to the dyadic level. They have two reasons for this. In the first place, the client's communication pattern is assumed to be serving some purpose or function in the interactions involving himself and his intimates. If it is changed without doing something about the problems for which it is a solution, then unpredictable consequences are likely to ensue in the relationships within that circle. Since the preservation of the intimate group—typically the client's family—as a functioning unit, preferably on a more workable basis, is usually seen as desirable, these therapists endeavor to include the larger social unit in the change process from the beginning. A second reason is that the nature and function of the client's communication pattern become more clearly evident in the interaction in the intimate group.

COMMUNICATION

From the point of view of a contextually oriented therapist, a problem is understood as something that people are doing to each other. In Haley's terms a problem is "a type of behavior that is part of a sequence of acts between several people. The repeating sequence of behavior is the focus of therapy. A symptom is a label for, a crystallization of, a sequence in a social organization" (1976, p. 2). That is to say, the problem is not to be thought of as something a person is doing, such as compulsive hand-washing or a tic, which might be accounted for as an acquired habit, but rather as a form of exchange between the individual and others. In symptomatic or pathological behavior there is a repetition of a particular kind of exchange which constitutes the problem.

In systems processes two kinds of exchange occur—energy exchange and information exchange. Information is a message that controls release of energy stored in the recipient of the exchange. The difference between energy exchange and information exchange is the difference between kicking a stone and kicking a cat. To the stone the kick is simply the transmission of energy; to the cat it is a message. In terms of the social processes with which the therapist is concerned, it is the information exchange—or communication—that is relevant.

Behavioral scientists, for the most part, have lacked a framework with which to approach the task of analyzing the communication process. Bateson (1972), whose ideas will occupy us in later chapters, is a notable exception. The differentiation between energy and communication provides an opportunity for orienting the reader to his thinking. He tells us:

> ... in the world of communication the only relevant entities or "realities" are messages.... The *perception* of an event or object or relation is real. It is a neurophysiological message. But the event itself or the object itself cannot enter this world and is, therefore, irrelevant and, to that extent, unreal. Conversely, a message has no reality or relevance qua message, in the Newtonian world: it there is reduced to sound waves or printer's ink.
>
> By the same token, the "contexts" and "contexts of contexts" upon which I am insisting are only real or relevant insofar as they are communicationally effective, i.e., function as messages or modifiers of messages.
>
> The difference between the Newtonian world and the world of com-

munication is simply this: that the Newtonian world ascribes reality to objects and achieves its simplicity by excluding the context of the context—excluding indeed all metarelationships—a fortiori excluding an infinite regress of such relations. In contrast, the theorist of communication insists upon examining the metarelationships while achieving its simplicity by excluding all objects [1972, p. 250].

Beyond alerting the reader to the issues that will concern us later, we will not pursue these abstract aspects of communication now. Our concern for the present is with what Watzlawick et al. (1967) call its pragmatics or practical effects. As these writers point out, all behavior carried out in the presence of others has communicational significance. Even inaction constitutes a communication. In consequence any behavior, whether silence, cheerful chatter, plaintive complaints, or vigorous activity, is a communication. So having a headache or a hallucination is a communication. This does not mean that either the headache or the hallucination can necessarily be reduced to its communicational significance, though it is possible that that may be its essential *raison d'être*.

Communication is the basis on which a social system functions. It is through communication that such systems both grow and change and also maintain stability and resist change. Growth and change occur as a result of deviation-amplifying—or positive—feedback, while stability or resistance to change results from deviation-countering—or negative—feedback within the system. Within any complex social network both forms of feedback loop are to be found. However, in the type of behavior which brings the client into therapy, it is typically deviation-countering feedback loops which call for attention. Symptomatic behavior is typically repetitive behavior maintained by negative feedback.

TYPES OF COMMUNICATION

Although all behavior has communicational value, there are differences between behavioral acts in terms of how the information is conveyed or exchanged. Watzlawick et al. (1967) and Haley (1976) distinguish between what they call digital and analogical communication. In digital communication there is a single clearly specified referent. When communicating digitally, the individual is communicating in a precise and logical way that avoids possibility of ambiguity. This is the language of science. In analogical communication, however, the language used is that of metaphor. There is more than one referent. What may seem to be the referent stands, in fact, for some other referent.

Both forms of communication have their appropriate place in information exchange. For the exchange of factual data the digital mode is most appropriate, but when the purpose is to deal with relationships between people, it is the analogical mode that comes into play.

Haley (1976) takes the example of two such situations as a man striking a nail with a hammer and a husband and wife having a quarrel. Both sets of events might be described by an onlooker in digital language. That is, he could give a precise account of the actual actions, verbal and motor, of those involved. However, while such a description will capture what is going on in the case of the man striking the nail, it will almost certainly fail to convey what is happening in the quarrel. If, for instance, the couple are quarreling about who is to pick up whose socks, it is highly improbable that picking up socks is the issue, which is most probably rather the nature of the relationship and the rules which govern it.

Haley indicates what is meant by analogical communication:

> When a message has multiple referents, it is no longer a "bit" but is analogic, in that it deals with the resemblances of one thing to another. It is a language in which each message refers to a context of other messages. There is no single message and single response but multiple stimuli and multiple responses, some of them fictional. Analogic communication includes the "as if" categories; each message frames, or is about, other messages. Included in this style of communication are "play" and "ritual," as well as all forms of art. The analog can be expressed in a verbal statement, as in a simile or verbal metaphor. It can also be expressed in action—the showing of how something is by acting it out. A message in this style cannot be categorized without taking into account the context of other messages in which the message occurs [1976, p. 84].

ANALOGICAL COMMUNICATION IN PSYCHOPATHOLOGY AND THERAPY

Within the contextual model, the interest in analogical communication centers on its use in pathological symptoms and their treatment. The child who has a phobia of school or of animals, the housewife who slashes her wrists, and the man who is subject to the fear of an imminent heart attack are all communicating analogically. The symptom is regarded, not as an attribute or affliction of the individual as an isolated entity, but in terms of its place in the system of relationships in which the individual participates. The symptom is a way of exerting influence within that relationship network. The particular function of any symptom can be determined only by examining the ongoing patterns of behavior in the intimate group, with particular attention being given to redundant features of the interaction. Typically, symptoms are seen as having stabilizing effects in the small social systems in which they occur.

The contextual model is not unique in treating symptoms as analogical. Psychodynamic systems of therapy also regard the symptom as a metaphorical communication. The psychoanalytic enterprise is based on the assumption that the "real" referent is something other than that given by a literal reading. Where the contextual model differs from other orientations is in seeing the symptom as functional in the working of a social system, usually serving the purpose of stabilizing or maintaining the status quo.

Haley (1976) gives us the example of a man who suffers from a fear of a heart attack although his heart shows no abnormality. In such a case the contextually oriented therapist would begin with the hypothesis that the communication about the heart is a way of managing a complex of social interactions and expectations in such areas as the behavior of children in the home, achievement at work, family outings, sexual relations, and the like. As such, the individual clearly has a high investment in the communication, but the contextual therapist would see it also as having a wider significance in the family system which would become apparent if a "cure" was effected and the fear eradicated.

Haley suggests that one way to treat such a symptom in individual therapy would be to impose a paradox by taking the analogical communication literally, agreeing the client is about to have a heart attack, and urging him to get on with it right away. This is done within a benevolent context in which it is clear that the symptom is not being taken seriously. The procedure requires trust in the therapist and acceptance of the fact that he is being helpful and is on the client's side. There is also a good deal of humor involved. As Haley points out, this method has been used by Frankl and Stampfl. It might also be noted here that in a slightly different form it has been developed also by Farrelly (Farrelly and Brandsma, 1974). Farrelly, who calls his method "Provocative Therapy," describes it as playing the devil's advocate. It is to be noted that in his practice he relies very heavily on the use of humor.

It can be seen that such an imposition of paradox by the therapist nullifies the attempt by the client to control the interaction with the therapist through his metaphorical communication. This forces him to give up that mode of interaction and adopt some other way of dealing with his situation. In principle, the procedure falls within the contextual model of influence. However, in terms of the practice of such systems-oriented therapists as Haley, it neglects to consider the consequences for the social system in which the symptom served a function. If, for instance, the symptom served the purpose of keeping the children quiet and orderly, of being a justification for very limited achievement at work, and of restraining the client's wife's aggression arising from her frustration over his incompetence or neglect, then the consequences of the cure might be uproar in the home possibly resulting in the disintegration of the family.

A more thoroughgoing approach would take note first of the family situation. The therapist would develop a trusting relationship with both spouses in which he would ascertain the functions of the symptom, particularly in respect of problems between husband and wife which are

avoided by the symptom. A first stage of treatment would involve helping the wife with these problems. When these had, in some measure,
been resolved and the wife was ready, the second stage could be enacted.
This could be carried through by getting the wife to take the metaphor
literally and handle it as the therapist might have done. Haley suggests
such action as taking each complaint as if it were an attack and summon-
ing medical help or an ambulance. Another procedure would be to visit
funeral parlors, get their literature on funerals, and leave this around
the house each time the husband complained about his heart.

What this achieves is an invalidation of the symptom as a means of
communication and hence a forcing of the couple to find new ways of
communicating with each other. The effects as Haley sees them are as
follows:

> The system has been forced into instability. One might think the husband
> would substitute another incapacitating metaphor, such as fear of cancer.
> However, this substitution does not occur in actual practice. The alliance of
> wife and therapist forcing the change in the heart metaphor also seems to
> force a change in that *class* of metaphor. Typically, the husband becomes
> angry and speaks more straightforwardly about various situations with his
> wife where the metaphor was previously used, such as sex life, recreation,
> and so on. The wife in turn expresses herself with another metaphor besides
> depressive behavior, and in the process the two of them work out changes in
> their behavior with each other and more "normal" marital communication
> [1976, p. 95].

CHANGE MANAGED IN STAGES

It will be noted, in the example just considered, that change is conceived
of as involving separate stages which are largely discontinuous with each
other. It can, of course, be said that all therapeutic change constitutes a
sequential process in which the patient's behavior passes through more
or less distinguishable stages. The psychoanalyst can predict a sequence
through which the patient will proceed in the course of his analysis, and
some of the earliest investigations of the therapy process carried out by
Rogers and his students at Ohio State University showed that change in
the client's behavior followed a predictable pattern. However, in these
and most other forms of therapy the therapist maintains a consistent
focus of intervention throughout, while in the problem-solving type of
intervention of the contextually oriented therapist it is very common for
the therapist to aim at intermediate targets which are necessary prereq-
uisites for the initiation of new moves designed to achieve the therapeutic goal.

In the very elementary example of the teacher with his group of defective readers outlined in the opening chapter, we have such a two-stage process. The teacher first sets up a situation and builds a relationship structure so that the children become very involved in an activity which seems to have nothing to do with reading, but which is under the teacher's control. Then the teacher introduces a reading component as part of the shared activity. In the more complex case of the heart complaint, the ground is first prepared to ensure that the consequences of the symptom removal will not be unduly disruptive of the intimate social network, and then the assault on the symptom is made from within that network. In reading accounts of Milton Erickson's handling of cases (Haley, 1974), one is struck by the frequency with which a separation into different stages can be noted. Therapy within this framework has the quality of a campaign carried through in accordance with a general strategy that requires, for its successful implementation, the achievement of intermediate tactical objectives. Such an approach introduces considerable flexibility into the therapeutic strategy. A goal for the client that may seem outside the bounds of possibility from the client's position at the beginning of therapy may become a realistic target if a "sideways" shift in the situation can be achieved.

Haley conceptualizes therapy in terms of such stages. In his model of family process, the aim of therapy is to remove constraints which impede the onward movement in the cycle of family life. In this cycle parents beget children, the children mature, become independent and involved with their peers, find mates, in turn beget children, and move into the roles of parenthood and grandparenthood. Pathology occurs when this onward process is impeded. A common interactional situation which gives rise to this is one in which one of the parents becomes excessively involved with the child and the other parent is peripheral. Such situations are frequently found in the case of schizophrenia in the child. In such a situation the immediate objective is to free the child from the entanglement with the parent so that he can become involved with his peers and find a mate. Since this leaves the problem between the parents, the second phase must be concerned with getting the parents interested in each other. What is involved is thus a progressive reorganization of the system of relationships in the family.

HIERARCHY IN FAMILY RELATIONSHIPS

Although we live in an era in which autonomy and equality have become catchwords, it is the nature of human society to function in terms of hierarchical organization. In Haley's words:

> If there is any generalization that applies to men and other animals, it is that all creatures capable of learning are compelled to organize. To be or-

ganized means to follow patterned, redundant ways of behaving and to exist in a hierarchy. Creatures that organize together form a status, or power, ladder in which each creature has a place in the hierarchy with someone above him and someone below him. Although groups will have more than one hierarchy because of different functions, the existence of hierarchy is inevitable because it is in the nature of organization that it be hierarchical. We may dream of a society in which all creatures are equal, but on this earth there is status and precedence and inequality among all creatures. . . . Everywhere the messages that creatures interchange in their repeating ways are messages that define positions in organizational hierarchies. If a group attempts to organize on the basis of equal status among the members, some members become more equal than others as organization develops [1976, p. 101].

Haley hastens to stress that

Although one must accept the *existence* of hierarchy, that does not mean one needs to accept a *particular* structure or a particular family hierarchy. One need not accept the status quo either in terms of the economic structure of society or the issue of a particular unfortunate hierarchy. Everywhere there are hierarchical arrangements that are unjust. One economic class suppresses another. Women are kept in a subordinate position in both family and work groups merely because they are female. People are placed in subordinate positions because of race or religion. Children are oppressed by their parents, in the sense of being restricted and exploited in extreme ways. Obviously, there are many wrongs that need righting that involve hierarchical issues, and any therapist must think through his ethical position [pp. 101–102].

It is also to be noted that hierarchical organization is maintained as much by those lower in the hierarchy as by those of higher status. Individuals who step out of line are just as likely to be put back in place by their peers as by their superiors.

Hierarchical lines are related to different functions. An expert in a particular area is likely to occupy a high position in the hierarchy when his particular expertise is salient, but at other times his status may be low. In families the generation line is the standard basis of hierarchical order. To quote Haley:

At the most simple level it is parents who nurture and discipline children, who in turn nurture and discipline children as the generations proceed over time. At any one moment there are, at most, four generations operating. Most commonly there are three: grandparents, parents and children. These three generations can be simplified into three levels of power, or status. In the traditional family, as still is evident in Asia, the greatest status and power resided with the grandparents; the parents were secondary and the children lowest in status. In the western world, particularly in this time of rapid social change, the status and power position of the grandparents is less. In the nuclear family living arrangement, the power often resides with the parents, and the grandparents are moved to an advisory, if not superfluous, position. Professional experts tend to replace the grandparents as authorities [1976, p. 103].

It is Haley's contention that when symptomatic behavior occurs, we will find confusion in the hierarchical arrangement. Different forms of confusion which give rise to symptoms include (1) the inability of the participants to know who are their peers and who are their superiors or subordinates, and (2) the consistent or repeated practice of a member at one level of the hierarchy forming a coalition against a peer (or against an immediate subordinate) with a member at another level (or with the subordinate's subordinate), thereby violating the fundamental rules of organization. That is, if one parent forms a coalition with the child against the other parent or if a grandparent forms a coalition with the child against the parent, there is a breach of the rules of organization. Such breaches, of course, are not confined to families. The manager who overrides a supervisor in his dealings with a worker or the supervisor who forms a coalition with a worker against a fellow supervisor is in breach of the basic rules of organization.

So-called "struggles for power" are better understood as attempts to clarify confusion regarding status positions in a hierarchy than as the expression of innate needs for aggression. To quote Haley, "When a child has temper tantrums and refuses to do what his mother says, this situation can be described as an unclear hierarchy. In such a case the mother is often indicating that she is in charge while simultaneously treating her child as a peer and so the hierarchy is confused" (pp. 103–104).

When there are breaches of the fundamental rules of organization, "the organization is in trouble and the participants will experience subjective distress" (p. 104). However, in the temporary interactions of psychotherapy, in which the aim is to reorganize family relationship patterns, it is often in the interests of therapy for the therapist to establish transitory coalitions with one or other of the participants.

SEQUENCES IN INTERACTION

The hierarchical order can be discovered by observing the interaction sequences and noting recurrent patterns. This is no easy task. Haley tells us it is difficult to note repeating patterns in a sequence of three or more events, particularly if the observer is also a participant in the events. "For example, a therapist may notice that a wife repeatedly provokes him. Perhaps he will even recognize a sequence of two actions by noticing that she provokes him after he has criticized her husband. Yet, it seems more difficult to notice that the child was rude, the father disciplined the child, the therapist reacted against the father, and then the therapist was provoked by the wife" (1976, p. 105).

This is a very interesting observation. Haley, however, appears to have missed an important point when he seeks to account for the difficulty by quoting Braulio Montalvo to the effect that "we have built into ourselves necessary amnesias for overlooking parts of sequences" (p. 105). In fact we usually do not have much difficulty in observing sequences as such. Observers at a sporting fixture (e.g., a baseball game) have little difficulty in observing and recalling several sequential events (e.g., that the pitcher threw a fast straight ball, that the batter drove it low and hard to left field, that the shortstop with great agility cut it off and threw it to first base where the batter was out, and that first base threw it to second in time to beat the runner, thereby effecting a successful double play).

Since it is not hard to observe and recall sequences of events of this kind, the question arises as to the nature of the difficulty in the situation Haley describes. The answer requires that we invoke the concept of context. Meaning is given to events in the game by the rules of baseball with which players and spectators are familiar and which provide a context for the relevant events. In the case of Haley's family interaction, however, we are dealing not with a single context, but with a hierarchy of contexts. In his example, it is necessary for the observer to note that it is in the context of the therapist criticizing the husband that the wife provokes the former and further that the husband disciplining the child is the context of the context in which the wife provokes the therapist.

Such hierarchies of context are extremely difficult for the human mind to grasp. The events involved are of the same nature as those occurring in reflexive processes expressed in such terms as "I see you seeing me seeing you. . . ." Consequently it is understandable that observers of family interaction experience difficulty in noting repeating sequences of three or more events. Their task is to find meaning in the sequence of exchanges, and meaning depends upon context and context of context. This theme of the significance of hierarchical order in communication, and hence in behavior, is central to the argument developed in this book. Haley's observation is consistent with predictions that could have been made from this conceptual frame which derives from the theory of logical types.

Historically, attempts to explain behavior pathology in children have gone through a series of changes. At one time the problematic behavior was attributed to the development of faulty habit patterns. Then attention was focused on the mother, who was seen as a causative agent because she was helpless and incompetent and the child was adapting to her behavior. Then the father was brought into the picture to explain the mother's behavior. When mother was competent, there was no function for the father, who withdrew from the family. When the mother was helpless, he became involved. Possibly also her helplessness was a way of supporting the father by giving him a sense of significance when he was feeling inadequate or depressed. Finally, the family network was seen as a system with all members playing a part in maintaining it. The attitudes and behaviors of father, mother, and child were now seen as constituting a circular self-maintaining system involving reciprocal causation.

For Haley the therapeutic aim is to intrude into the established interaction pattern in such a way as to prevent its continuing. He suggests that changing any *one* of the steps in the circular sequence, or changing the behavior of any one of the three participants, is not enough to change the pattern. It is necessary to change at least two of the behaviors. Furthermore, such change typically produces conflict between the parents as one of the stages of the treatment process.

The family therapist making such an intrusion should be able, he tells us, to think in terms of three steps of a sequence and three levels of an organizational hierarchy. Having put together sequence and hierarchy in the particular case, the therapist is then in a position to apply a rational procedure. His basic strategy must be to prevent coalitions across generation lines. Subjective distress will end when coalitions between one parent and child against the other parent end.

The term "coalition" is used to describe combined action against a third party and not a situation where two people share an interest which is not shared by a third. Transitory coalitions which are dictated by situational events (e.g., one supervisor may intervene on behalf of a worker with another supervisor over a particular incident, or a mother may protect a child against the father as occasion requires) do not cause problems. It is when coalitions become a chronic feature of the interaction, when they are repeated again and again so that they become a way of life, that the organization is in trouble. The trouble will be most severe when the coalition is not acknowledged, but is concealed or denied.

Haley provides accounts of different types of two-generation and three-generation violation of the rules of organization. A three-generation situation is common among one-parent families. Typically this is found among the poor, or in middle-class families where the mother has divorced and gone back to live with her mother. "In the classic example, the grandmother tends to be defined as dominating, the mother as irresponsible, and the child as a behavior problem" (1976, p. 110). In such a situation a typical recurring sequence consists of grandmother accusing mother of irresponsibility and taking over the care of the child, the mother withdrawing, the child misbehaving, grandmother protesting that the mother should look after her own child, mother beginning to take care of the child, grandmother accusing the mother of irresponsibility and taking over the care of the child, mother withdrawing, child misbehaving, and so on again around the circle.

Substituting the therapist for the grandmother, Haley sees a somewhat parallel situation occurring in long-term family therapy. Another three-generation situation occurs in the training of therapists, where supervisor, trainee, and client form a three-generation hierarchy.

REJECTED THERAPEUTIC INTERVENTIONS

Given the recurrent sequence of interaction, what are the options open to the therapist? Among the possible courses which Haley considers and discards are these:

Asking for Expression of Emotion. Expression of emotion is not likely to produce change unless the person expresses it in a way that is new or different from his habitual pattern. If a new mode of expression occurs, it will force change in the way others respond to him, and this in turn will cause him to change his communication pattern. In other words, a change in a way of communicating means a change in the interaction system—that is, in the overt behaviors exchanged. It is to be distinguished from the cathartic process of release of feelings within the individual. Haley thinks a therapist should not ask, "How do you feel?" Rather he should provoke the client into communicating in a new way—perhaps by making him angry.

We might note here that for the person who has not had the experience of being listened to, a therapist who listens attentively and empathically can be expected to initiate a new mode of interaction on the part of the client. This would account for the often remarkable changes in communication patterns of clients that are observed in client-centered therapy.

Providing Explanations in Terms of Past History. Learning how his past experience is making him behave as he does makes little contribution to helping a person to change his behavior pattern. The belief that he is programmed by his past tends to provide a justification for behavior rather than a cause for change. For Haley "the theory of repression is a handicap of one is thinking about how to change sequences" (p. 118). He would argue that insofar as psychoanalytic interpretation effects change, it is because the paradox-imposing behavior of the analyst forces change in the patient's communication pattern.

Showing the Individual His Part in the Interaction Sequence. Though it might seem that the person who is shown what is going on in the interaction sequence would be able to change his behavior, the evidence is that such does not occur. The person resists such efforts. Both Erickson and Haley regard attempts to give the clients insight into the interaction patterns in which they are enmeshed as being misguided and counter-productive.

EFFECTIVE STRATEGY

Since the foregoing options are rejected, the question arises as to what the therapist can do. The answer is that he must intrude into the on-going sequence of interaction and effect changes in it. He is able to do this because, as the professional expert, he is at the top of the power hierarchy over any of the family members.

From this power position, he can give directions or form temporary cross-generational coalitions, as appropriate, and thereby change power balances and interactional processes. Since to do this is to assume considerable responsibility, it is necessary that the therapist have both a general policy applicable to all cases and a particular plan for implementing the policy in each particular case.

The general policy, as indicated earlier, is to locate and interdict, or eliminate, chronic cross-generational coalitions. The typical cross-generation coalition in a two-parent family is a close or intense relationship between one parent and a child that alternately includes and excludes the other parent. In the single-parent case, the typical cross-generational coalition involves a grandparent having an intense relationship with the child and the single parent being intermittently included and excluded. Other situations which occur involve a failure to make generation lines clear. This latter occurs in those cases where the parent has no control over the child.

While the policy of keeping generation lines clear and avoiding cross-generational coalitions is easy to formulate, it may not be so easy to implement. The therapist will have to develop his tactical plan in accordance with the particular circumstances. Ordinarily a plan will involve two phases. Thus in a two-parent family where the plan is to involve the child with his peers and the parents with each other, two steps will be required. In the first the child is liberated from the involved parent, usually the mother. This may be achieved by using the peripheral parent to form a working group with therapist and child while the involved parent is pushed to the periphery. When this step is accomplished and the child freed, the second phase of involving the parents with each other can be embarked upon. Having been cut off from the intense relationship with the child, the formerly overinvolved parent is likely to be responsive to such efforts. As this is accomplished, "the therapist must disengage and get out, leaving the parents involved with each other and the boy involved with his friends" (p. 136).

While the principles are simple and clear, the planning and execution of the policy in any particular case require a high level of expertise. It is necessary to keep the parties together and to avoid alienating the party against whom the coalition, at any given time, is formed. The therapist must remain in control. One feature that needs to be noted is that triangular interaction patterns are more stable than dyadic patterns. Third parties, such as children, play a stabilizing role. When a child is freed from such a role as suggested above, the therapist must take his place as a stabilizing element in the system until a new and more effective mode of interaction between the parents can be developed.

THE RELEVANCE OF GROUP THEORY AND THE THEORY OF LOGICAL TYPES

Haley is primarily concerned with groups which have a history and form stable communication patterns. His particular interest is the family as a communication system. He views hierarchical control systems in terms of such social units. The critical reader may consider that, in his analysis of pathological behavior and its consequences, he overemphasizes the part of the family interaction pattern. How, it may be asked, can we account for the stability of the behavior of the individual who not only leaves his family, but moves around from one social context to another recreating the same interactional patterns?

Those who would ask such questions will be interested in the slightly different perspective on the systems approach provided by Watzlawick et al. (1974). These writers have much in common with Haley, but instead of his presentation of control systems in terms of social organization, they present them in terms of mathematical and logical formulations. Haley's generation lines correspond to their logical levels or classes. Just as generation levels must not be confused, so classes and their members must not be confused. The theory of logical types is basic to both perspectives.

Watzlawick et al. draw upon two abstract and general theories from mathematics and logic for an understanding of the complexities and paradoxes of human interaction. These are (1) group theory, a branch of mathematics that traces back to the work of Galois in the early part of the nineteenth century, and (2) the theory of logical types. In their words:

> Group Theory gives us a framework for thinking about the kind of change that can occur within a system that itself stays invariant; the Theory of Logical Types is not concerned with what goes on inside a class, i.e., between its members, but gives us a frame for considering the relationship between member and class and the peculiar metamorphosis which is in the nature of shifts from one logical level to the next higher. If we accept this basic distinction between the two theories, it follows that there are two dif-

ferent types of change: one that occurs within a given system which itself remains unchanged, and one whose occurrence changes the system itself [1974, p. 10].

They refer to the former type of change as first-order change and to the latter as second-order change. As an example of the former they cite the different things a person might do in a nightmare such as fight, run, hide, or knock somebody down—that is, the person may change from one activity to another, but all within the nightmare. To escape from the nightmare he must wake up, and that would be a second-order change.

First-order changes are of everyday occurrence and resolve many difficulties. If a person is cold, he can put on more or warmer clothing. He can keep putting on more or warmer clothing until he no longer feels cold. If he is weary he can rest, and if a short rest is not sufficient he can take a longer rest. If he is walking and is likely to be late, he can walk faster or he can run. In a lot of situations, he can resolve a difficulty by trying harder or by trying some variation of what he is doing. Common-sense solutions to difficulties are first-order solutions.

But there are situations in which attempts at first-order solutions are counterproductive. If one has difficulty in falling asleep, then trying harder to go to sleep will ensure insomnia. Similar effects occur in any behavior such as sexual response or feelings of affection, which of their nature are "spontaneous."

In interpersonal processes, trying harder or applying more of the same is commonly a recipe for a deteriorating relationship. The spouse who wants openness in the marital relationship is likely to drive the partner toward seclusiveness, and the harder he or she tries, the more seclusive the partner is likely to become. The wife who tries to control her husband's drinking is likely to drive him to alcoholism by her efforts. Consider the following incident involving a married couple in which the husband regarded his wife as dominating and she regarded him as irresponsible. On one occasion he won a bottle of sherry in a competition, and, taking it home proudly, he suggested they have a drink before dinner. His wife replied tersely to the effect that she would not touch the stuff. "So," he related, describing the event, "I told her if that was how she felt, I'd drink it all myself, and I sat down and drank it all, though it damned nearly killed me."

In such cases we have the process of deviation-amplifying feedback at work. Watzlawick et al. draw the analogy of two people in a sailboat on a calm day trying frantically to steady it by leaning out on opposite sides. The more one leans out on his side, the more the other has to lean out on the other side to stabilize the boat. As they comment, "It is not difficult to see that in order to change this absurd situation, at least one of them has to do something seemingly quite unreasonable, namely to 'steady' *less* and not more, since this will immediately force the other to also do less of the same" (p. 36). However, this is a very unusual sort of thing to do in the type of situation under consideration.

It is not only individuals that get caught in such "more of the same" situations. Armament races between nations provide an example of the process at the international level, and restrictive legislation on alcohol and drugs of the milder type seems to produce more difficulties than it resolves.

In addition to the pathologies arising from the "more of the same" policy, there are also those arising from "terrible simplifications," "the utopia syndrome," and the generation of paradox in attempts to produce change. These all involve modes of interaction in which attempts to produce change from within the frame of the group create or magnify difficulties. Thus the quest for utopia prevents the individual from attaining the gratifications that are accessible to him—the search for meaning from life prevents him from enjoying what life has to offer. In discussing such "syndromes," the authors relate the behaviors and their consequences to the mathematical properties of groups. It is, unfortunately, not possible in the space available here to do justice to their subtle and penetrating analyses of such issues.

Where attempts at first-order change frequently aggravate or even create pathology, a move to a second-order change may resolve the problem. It is to be noted here that Watzlawick et al. make a distinction between those matters which can be resolved at the level of first-order change, which they call *difficulties,* and those for which it is necessary to move to second-order change, which they call *problems.* Difficulties respond to commonsense methods; problems require the exercise of uncommonsense methods which on the surface may appear irrational, but which can be demonstrated to have their own rationality based on the theory of logical types. Since this theory, to which we have made frequent reference, is regarded as being of fundamental significance, an excerpt from *Principia Mathematica* outlining the nature of the argument of Whitehead and Russell appears as an Appendix.

Like group theory, the theory of logical types is concerned with collections of items which share a common property. The totality of such a collection is called a class, and each item in the collection is called a member. A critical axiom of the theory of logical types is that "Whatever involves all of a collection must not be one of the collection" (Whitehead and Russell, 1910, p. 40). In amplifying on just what this axiom states, Bateson says:

> . . . the theory asserts that no class can, in formal logic or mathematical discourse, be a member of itself; that a class of classes cannot be one of the classes which are its members; that a name is not the thing named; that "John Bateson" is the class of which that boy is the unique member; and so forth. These assertions may seem trivial and even obvious, but . . . it is not at all

unusual for the theorists of behavioral science to commit errors which are precisely analogous to the error of classifying the name with the thing named—or eating the menu card instead of the dinner—an error of *logical typing.*

Somewhat less obvious is the further assertion of the theory: that a class cannot be one of those items which are correctly classified as its nonmembers. If we classify chairs together to constitute the class of chairs, we can go on to note that tables and lampshades are members of a large class of "nonchairs", but we shall commit an error in formal discourse if we count the *class of chairs* among the items within the class of nonchairs [1972, p. 280].

The theory thus draws a sharp distinction between the totality and its members. The totality is of a higher order than its members and provides a frame or context which defines or gives meaning to the members. Changing the totality changes the meaning of the members.

The points at issue are complex and difficult to convey. Watzlawick et al. resort to analogy. One example is an automobile with a gear shift. There are two ways of manipulating the performance of the automobile: (1) by the use of the accelerator, which controls the fuel supply to the engine, (2) by shifting gears. At any given gear the behavior of the car—within certain limits—can be changed by the use of the accelerator. "But if the required performance falls *outside* this range, the driver must shift gears to obtain the desired change. Gear-shifting is thus a phenomenon of a higher logical type than giving gas, and it would be patently nonsensical to talk about the mechanics of complex gears in the language of the thermodynamics of fuel supply" (1974, p. 9).

They go on to quote Ashby (1956, p. 43), on the cybernetic properties of a machine with input: "It will be seen that the word 'change,' if applied to such a machine can refer to two very different things. There is the change from state to state, . . . , which is the machine's behavior, and there is the change from transformation to transformation, . . . , which is *a change of its way of behaving,* and which occurs at the whim of the experimenter or some outside factor. The distinction is fundamental and must on no account be slighted."

The position can be summed up by saying that the theory of logical types, in requiring a sharp distinction between logical types or levels, necessitates a discontinuous leap or transformation in moving from one level to the next. As the authors say, this is of great practical and theoretical importance, for it offers a way out of the problem situation.

This raises the question of the practical application of the principle to human problems. Watzlawick et al. approach this by first giving some illustrations in which second-order change occurs. Two of their examples will indicate the nature of their approach. The first concerns a four-year-old child on her first day of kindergarten, who was so upset when her mother was going to leave that the mother stayed all day. This pattern was then repeated, despite attempts to correct it, until one day when the mother was unable to accompany the child; the father took her, dropped her off, and left her. The child soon calmed down, and there was no recurrence of the problem. In the other case a man, living alone and afflicted with an agoraphobia that was progressively reducing his anxiety-free territory, decided to end it all. "He planned to get into his car and drive in the direction of a mountaintop about fifty miles from his home, convinced that after driving a few city blocks his anxiety or a heart attack would put him out of his misery. The reader can guess the rest of the story: he not only arrived safely at his destination, but for the first time in many years he found himself free from anxiety. He was so intrigued by his experience that he wanted it to be known as a possible solution for others who suffered from the same problem" (1974, p. 80). Five years later he not only was still free of his phobia, but had helped a number of other phobics with their problems.

From such examples, the authors derive four propositions about second-order change:

a. Second-order change is applied to what in the first-order change perspective appears to be a solution, because in the second-order change perspective this "solution" reveals itself as the keystone of the problem whose solution is attempted.

b. While first-order change always appears to be based on common sense (for instance, the "more of the same" recipe), second-order change usually appears weird, unexpected, and uncommonsensical; there is a puzzling, paradoxical element in the process of change.

c. Applying second-order change techniques to the "solution" means that the situation is dealt with in the here and now. These techniques deal with effects and not their presumed causes; the crucial question is *what?* and not *why?*

d. The use of second-order change techniques lifts the situation out of the paradox-engendering trap created by the self-reflexiveness of the attempted solution and places it in a different frame [pp. 82–83].

Second-order change methods are exemplified in such practices as encouraging the depression of a depressed person, or "helping" a person who is being angry and irrational to express his "unreasonable" ideas. Such procedures contrast sharply with behavior dictated by the commonsense approach of first-order change.

Other examples of second-order change procedures can be grouped under the heading of prescribing the symptom. So a sufferer from insomnia may be directed to try to stay awake, or a person who has a fear of fainting may be directed to faint.

But insofar as our interest is in conceptualizing change at the second level, the most interesting of the uncommonsense change techniques is the use of reframing. By this is meant a transformation of the meaning or significance of the behavior by a process of reclassification. This involves a contextual change in which the old facts are given a new significance. When a client on termination says in a somewhat puzzled tone, "Things are going a lot better, I don't quite understand it because objectively the situation is much the same, but somehow I feel quite differently about it," he is talking about a change in his way of conceptualizing events which have not themselves changed—that is, he is talking about a change in the way he frames them.

It must be appreciated that, as Epictetus expressed it nearly two thousand years ago, and as Albert Ellis likes to remind us, "It is not the things themselves which trouble us, but the opinions that we have about those things." As Watzlawick et al. note, "The word *about* in this quotation reminds us that any opinion (or view, attribution of meaning, and the like) is *meta* to the object of this opinion or view, and therefore of the next higher logical level" (p. 95). (Note: the reader is asked to keep this point in mind in the next chapter, when we consider Rogers's [1957] statement of "The necessary and sufficient conditions of therapeutic change.")

While, in the light of the theory of logical types Epictetus's point is obvious enough, its relevance seems to have eluded many psychotherapists, who talk glibly about adaptation to reality as the sign of normality. Reality, in the sense in which psychotherapists ordinarily use that term, is what some prevailing consensus defines as real. As Watzlawick et al. (1974) tell us, "the agreed-upon definition is reified ... and is eventually experienced as that objective reality 'out there.'" [p. 96]

Reframing is a process of changing "reality" in the sense of how events are conceptualized or defined. It is at a meta level in relation to the events. To quote Watzlawick et al.:

> ... the Theory of Logical Types permits us to conceptualize this more rigorously: As we have seen, classes are exhaustive collections of entities (the members) which have specific characteristics common to all of them. But membership in a given class is very rarely exclusive. One and the same entity can usually be conceived as a member of different classes. Since classes are not themselves tangible objects, but concepts and therefore constructs of our minds, the assignment of an object to a given class is learned or is the outcome of choice, and is by no means an ultimate, immutable truth. ... A red wooden cube can be seen as a member of the class of all red objects, of the class of cubes, of the class of wooden objects, of the class of children's toys, etc. [p. 97].

The class to which an object or event is assigned is determined by choice and circumstances, but once the assignment has been made, it can be very difficult to see it in terms of a different but equally valid class. Items of food provide excellent examples. What constitutes a gourmet's delight for members of one culture may be regarded with revulsion by members of another culture. Very dire circumstances are necessary before some items of very nutritious food are reclassified as "edible material" by some people.

It will now be apparent that

> In its most abstract terms, reframing means changing the emphasis from one class membership of an object to another, equally valid class membership, or, especially, introducing such a new class membership into the conceptualization of all concerned. If, again, we resist the traditional temptation of asking *why* this should be so, we can then see *what* is involved in reframing:
>
> 1. Our experience of the world is based on the categorization of the objects of our perception into classes. These classes are mental constructs and therefore of a totally different order of reality than the objects themselves. Classes are formed not only on the basis of the physical properties of objects, but especially on the strength of their meaning and value for us.
>
> 2. Once an object is conceptualized as the member of a given class, it is extremely difficult to see it as belonging also to another class. This class membership of an object is called its "reality"; thus anybody who sees it as the member of another class must be mad or bad. Moreover, from this simplistic assumption there follows another, equally simplistic one, namely that to stick to this view of reality is not only sane, but also "honest," "authentic," and what not. "I cannot play games" is the usual retort of people who are playing the game of not playing a game, when confronted with the possibility of seeing an alternative class membership.
>
> 3. What makes reframing such an effective tool of change is that once we do perceive the alternative class membership(s) we cannot so easily go back to the trap and the anguish of a former view of "reality" [pp. 98–99].

Once an issue has been reframed and a solution arrived at, as happens, for instance, in "breakthroughs" in scientific discovery, it is virtually impossible to revert to the earlier perception of the situation. Such "breakthroughs" are liberating intellectually and practically. Watzlawick et al. (1974, p. 100) quote Howard (1966), a games theorist, to the effect that "if a person comes to 'know' a theory about his behavior, he is no longer bound by it but becomes free to disobey it." As a simple example of this, it can be noted that inmates of mental hospitals and corrective institutions who are aware of the principles of token economies can—and often do—refuse to be bound by such tactics when the latter are applied to them. Some of the issues that arise in this regard will be considered in the next chapter when Lefebvre's reflexive polynomials are discussed.

These considerations bear on the role of "insight" in psychotherapy. Much confusion over this matter arises from different meanings given to the term "insight." Watzlawick et al. and Haley reject insight as a means of resolving problems, but in their usage the term typically refers to explanations of the problem as the result of historical events. It can be agreed that the ability of an individual to explain how he got to be the way he is contributes little to changing the way he is—indeed it is more likely, in itself, to provide a justification for his present predicament. On that basis there can be no dispute with the authors concerned.

However, there is quite another usage of the term "insight." When gestalt psychologists talk about insight, they are talking about something quite different from explanations as to how things have come to be as they are. They are talking about a new way of conceptualizing a problem or issue. In other words, gaining insight in this sense is a matter of reframing the matter under consideration. When Kohler's (1926) ape stumbled upon the solution of joining two sticks to reach a banana that could not be reached with either stick separately, she did a bit of reframing.

When psychotherapists talk about "real" insight, what they are talking about, although they do not seem to know it, is this kind of higher-level reframing of the problem. This kind of insight is highly potent in effecting change. Indeed it is central to the development of our understanding of our world and is the basis of the changes that have taken place in that understanding over the milennia. The consequences, in terms of increasing control and increasing freedom resulting from such insight, hardly need emphasis.

Haley and Watzlawick et al. are obviously correct in saying that insight is not essential for people to perform effectively in the area of human relationships. After all, people perform effectively in many areas without insight into what they are doing; for instance, a six-year-old child can speak a language fluently without having much insight into how he is doing it. And they are, almost certainly, also right in taking the view that focusing on getting their clients to understand their life situation is going to interfere with the latter living it and making the most of it. If one wants to enjoy playing football, it is better to get out on the field and start playing it than to go to lectures on the theory of the game. But all this does not mean that theory is not valuable. It simply means that for the practical problems with which therapists are called upon to deal, a focus on insight is usually inappropriate.

Therapists who, nevertheless, do want to focus on insight should concentrate on the axioms on which the individual is basing his strategy of living rather than on the antecedents of his current situation. In other words, one way of doing therapy is to get the individual to question what Frank (1973) calls his "assumptive system." And for the person who is chronically unhappy and wants to lift himself by his own bootstraps, a piece of advice would be for him to ask himself what belief he holds most strongly and then to question it. For instance, if he is distressed because he cannot find a purpose in life, he should ask himself what he means by having a purpose.

EVALUATIVE COMMENTS

The ecological model is in many ways the most powerful conceptually and practically of those available. It is free of the logical problems which are embedded in the other models. The divergence between Haley with his emphasis on family systems and Watzlawick et al. with their broader theoretical concerns seems likely only to enrich the model as they explore its many ramifications. Both approaches claim inspiration from the same sources—from the conceptual genius of Gregory Bateson and the practical genius of Milton Erickson.

PART III
The Conceptual Base

CHAPTER 7
Interpersonal Understanding

THREE MODELS WHICH, together, cover the broad spectrum of psychotherapy as it is currently practiced have been outlined and their main features exemplified in the application of therapy within extant systems. It is now proposed to undertake a more theoretical and more radical analysis of the processes involved.

The point at issue is influence. Within each of the three models the goal is the same: to exert influence over the thought processes and overt actions of the client. The therapist's objective is very similar to that of the parent who wants his child to want to be industrious, cooperative, considerate, friendly, and well organized. The typical therapist wants the client to be, and to see himself as, competent, lovable, reliable, and in control of himself and of the situations with which he has to deal. Such objectives cannot be achieved by simply exerting pressure or power. The problem for parent or therapist is to arrange conditions so that the child or client will acquire the desired thought and action patterns.

If any attempt to move the person in the desired direction is to be effective, it must be based on some understanding of the person. How such an understanding is to be arrived at has posed problems which have exercised philosophers and social scientists over a long period. In raising the issue once more, O'Neil's (1972) statement provides a good starting point. He tells us:

> The study of the person presents contemporary psychology with a dilemma, indeed a double dilemma. In so far as psychology tries to be scientific on the model of the successful natural sciences it tends to block itself in its attempts to study the person. In so far as it tries to grapple with the person, no holds barred, it tends to depart from the model provided by the successful natural sciences. There are two parts to the dilemma. The first concerns the data which may be used and the second concerns . . . the interpretative mode or strategy to be adopted [p. 73].

The first part of the dilemma relates to objectivity of observation. Natural science requires that different observers have equal access to the data and be able to observe and report them with "a fair degree of agreement and consistency." This presents difficulties to the psychologist who is investigating such phenomena as a person's "feeling of depersonalization or personal discontinuity," which are not amenable to consensual validation. O'Neil believes that "this is not as serious a problem as it is often made out to be, especially when we find different observers (of admittedly separate events) making congruent reports," though he also indicates that it cannot be dismissed.

It is, however, the second part of the problem that exercises him and which is of interest to us. This relates to the nature of explanation.

He identifies two modes of explanation. The natural sciences, he tells us, explain events "by showing that (i) certain laws (or law-like statements) taken in conjunction with (ii) certain specified circumstances jointly logically imply the events to be explained (the *explananda*)" (p. 74). So Newton's laws of motion and his law of gravitation, taken in conjunction with certain data on the solar system (masses, velocities, distances, etc.), yield an "explanation" of observed planetary motion.

The question is whether this type of explanation, called the covering law model by Hempel, is appropriate to account for the behavior of the person as an integrated totality. Dilthey, Weber, and other German philosophers of the nineteenth century argued that a different form of explanation was required if we were to understand the individual behavior of our fellows. They proposed that an understanding of an empathic kind, called *Verstehen*, was the appropriate method for this purpose. This procedure involves careful observation of the individual, combined with putting oneself in his situation, so that we have a sense of his values and perceptions which will enable us to "understand" why he acts as he does.

It may be asked whether these approaches are discontinuous or merely represent polar positions on a continuum. O'Neil, after examining various aspects of the two models, appears to come down in favor of the latter view, which he qualifies in the following terms:

I do, however, suggest that there is an important difference where the "covering laws" can be specified other than in a vague way so that they enable genuine inferences open to objective logical tests from those cases where only a "psychologic" can be applied.

On these scores I should like to defend the covering law model on the ground that it exposes itself to falsification whereas "understanding" scarcely does so. The latter is largely protected from falsification by subsequent observation for reasons I have hinted at.

Finally, I admit in practical terms, the covering law model though fairly successful in dealing with part psychological processes has not been very successful to date in dealing with the person. Those of us who have to deal with persons in our day-to-day work seem to be much more helped by a humanistic approach with its intuitive judgments of the concrete situations and its empathetic judgments of what follow from them [pp. 88–89].

The following two points emerge from O'Neil's analysis:

1. If the aim is a precise explanation of behavior in the tradition of the natural sciences, the covering law model constitutes the ideal and is at the other pole from the intuitive empathic approach of the humanist.
2. If the aim is to understand, to influence, and to work in harmony with others in the practical affairs of life, the intuitive empathic approach of the humanist is to be preferred.

This hiatus between what "works" in practice and "the interpretative mode or strategy" favored by the prevailing concept of science in the behavioral sciences constitutes an anachronistic situation that can hardly endure. If the situation is to be resolved, it would seem that there must be either a change in the accepted model of science or increased sophistication and precision in the application of the *Verstehen* approach, or possibly in both realms. In the remainder of this chapter the concern will be with developing the *Verstehen* orientation, while the following chapter will be concerned with the consideration of fundamental strategies in science—that, is with epistemological issues.

The *Verstehen* perspective involves trying to replicate the thought processes of the other. One term for this activity is "reflexion."

REFLEXION

The issues involved are complex. An illustration from a very well-known theoretical contribution will serve as an entry point into the matters which are of concern. Rogers (1957) published a paper on "The Necessary and Sufficient Conditions of Therapeutic Personality Change" in which he listed six conditions that had to be met for such change to occur and which, if met, would ensure such change. For the purposes of the present exposition, conditions 1 and 2 may be ignored. Conditions 3, 4, and 5 required respectively that the therapist (or other change agent) be congruent, warm, and empathically understanding in the relationship. Condition 6 required that the client (or change target) perceive, in some degree, these conditions being met by the therapist or other change agent.

This was an extremely influential paper. It stimulated a very large volume of research, gave rise to a substantial body of literature, and became the basis for numerous training programs in the practice of therapy. Yet the paper contains an important logical anomaly which seems largely to have escaped attention.

The anomaly is (Pentony, 1972) that condition 6 makes conditions 3, 4, and 5 redundant. If condition 6 is met, it is irrelevant whether conditions 3, 4, and 5 are met, and if condition 6 is not met, then it is also irrelevant whether 3, 4, and 5 are met.

It may be argued that 6 cannot be met if 3, 4, and 5, are not met. This is debatable because there is such a thing as being a good actor, and apparently it was envisaged that 3, 4, and 5 could be met without 6 being met. Otherwise there would have been no point in including 6. If error can occur in one direction, then presumably it can occur in the other. But these are minor issues. What concerns us is of a more profound and significant nature. The important question is how 6 comes to have the power to override 3, 4, and 5.

The impatient reader, who may regard the answer as obvious and the question as frivolous, is asked to think again. The obvious can require explanation.

The answer lies in the fact that communication is a multilevel phenomenon and the issue in question is one of communication. Any attempt to understand thought, the nature of mind, or processes of human interaction inevitably involves the analysis of communicational processes. The position has been well expressed by Bateson (1972):

> A priori it can be argued that all perception and all response, all behavior and all classes of behavior, all learning and all genetics, all neurophysiology and endocrinology, all organization and all evolution—one entire subject matter—must be regarded as communicational in nature, and therefore subject to the great generalizations or "laws" which apply to communicative phenomena. We therefore are warned to expect to find in our data those principles of order which fundamental communication theory would propose. The Theory of Logical Types, Information Theory, and so forth, are expectably to be our guides [pp. 282-283].

In the case under consideration, the reflexion in the "mind" of the client (or change target) of the intentions and purposes of the therapist (or change agent) is of a higher logical order than those intentions and purposes and overrides them insofar as we are concerned with the client's behavior.

Lest it be considered that such questions and their analysis constitute academic hair splitting that is irrelevant for practical affairs, consider the widely used practice of focusing on the "here and now" in individual and group therapy and in encounter groups. When a "here and now" response takes the form of being what the speaker hears another say, it is a reflexive act and of a higher logical order than that which it reflects. An example may illustrate what is at issue.

Mr. X, who was at the time a member of an encounter group being led by Dr. Y, a leading exponent of the client-centered orientation, drew attention to what he regarded as an inconsistency in papers written by Y. The latter responded by saying that three things came to mind as he listened—first that X understood his position, second that X was trying to go past that position, and third that in order to do so, he had to prove Y wrong. As might be expected, this took the discussion away from the point X was trying to make and focused attention on what he was doing in the "here and now."

Here we have a case of the issue of levels being utilized to control an interaction. Dr. Y's response expressing the reflexion in his mind of the processes in X's mind overrode, for the group, the contents of the latter's statement. It framed X's statement and defined the nature of the subsequent interaction.

What we have here is a conferring of meaning on events. Meaning is a function of context. Context is of a higher logical level than that for which it is the context. In making a statement charging Y with inconsistency, X was making a bid to define the context as one dealing with the truth or falsity of certain propositions. In responding with a reflexion, Y defined the context as one in which the behavior of X was the issue.

It has already been pointed out in the discussion of client-centered therapy that the reflexion of feeling response, which has been the most distinctive feature of that school, is of a higher logical level than the client statement which it is a response about. Similar remarks apply to the psychoanalytic interpretation. It too is a reflexive statement and, like the reflexion of feeling response, is of a higher logical level than that which it interprets, and, consequently, it defines the context of the interaction.

The argument to this point has been concerned with the fact that communication is a multilevel phenomenon and that the higher level has precedence over the lower level. This is what Watzlawick et al. (1967) mean when they say that the person who metacommunicates defines the context of the interaction. For the person who wants to contest the definition of the context, the appropriate response is to metacommunicate about the metacommunication—that is, to meta-metacommunicate.

In the case described above, X might have responded by reflecting Y's reflexion. In simpler terms, he could have pointed out what the leader was doing.

However, it is not always easy to do this. In part, the difficulty arises through ignorance in that the "victim"—or often both parties—may be unaware of what is actually occurring. In part, the difficulty may arise because such behavior may be regarded as inappropriate in view of the respective roles and power of the participants. A subordinate is not supposed to metacommunicate in respect of his superior's communications—that is, he is not supposed to point out to the superior how the latter is managing the interaction.

These and related points were brought out in the "double bind" hypothesis proposed by Bateson et al. (1956). They included in their discussion the problem of paradox. As they presented their theory of the etiology of schizophrenia, the "victim" who became schizophrenic was placed in a paradoxical situation from which he could not escape but to which his schizophrenic behavior was a solution.

Paradox is not a necessary feature of metacommunication in any particular case. Metacommunication is an inevitable and pervasive aspect of all human interaction. Paradox arises only when the multilevel nature of communication is ignored and one of the participants to an interaction contravenes the "law," as formulated by Whitehead and Russell in their theory of logical types, that whatever involves all of a collection cannot be one of the collection. Equally paradox arises when there is violation of the rule that a reflexion must not be confused with that which it reflects; or that a class of behaviors (e.g., being spontaneous) must not be confused with the behaviors which constitute it; or that a context must not be confused with the events occurring within it. Such violations are of frequent occurrence in psychotherapy and encounter groups. Attention has been drawn, in an earlier chapter, to such a violation's occurrence in the psychoanalytic process of requiring the patient to control himself to be uncontrolled in his free associating—a case of confusion between a class of behaviors and the behaviors which constitute the class.

An example of the posing of paradox is the action of a leader who intimates to the group that he is not going to direct it. Essentially his message to the group is "Treat me as someone who is not going to give you directions." But such a message is itself a direction. If the members of the group accept that direction, they place themselves in a paradoxical situation somewhat comparable to that of a hypnotic subject. They are precluded from perceiving subsequent directions from the leader as directions emanating from him. Similarly, the group leader who defines himself, verbally or otherwise, as an "ordinary" member of the group at some point in the group's life poses a paradox. What is happening in such cases is that the leader is simultaneously addressing the group and placing himself in the group being addressed.

The discussion so far has been focused on certain aspects of interpersonal control as these are exerted in the specialized area of psychotherapy. However, this chapter began with the issue of understanding the other with a view to exerting influence on him, and it is now time to come back to that point.

There is a general recognition of the fact that people, whether they seek to or not, influence the thoughts and actions of those with whom they are in contact. There is no way they can avoid doing so. One cannot not communicate. The task is to develop a systematic account which makes clear the full implications of what is involved. For such an account we are indebted to Lefebvre (1972, 1977).

Lefebvre's Reflexive Structure

Lefebvre is exercised by the issue, which has been of concern to us, that in human interaction each participant is observing and trying to understand someone who is observing and trying to understand him. He points out that the problems at issue go far beyond those which have been raised in the area of subatomic physics. In the case of the latter:

> ... the findings obtained by the investigator depend upon or are even the results of interaction between the object and the investigator's apparatus; but the findings do not influence the properties of the physical process which they reflect. Thus, Planck's constant does not depend on the fact that it was published. The scientific conception, not being a physical event, is not a property of the apparatus [1977, pp. 39–40].

In human interaction, the conception of one of the participants can, and often does, influence the properties of the process it reflects. This is shown in placebo effects and in the co-constitution of reality, but the aspect of main interest to Lefebvre is competitive behavior.

> The relations between objects-investigators manifest themselves most clearly in conflicts. For this reason, conflict is of interest in the study of interactions between an investigator and a system comparable to or superior to himself. It becomes vitally necessary to penetrate into the opponent's plans, that is, to analyse his thought processes. The very situation itself forces each participant in a conflict to investigate the inner world of his opponent and to construct an appropriate theory. This is an unusual interrelation between an object and a theory about it. The object constantly tries to "escape" from the theory, that is, to falsify it.
>
> In studying social-psychological phenomena the investigator becomes one of the personae in a specific game which we shall call a *reflexive* game. To the extent that the investigator cannot exclude the possibility of contact with

the other personae studied, his theoretical constructions, being assimilated by those other personae, may change radically the behavior of the whole system. On the other hand, the researcher may find himself a prisoner of his object: His conception may be imposed on him by the object [p. 43].

Thus while his primary concern is with phenomenological psychology, much of Lefebvre's discussion is oriented toward issues of games theory. His book has been translated from the Russian by Rapoport, who, in an instructive foreword, points out that as a competitor with games theory in the latter's domain—rational decision making—Lefebvre's approach is at a disadvantage. In that area, the mathematics of games theory constitute a much more powerful analytic tool. Nevertheless, as Rapoport goes on to tell us, since games theory does not take into account the thought control processes which Lefebvre discusses, the two systems are not in direct competition. Though he reserves judgment on the long-term utility of Lefebvre's contribution, he clearly regards it as deserving of serious attention. In a summarizing statement he tells us:

> Two concretely "scientific" contributions are offered in this book. One is a formal notation to register the extent to which in a given situation a number of actors "assimilate" or "replicate" each other's inner worlds and the underlying reality. The other is an experimental method designed to assess the possibilities of "inducing" in subjects certain hypotheses with the view of "exploiting" them in a game of strategy [p. 36].

The first of these "scientific" contributions is the development of a formal system, modeled after mathematics and formal logic, that will enable reflexive propositions to be translated into abstract symbols by means of which it is possible to carry out operations far more complex than can be carried out in natural language. Like Laing et al. (1966), whose position in certain respects has much in common with that of Bateson and his former associates at Palo Alto, Lefebvre is interested in such reflexive statements as "A believes that B believes that A believes. . . ." His approach, however, is different. Whereas Laing et al. are concerned with the content that is reflected, Lefebvre is interested in the reflexive structures whereby the content is processed. He has developed a system of algebraic polynomials that enables him to represent these structures and their functioning without having to take into account the content material that is reflected. This permits a deductive procedure for reflexive processes comparable to that made possible by the use of mathematics in the physical sciences. The problem which remains is that of relating the observational data to the symbolic system. The extent to which this can be accomplished is the critical issue.

The nature of the second contribution may be approached by considering one of the experiments based on this approach. In this experiment the subject faces a map of a maze with two lights—one green and one yellow—at each intersection. He is told that at the center of the maze there is a traveler who is trying to escape from the maze. There are five exit points. The traveler does not know the way and has no memory, so that he does not know where he has been. The subject's task is to prevent the traveler from escaping while ostensibly guiding him. He guides the traveler by lighting up a green light at an intersection adjacent to the one where the traveler is located. The traveler's position at any time is indicated by the lighting up of a yellow light. The traveler has the choice of two moves—he can move toward the green light or in the opposite direction. The choice is, in fact, preprogrammed.

Now the interesting point is that when this experiment was conducted using thirty-two engineering students each playing twice, the mean number of moves taken by the traveler to escape was fifteen on the first trial and eighteen on the second. For purposes of comparison, on the basis of a random choice at each intersection point, the number of moves required to escape would be 25. In other words, the attempts by the subjects to prevent the escape hastened it.

This peculiar result, which Lefebvre calls "turning apprehension into reality," occurs because the subject tries to "read" the traveler's "mind". That is, the subject tries to guess whether the traveler will obey the guide and move toward the green light or disobey and move in the opposite direction. The traveler is preprogrammed to begin by obeying, for a few trials, then to switch to disobeying, and then to switch again to obeying, and so on until he escapes. The subject typically adjusts his tactics too slowly to keep up with the traveler.

Given sufficient trials the subject will, of course, learn the traveler's response pattern and thereafter will have no difficulty in keeping him in the center of the maze. Even one trial was enough to make an appreciable increase in the average number of moves required to escape. That is to say, as the subject comes to construct a model of the traveler's strategy corrected by feedback, he will be able to anticipate the latter's moves.

Of more interest is the situation from the traveler's perspective. As Lefebvre says, if we anthropomorphize the traveler, we can say that he forms a model of the subject which includes the fact of the latter's reflexive awareness and consequent ability to change his strategy in the light of feedback. Using this model, the traveler can then predict the subject's responses to his moves. Of course, since the traveler is preprogrammed, the model formation is in fact carried out by the programmer.

What Lefebvre is saying is that interpersonal control is exerted by utilizing knowledge of the subject's model-forming propensities. Human interaction is thus presented as a process of mutual model manipulation by the participants. In this process, levels of reflexion play a significant part.

But competitive interaction is only a part of the story. Cooperative effort equally requires reflexive awareness. For two persons to coordinate their efforts in some task, it is necessary that each have a model of the situation and also a model of the partner, which must include his model of the task. In other words, each must be able to see the task through the other's eyes. From this it will be possible to develop a plan for performing the task.

Lefebvre has some interesting things to say about human organizations and similar collectives which might be encountered in the course of space travel. He calls such collectives "civilizations." A civilization is distinguished from a subhuman collective such as the colonies of cells that constitute a multicellular organism, or colonies of individuals such as a beehive or an ant hill, in that the members have to some extent an awareness of the contents of each other's awareness. In his more precise language, the distinctive feature of a civilization is that it can be represented by a reflexive polynomial. He goes on to point out that there is no necessary connection between a civilization as he uses that term and an advanced technology. A school of dolphins would be a civilization if these mammals are capable of reflexive awareness—that is, if they are capable of looking at the world through each other's eyes.

In his discussion of the functioning of a civilization—that is, of a collective in which the members have the ability to replicate the decision procedures of their fellow members—Lefebvre makes it clear that the collective requires a leader who stands out from it and over it. He has a special task of coordinating the activities of the members, and to do this he must have a model (or image) of the group as a totality and, within that, of the individual members and their tasks. He may, of course, perform some of the tasks which individual members perform, but this is in addition to, and not in lieu of, his function as leader and must not be confused with it. There is no place in Lefebvre's scheme for leaderless groups or groups in which the leader is just an ordinary member.

TESTING THE SYSTEM

Lefebvre has formulated and articulated in precise terms a scheme for approaching the difficult problem of consciousness. His development of a formal logical system for manipulating symbolically states of awareness impresses as being a very significant step in the understanding of psychological phenomena. The critical question, as Rapoport points out, is how the observations can be related to the formal system.

There are obvious difficulties in directly observing reflexive processes, and it is not clear how, within the traditional strategy of the application of the scientific method to psychological data, such relating of observations and symbols can be achieved. However, as Rapoport suggests, the idea of "reflexive control" might be incorporated into the designing of game-playing machines. As he comments, this would probably be an innovation in this area.

Such machines would operate on the principle of playing the opponent rather than the board. Thus a chess-playing machine might rank the moves available to the opponent at each decision point and, by comparing the actual moves made with this order, arrive at an estimate of the caliber of its opponent. It could then develop its own strategy in the light of this assessment. The basis on which the moves available could be ranked could cover such aspects as quality (how good the move is as determined within the machine's limitation) or the degree to which it constituted an aggressive, risk-taking strategy. A machine playing the opponent rather than the board in this way would, of course, be open to a counterstrategy in which the opponent begins with moves that suggest lack of skill or a particular strategy and the switches to a different pattern. While such machines would initially function at a relatively simple level, the processes involved would, in principle, conform to the reflexive control employed in human interaction.

Lefebvre's system of reflexive polynomials should aid in the design of such machines. The fact that his mathematical system allows for the specification of reflexive processes to infinite limits raises interesting questions concerning the theoretical limits of the reflexive power of such machines. If, as would seem to be suggested by Bateson's analysis of the learning process to be discussed in Chapter 9, there is an intimate relationship between reflexive capacity and learning, it should, in principle, be possible to construct machines with a high level of adaptability or capacity for learning.

It is obvious that there would be great practical difficulties in making machines of the complexity that would be required. Our concern here is with the principles and whether they can be shown to hold in relatively simple cases. From a scientific point of view to be able to construct apparatus which will replicate the phenomena being investigated is strong supporting evidence for the validity of the theory which provided the basis for the construction of the apparatus. This takes the discussion into the realm of epistemology, to which attention can now be turned.

CHAPTER 8
On Epistemologies

AN APPROACH to the practice and theory of psychotherapy which views the process as an exercise in influence and which proposes three models has been outlined. In reviewing the ground covered, the following points emerge:

1. Influence is a reciprocal process. This mutual causation aspect is evident whether the phenomena are viewed from a competitive point of view and seen in terms of a power struggle, or from a cooperative point of view and seen in terms of a co-constitution of reality.
2. The reciprocal nature of influence poses problems of power and its management, for the therapist, in the interests of the therapeutic objective.
3. The communication process has a hierarchical structure which can be expressed in terms of context and context of context and so on in infinite regression. Equally it can be expressed in terms of classes and classes of classes or of reflexions and reflexions of reflexions in infinite regression.
4. The strategic stance of the therapist is typically based on this hierarchical order, with the therapist communicating at a higher

logical level than the client. This enables the former to avoid being bound by the client's message.

Ideally, it would be time to turn to social psychology in the attempt to integrate such observations into the main body of theory. It is, however, fruitless to attempt to do so. Social psychology has little more to offer than a collection of unrelated descriptive statements of low generality. There is nothing in social psychology—or in psychology in general—that bears a resemblance to a general principle comparable to those of the established sciences.

It is no secret that there is considerable soul searching taking place among the more thoughtful workers within the discipline of psychology. The hundred years which have elapsed since Wundt opened the first psychological laboratory have seen remarkable little progress in the direction of scientific "discovery." Such innovations as have occurred and contributed to the content of the discipline have come, for the most part, from workers who have received their training in other fields. The payoff for a vast expenditure of resources in psychological training and research can only be described as meager.

Such attempts as have been made to chart new paths have not been promising. Humanistic psychology, which began by protesting the inadequacies of more traditional approaches in the discipline, is developing into a body of technology of highly dubious quality and validity. Farson (1978), in a pungent paper, has drawn attention to the wide margin between early aspirations and current practice within this orientation. His strictures on the dearth of scientific and scholarly work conducted by "humanistic" psychologists suggest that present activities in this area will be unlikely to make a serious contribution to the discipline.

Psychologists pride themselves upon their strictly empirical, inductive approach. The dangers of such an approach are that, in the absence of guiding principles, it leads to what one scientist called "postage stamp collecting" rather than science. No doubt the desire of psychologists to differentiate themselves from philosophers has played a part in the emphasis on the empirical and the reluctance to engage in speculative discussion. Nevertheless, the psychologist as a scientist must keep in mind how his method of investigation and his findings relate to what Bateson calls "the network of scientific fundamentals" (1972, p. xix). In this regard it would seem to be worthwhile to consider the epistemological basis of psychology and other sciences.

We may adopt the position outlined by Maruyama (1977). He defines epistemology as "structure of reasoning and structure of universe resulting from that reasoning." He identifies the three levels of theories, logics, and epistemologies. So Euclidean geometry is one theory, and non-Euclidean geometry is another theory, and both are in the one bivalue logic (true-false, equal-unequal). In turn bivalue, multivalue, and continuous value (as in physics) logics are different logics "within the same epistemology which is deductive and has a hierarchical universe in which values can be rank-ordered or quantitatively compared, usually obeying the transitive law. On the other hand, the non-reciprocal causal logic and the reciprocal causal logic belong to two different epistemologies" [1977, p. 121 footnote].

Epistemologies of Modern Science

There are several epistemologies in current scientific research. Maruyama lists five, but four seem to be relevant to modern psychology and particularly to the psychology of influence. These he calls:

1. Hierarchical and nonreciprocal causal epistemology
2. Independent event and random process epistemology
3. Homeostatic and morphostatic epistemology
4. Morphogenetic epistemology

Hierarchical and Nonreciprocal Causal Epistemology. This is the epistemology that prevailed in science up to and including Einstein's theory of relativity. It continues to enjoy favor among philosophers of science and in the social sciences, but the physical and biological sciences are moving out from it. Its essential feature is:

> . . . a nonreciprocal flow of influence from the "cause" to the "effect." The influence occurs with some probability rather than with certainty. "Effect" can be predicted from the "cause" with some probability, and the "cause" can be inferred from the "effect" with some probability. Complete information can never be obtained even on the present condition because of the fact that the information-collecting instrument interferes with the observed phenomena and the act of information-collecting disturbs the phenomena. The "scientific method" consists in discovering the probability distribution in the "effect" when the cause is hypothetically specified (neither cause nor effect can be completely accurately measured), and in establishing the limits of accuracy of observation. Multivariate statistical analysis such as factor analysis, correlation analysis, regression analysis, etc. can be attempted in the study of phenomena which are not completely amenable to laboratory experiments, such as weather, tropospheric scattering of electromagnetic waves and social revolution. If statistical relations between two variables are found, this may be due to one of the following nonreciprocal causal relations: a) one causes the other with some probability either directly or through other intermediate variables; or b) both are influenced by some common cause with some probability. The causal direction cannot be known from statistics alone, and must be determined by logical consideration [1977, pp. 123–125].

The patient reader will recognize this as a description of science that has been fostered in the minds of countless students of psychology. For many it is seen as the only way to be scientific. It does not seem to have been a particularly fruitful epistemology for psychology, particularly for social psychology. It is true that there have been attempts to formulate theoretical positions based on other epistemologies. Functionalist, holistic, gestalt, and field theoretical positions (MacDougall, 1915; Spencer, 1900; Koffka, 1935; Lewin, 1936) are examples of orientations that have, at various times, called into question the hierarchical and non-reciprocal causal perspective. Systems theory may be said to have emerged from such thinking. Nevertheless, the hierarchical and non-reciprocal causal epistemology has remained dominant in the behavioral sciences, particularly in North America. To the extent that it is seen as constituting *the* scientific method, departures from it tend to be regarded as requiring the surrender of hope of a rigorous intellectual approach to human behavior.

Independent Event and Random Process Epistemology. This is the epistemology of the second law of thermodynamics and Shannon's information theory. It is an epistemology of a *decaying* universe. It is of interest to psychologists and other social or behavioral scientists because the second law of thermodynamics has been interpreted as requiring the decay of isolated systems. Psychologists are concerned with systems—organisms and organizations—which grow and develop and hence seem to defy this law.

This epistemology arose with the theory of equilibrium dynamics of the nineteenth century and is based on a principle similar to that of tossing coins. In tossing a coin, each toss is taken to be independent of other tosses. If a fair coin is tossed 1,000 times, the most probable outcome is approximately 500 heads and 500 tails. A highly improbable outcome would be 1,000 heads and zero tails or zero heads and 1,000 tails. Similar considerations apply in the case of temperature. If left alone without outside interference for a long time, the most probable distribution of temperature in a nonliving isolated object is homogenous distribution. In Maruyama's words:

> If an isolated system is found in a state in which the temperature distribution is not even, it is thermodynamically in an improbable state. The more uneven the distribution of the temperature, the more improbable its state.... The system *tends* to change from a low-probability state to a higher-probability state. ...
> This tendency is called the law of increase of thermodynamic entropy. Entropy is *defined* in such a way that the higher the degree of homogeneity of the distribution of temperature, the higher the entropy [1977, p. 126].

Shannon's information theory also is based on the principle of improbable states. In his work with Bell Telephone Laboratories he was interested in minimizing the effect of random movements of electrons, caused by the amplifier, on the amount of information transmitted. He defined the amount of information as the degree of nonrandomness of the patterns. Not surprisingly, the mathematical formula for the amount of information thus conceptualized turned out to be the same as the mathematical formula for thermodynamic entropy, except that, because of the way information and entropy were defined, the relationship was inverse. That is, the greater the randomness, the greater the entropy but the less the information.

Maruyama is at great pains to point out that

> . . . *neither* thermodynamic entropy *nor* amount of information is a quantity which persists like energy or matter, and that there is *no* physical conversion between thermodynamic entropy and amount of information (while energy is convertible to and from matter), *nor* is entropy or information convertible to and from energy or matter.
>
> The first law of thermodynamics is the law of conservation of energy. The second law is the law of increase of entropy, in other words law of homogenization. They are two *logically independent* and *physically independent* laws [1977, p. 127].

It is essential to grasp the significance of this distinction. Information must not be confused with energy, as so often happens. They are conceptually and practically quite different things. Information is degree of improbability, not an entity sent through space. Information belongs in the communicational world, energy in the Newtonian.

Shannon's work has been important in science. In Maruyama's words:

> The purpose of science based on Shannonian information theory is to identify the amount of information, the type of coding and decoding, and the mode of transmission in living organisms and in man-made control and communication devices. Since noise and overloading of channels result in loss of information, and since information can never be increased, the primary concern of this type of science was the *economy* and the *efficiency* in the coding and decoding as well as the *maximum* use of channel capacity without creating overloading.
>
> Examples of fields of specialization which flourished under this epistemology are: the study of so-called genetic codes; neurophysiology; coded data transmission in space technology; data bank and information retrieval [1977, p. 128].

Mutual Causation

The third and fourth epistemologies are both based on the feedback loop principle and share in the radically new element of reciprocal causation. While they are both of recent origin, Maruyama sees two time phases involved:

a. The phase of the deviation-counteracting and equilibrating reciprocal causal epistemology. This phase occurred in the period extending from 1940's to the 1950's.

b. The phase of the differentiation-amplifying and heterogeneity-increasing reciprocal causal epistemology extending from the early 1960's to present. There may yet be the third phase to develop, characterized by mathematical elaboration of the diversity-symbiotizing reciprocal causal epistemology [1977, p. 129].

He gives the name "homeostatic and morphostatic epistemology" to that occurring in phase (a) and the name "morphogenetic epistemology" to that occurring in phase (b).

Homeostatic and Morphostatic Epistemology. Relatively simple self-regulating devices have existed for some time, but the development of a science based on the feedback principle may be dated from the mathematical formulations employed in weapon control systems in the Second World War. Since then, there has been widespread application of a general mathematical model of deviation-counteracting feedback networks to an array of events and processes which include automatic steering devices, economic processes, the regulation by the body of its temperature, and thermostats. The essential feature is that "a pattern of heterogeneous elements is arrived at regardless of the initial condition and is maintained by means of reciprocal interaction. It converges to a fixed heterogeneous pattern" (1978, p. 454). This epistemology has been invoked by those research workers we have identified above as favoring a contextual model of influence in their view of the family as a system. Don Jackson (1957) expressed it when he coined the phrase "family homeostasis."

Morphogenetic Epistemology. Social scientists, including psychologists, as yet have not given much attention to the developing area of work in respect of those events and situations in which the mutual causal effects are deviation-amplifying. Such events are widespread and are found in all areas of activity. They include such processes as the growth of an organism, the rise of a culture, the accumulation of capital in an industry, the growth of a city, the evolution of living organisms, the growth of friendship or hatred, the interpersonal processes that lead to mental illness or recovery, and indeed all that broad class of events which are termed "vicious (or virtuous) circles." That is, they include all processes of mutual causal relationships that amplify an event, which may be of an accidental or insignificant nature, producing a building up of deviation and divergence from the original condition.

Maruyama dates the beginnings of a science based on this "second cybernetics" to a paper read by Ulam, a mathematician, at Stanford in 1960. The point he made, and which Maruyama (1963, 1969) has also demonstrated, is that information can be generated in a system in the absence of information input from outside the system. This position is in direct opposition to inferences drawn from the second law of thermodynamics.

The case in point is that of the "genetic code." There has been some question as to whether this code could contain all the information necessary to constitute a blueprint of the mature organism. Ulam and Maruyama demonstrate that it does not need to. All that is required is that the code contain a set of rules determining the interactional behavior of the dividing cells. By following such rules, the interacting cells will form the mature organism. The amount of information required to specify the rules is relatively small compared with that necessary to specify the complete organism. This means that the information that is required to produce the organism is less than the information that is required to describe it. Thus information can be generated within the organism system—information can grow.

At first glance there may seem to be nothing remarkable about this, After all, the organism is an open system, and it can therefore take in negative entropy—presumably in the form of food—which provides the basis for growth. This, of course, misses the whole point of the independence of the first and second laws of thermodynamics. This confusion between energy and information has clouded thinking in this matter. It is a confusion between the communicational and Newtonian worlds.

Maruyama makes the point clear:

> This solves one of the puzzles of science. Thermodynamics based on the independent-event and random process epistemology could not explain how living organisms decreased the entropy (increased temperature differentiation). It simply begged the question by saying that living organisms are not isolated systems. But this question-begging was as unsatisfactory as the attempt at explaining how a computer works by saying that it works because it is plugged into a power source. A more satisfactory explanation lies in the recognition that the biological processes are reciprocal causal processes, not random processes [1977, p. 130].

There are implications here for those who would argue for growth forces in the universe or the converse. The writer is less interested in such questions than in the possibility of steps toward the development of a paradigm for the study of interpersonal processes. What Maruyama has told us is that the scientist can survey a range of epistemologies, all of which have their utility and validity, and select the one (or more) that seems most promising for his particular purposes. He is not confined to any particular one among the selection available. The fact that the physical and biological scientists are moving out of the hierarchical and nonreciprocal epistemology does not mean that the social scientist must do likewise, but it does suggest he might think about it.

Relevance for Psychology

Psychologists, in general, have accepted the hierarchical and nonreciprocal causal epistemology. The favored experimental design employing the dependent and independent variable model is based on it. Nevertheless, the weight of observational data has forced some departures from it in the formulation of theory. Both reinforcement theory and drive reduction theory, which tend to "explain" antecedents by their consequents, imply a circular causation process. What has been lacking has been an explicit acceptance of a reciprocal causal epistemology. Those behavioral scientists who have developed the contextual model of therapy have made the reciprocal causal epistemology explicit. Their work has already been discussed in some detail and needs no elaboration here. The relevance of the morphogenetic epistemology for some of Bateson's early work may be noted, and a plea by Wender (1968) for the application of this epistemology to psychotherapy deserves attention.

BATESON

Bateson (1936) appears to have been the first to discuss, in a systematic way, change as a process of reciprocal influence. In a discussion of the function served by a tribal ritual known as Naven which he observed among the Iatmul, a tribe in the Sepik district of New Guinea, Bateson (1936) proposed the term "schismogenesis" to refer to a process of change in the interaction of individuals *in the absence of interference from outside.* His point was that when two people—or two groups—are interacting, it is not sufficient to note a single exchange between them, but rather one must view interaction as an, at least potentially, escalating process in which the response of B to A's behavior affects A's next move and this in turn affects B's later response. Bateson thought that this sequential effect was of such significance that social psychology might be defined as the study of the reactions of individuals to the reactions of others. He comments:

> It is at once apparent that many systems of relationship, either between individuals or groups of individuals, contain a tendency towards progressive change. If, for example, one of the patterns of cultural behavior, considered appropriate in individual A, is culturally labelled as an assertive pattern, while B is expected to reply to this with what is culturally regarded as submission, it is likely that this submission will encourage a further assertion, and that this assertion will demand still further submission. We have thus a potentially progressive state of affairs, and unless other factors are present to restrain the excesses of assertive and submissive behavior, A must necessarily

become more and more assertive, while B will become more and more sub-missive; and this progressive change will occur whether A and B are separate individuals or members of complementary groups.

Progressive changes of this sort we may describe as *complementary* schis-mogenesis. But there is another pattern of relationships between individuals or groups of individuals which equally contain the germs of progressive change. If, for example, we find boasting as the cultural pattern of behavior in one group, and that the other group replies to this with boasting, a compe-titive situation may develop in which boasting leads to more boasting, and so on. This type of progressive change we may call *symmetrical* schismogenesis [pp. 176–177].

Richardson (1960), who was working on his mathematical models of war in the late 1930s and early 1940s, discussed the ideas and pointed out the similarity to his own position, but otherwise they do not seem to have received much attention until the 1950s. In that decade their relevance for the conceptualization of interaction processes, particularly within the family group, became apparent.

It is to be noted that Bateson and others following him have tended to see the consequences of deviation-amplifying feedback predomi-nantly in terms of the development of pathology. Their focus has been on one aspect of a more general process. Wender (1968), who was famil-iar with Maruyama's earlier writing, treated the issue on a more general level.

Wender

Wender first outlines the nature of deviation-amplifying feedback (DAF), giving illustrations of its occurrence in both physical systems (e.g., feedback in electronic systems such as hearing aids and public address systems) and organic systems (e.g., in some forms of hyperten-sion involving diminished renal blood flow). He goes on to discuss why the amplification does not proceed to infinite dimensions by pointing out that in physical systems, limits are set by the amplifying strength of the components, while in life processes, amplification sooner or later brings into play deviation-counteracting feedback mechanisms. So a line of evolutionary development may come to an end because the excessive specialization results in maladaption, particularly if the environment changes. The growth of a city in which increasing size leads to further increase in size (e.g., more people make it more attractive for industry and more industry makes it more attractive for people who seek work) may result in bringing into play counteracting feedback such as strain on natural resources, environmental pollution, restrictive legislation, and similar stabilizing effects.

Following Maruyama, Wender proceeds to list some formal properties of deviation-amplifying feedback systems, which are illustrated with accompanying diagrams. As he indicates, this can only be taken as illustrative material and not as providing a logically precise scheme. The notable feature of deviation-amplifying feedback is that any prediction of amplifying or dampening effects in natural systems requires a detailed knowledge of the specific elements in the system. That is to say, if one wants to predict whether or not a given city will continue to grow or the population of a given country will rise or fall, or whether a given individual will gain confidence and become more capable of managing his affairs or lose confidence and become increasingly helpless, it will be necessary to make a detailed analysis of the relevant factors in each case and assess the likely effect of changing events on these factors.

Wender cites a number of syndromes and situations which he considers are best understood in terms of deviation-amplifying feedback. These include (1) depression, which leads to decreased coping ability, which leads to negative self-evaluation, which leads to increased depression; (2) decreased coping ability, which "forces" others to provide assistance, which generates a self-perception of dependence, which leads to decreased self-evaluation, which leads to depression; (3) the shut-in schizophrenic reaction type in which social incompetence leads to withdrawal and withdrawal leads to social incompetence; (4) the psychiatric breakdown syndrome, in which a transient disturbance leads to a definition of sickness, which acts back to amplify the disturbance, resulting in long-term disability; (5) the situation of an uncontrollable child, in which a more complex amplification chain operates, where laxity by a parent leads to limit testing by a child, which results in excessively punitive parental behavior, which in turn gives rise to guilt in the parent, which is then assuaged by laxity (less restrictive control) with the child, and the whole cycle begins again; (6) the corrective emotional experience in which an unexpectedly positive encounter with another (the prototype is Jean Valjean in Victor Hugo's *Les Miserables*) sets in train a new pattern of interaction with others; (7) the working through of a transference neurosis in a Kleinian psychoanalytic model; (8) the application of Ellis's Rational Emotive Therapy; and (9) the self-fulfilling hypotheses of Eric Berne's games players.

As he points out, "The mechanism of DAF explains how small causes can become associated with large effects—how small, perhaps chance, variations in experience can generate chains of events which culminate in gross alterations" (p. 321). He goes on to suggest that the problems psychologists have in predicting later personality attributes from earlier measures, even though no significant intervening experiences would seem to have occurred, can almost certainly be attributed to the amplification of small variations in experience over time.

> It is inevitable that the process of DAF and happenstance will produce variations. To the novelist this is "old-hat" but to the scientific psychologist it is unsettling. Teachers, friends, spouses, and others met by chance often produce profound and lifelong changes in one's values and direction, changes that survive a brief contact, and, seemingly, are of much greater intensity than the initial events seemed to warrant. Furthermore, memory of such contacts—"random perturbations"—may later seem to have disappeared, not because of repression but because of the initial apparent triviality of the contact [p. 321].

Wender's theme is that it is time for behavioral scientists to recognize what is obvious to everyone. He argues for an interaction perspective. "Repeated actions and reactions do not fit a unidirectional causal model, are difficult to describe—except historically—and do not lend themselves to simple generalizations pretty to exposit. ... It is unfortunate, perhaps, but it seems that in many respects history provides a better model for psychology than does physics" (p. 321–322).

His comments on the relevance of deviation-amplifying feedback to psychotherapy are simply a statement of the position of the exponents of the contextual model, discussed elsewhere. Perhaps of more importance is his point that accepting the deviation-amplifying feedback principle will not be easy for those who, in the traditional "scientific" style, believe that large variations in outcome must derive from large antecedent causes, and who hope for the discovery of a few simple rules to explain many social events. In other words, he is saying that the acceptance of the deviation-amplifying feedback principle calls for a radical reorientation in thinking from those behavioral scientists who are concerned with understanding social behavior.

BROADER IMPLICATIONS

The behavioral scientist who accepts the case for the reciprocal causal epistemology will want to know what its implications are for theory and practice in his field. This raises issues which will be addressed in Part IV. For the present we can note Maruyama's comment that

> ... the structure of research will be different. In the traditional logic, it is assumed that similar conditions produce similar results. Therefore, if the results are dissimilar, the conditions must be dissimilar, and research is designed to find the differences. In a differentiation-amplifying reciprocal

causal process, however, similar conditions may lead to dissimilar results. Therefore, instead of looking for different conditions, one must study amplification loops [1978, p. 454].

It is apparent that the reciprocal causal epistemology will require the development of new research strategies in the social sciences. Some developments in this direction seem to be taking place, as, for example, in the use of videotape to study mother-child interaction patterns. In view of the increasing interest in situational and contextual factors in human behavior we can hope for further developments of this kind.

CHAPTER 9
On Mind

THE DISCUSSION has proceeded to the point where it is time to make as explicit as possible the stance being taken on the age-old question of the nature of mind. If it were necessary to state this in a few words, the short answer would be that mind—in the case of an individual—is coextensive with the system of control circuits that govern his behavior. Another way to put this would be to say that mind extends beyond the body and includes environmental processes that participate in the circular control system. The position taken is in line with that of Gregory Bateson, who has expressed it by saying that he has never made a free choice in his life.

Since such a formulation calls for justification and explanation, this chapter will be devoted to trying to outline a position on the nature of mind and its mode of operation. In addition to Bateson (1972), we are indebted to Boulding (1956), Hayek (1952, 1969), Koestler (1964, 1969), Lefebvre (1977), Miller et al. (1960), Waddington (1969), and Weiss (1969).

Among the ideas which emerge from such writing, perhaps the most important is that of hierarchical organization. This is a recurrent theme irrespective of the area of investigation and discussion. There appear, however, to be, at first glance, two types of hierarchy:

1. The hierarchy which is a feature of the algorithm and the mechanics of which, in control systems, have been detailed by Miller et al. in their brilliant discussion of the Plan
2. The hierarchy of awareness which the theory of logical types illuminates and which is discussed in terms of contexts (Bateson) and reflexions (Lefebvre)

In fact the two hierarchies reduce to different aspects of one hierarchy, but for the purposes of discussion it is convenient to treat them quite separately for the present.

ALGORITHMIC HIERARCHY

An algorithm is simply a set of instructions for carrying out some task in a step-by-step process. The most obvious example of an algorithm is a cook's recipe, in which each step in the process is spelled out in detail in the order in which the steps are to be executed. In a typical recipe some of the steps are grouped. Thus some of the ingredients must be prepared and mixed with other ingredients before being included in the main mixture. That is, the sequence is punctuated or bracketed so that certain groups of steps form subsequences within the larger sequence. The hierarchical structure derives from such bracketing in which there are subsequences within the whole, and the subsequences may be broken up further into sub-subsequences and so on until basic units are reached. Miller et al. (1960) have described the basic step or unit in such a hierarchical order—the feedback loop or TOTE unit—and shown how the higher-level units or subsequences and, ultimately, the whole sequence that constitutes the complete task are themselves TOTE units containing the lower units within them. That is, the whole series of steps to complete a task—or execute a Plan—is controlled by a hierarchical structure of TOTE units.

The program for a computer is an algorithm which specifies the sequence of TOTE units for the completion of the computer task. The Plan is an analog in human behavior of the computer program. A Plan is defined as "*any hierarchical process in the organism that can control the order in which a sequence of operations is to be performed*" (1960, p. 16). In principle, it would be a relatively easy matter to program a computer to control the operations of baking a cake—that is, of following the Plan the cook uses to bake it.

The differences between the Plan an individual executes when he performs some task (e.g., writes and mails a letter) and a computer program are (1) that the individual formulates the Plan he executes, whereas the program which the computer executes is prepared by a

human intelligence; and (2) that the individual formulating and execut-
ing the Plan does not *consciously* specify the numerous substeps (the
many muscle movements which are carried through at a subconscious or
unconscious level), whereas it is necessary to specify these in precise
detail in the case of the computer program.

The Plan is an explanatory concept of great power and clarity. It can
account for the control of a wide range of behavior including the operation of the genetic code, instinctive behavior, learned habits, and purposive action. What is not clear from the account is the nature of the
relation of the Plan to awareness. Miller et al. are primarily concerned
with action and seek to explicate how action is controlled and directed.
They regard their work as complementing a cognitive perspective outlined by Boulding (1956), who employed the metaphor of the Image to
represent what the individual knows about his universe. While Miller et
al. tell us that "the central problem of this book is *to explore the relation
between the Image and the Plan*" (1960, p. 18), it is precisely the nature of
this relationship that is most obscure.

The problem in relating the Plan to the Image seems to reside in the
way the Image is formulated. Boulding provides us with a broad survey
of many fields of knowledge couched in expressive language, but tells us
little about how the Image functions. It is questionable whether the
pictorial metaphor can lend itself to the explanation of a working system.
In at least one important area, the metaphor would seem to be misleading. This concerns Boulding's discussion of the genetic code. In discussing the genes and their role in the formation of the adult organism, he
tells us that they act like a blueprint, and he uses the analogy of the
blueprint of a building toward which the builder works. There are,
however, very good reasons for believing that the genes do not act like a
blueprint. It is highly improbable that the genes could contain the information necessary to specify the adult organism. In any case, as has
been indicated in the preceding chapter, Ulam and Maruyama have
demonstrated that they do not need to. All they need to do is to provide
a set of rules of interaction for the dividing cells, and this, in conjunction
with the operation of deviation-amplifying and deviation-counteracting
feedback processes, will result in the formation of the mature organism.
Szent-Gyoergyi (1974), who considers that the genes cannot possibly
contain all the information necessary to describe the mature organism,
tells us that the genetic code cannot be a blueprint, but must rather be a
manual of instructions.

Since the Image metaphor does not appear to provide a useful approach to an understanding of the nature of knowledge on which planning is based in the scheme proposed by Miller et al., a new approach
seems to be required. For this purpose, the second type of hierarchy—
the hierarchy of awareness—would seem to be a possible candidate.

THE AWARENESS HIERARCHY

The concern here is with levels of awareness. In the discussion of this hierarchy, we are concerned with the processes of learning and knowing. We can approach the issues that are involved in terms of classes, contexts, or reflexions. The three terms are, for our purposes, synonyms. For purposes of exposition, it would seem to be most convenient to think in terms of reflexions.

It is well appreciated that a person may be aware of some object or event, that he may be aware of his awareness of that event, and that he may be aware of his awareness of his awareness of that event. Beyond that point it is well nigh impossible for the individual to grasp the meaning of such statements, and even this statement would pose difficulties for most people. It is easier to grasp what is meant if the statement is rephrased in some such form as "John is aware that he knows he is observing a very unusual event."

The problems posed by the hierarchical structure of organismic events were central in the discussions at the Alpbach Symposium (Koestler and Smithies, 1969). In the exchange which took place between Koestler and Hayek after the latter's paper, an important issue which is relevant for our considerations was raised, but apparently not fully developed and resolved. In his paper Hayek's main point was that organismic development proceeds from the general to the particular and hence what is most primitive is most abstract. There was broad agreement on this, though different speakers formulated the principle in slightly different terms (e.g., as progressive differentiation).

As long as the discussion was concerned with such processes as embryological development, instinct rituals, or the development of language, no problem arose. Such processes exemplify the Plan of Miller et al. They fit the algorithm. As Waddington noted: "When you go from the general to the particular, the thing that carries you has got to have the character of an instruction. It is a rule of the game, in fact an algorithm" (in Koestler and Smithies, 1969, p. 330).

However, there are obvious problems when awareness and learning are brought into the discussion. It is apparent that at the level of awareness it is not true that the most abstract is most primitive. The thought processes of the mathematician as he plays with highly abstract ideas are obviously not more primitive than those of the individual who thinks in "concrete" terms. As Koestler pointed out, "when we learn a new skill like piano-playing or chess, then there is no primacy of the abstract" (Koestler and Smithies, 1969, p. 326). While a skill, once mastered, can be said to conform to the algorithm in its operation, the acquisition of the skill is quite another matter. Hayek effectively conceded this in agreeing that there were learned rules. However, his statement that "We could not explain the process of learning if there weren't other rules which had not been learned" (p. 326) does little to resolve the issue.

Koestler has a more complete grasp of the issues in his generalization that "*the output hierarchy concretizes, the input hierarchy abstracts*" (1969, p. 201). The learning which enables the skill to be acquired constitutes a different process from that which governs the practice of the skill once the acquisition has occurred.

In Koestler's scheme, the output hierarchy is that of the Plan or the algorithm that is being executed. Examples of its operation, as indicated above, are embryological development, the performance of skilled acts, instinct rituals, and purposive action. Input hierarchies, on the other hand, relate to the acquisition of knowledge and skills—that is, to learning how the universe or some aspect of it "works" and how to perform tasks. As he presents his position, *the input hierarchy is the output hierarchy in reverse.* The reflexive awareness begins with the concrete and arrives at an understanding of the Plan or algorithm governing an orderly sequence of events. The procedure is basically inductive or empirical, but allows for, and is greatly aided by, deductive "hunches" or hypotheses which constitute quantum leaps of the "insight" variety.

The input hierarchy is the awareness hierarchy. It is possible to see now the nature of the relationship between the two hierarchies. The awareness hierarchy takes shape in the process of backtracking on the executed algorithm. It is a model building process involving a reconstruction of the sequence of events.

Such back-tracking is a difficult process. As we noted, it is difficult to grasp the meaning where three levels of the awareness hierarchy are involved ("John knows that he knows he is observing a significant event"). The reader will recall that Haley commented on the difficulty observers experienced in noting three sequences occurring in an interaction pattern (Chapter 6). We suggested that the explanation for the observed difficulty lay in the fact that what is called for in such a case is a backtracking process in a sequential series involving three levels. That is, the observer has to note that the third or last response in the sequence occurs in a context set by the penultimate response, which in turn is a response in a context.

The question then arises as to whether the different levels of awareness—the reflexions or the contexts—match up with the different levels of the algorithm. That is, do subsequences of subsequences within the algorithm match up with the awarenesses of awareness or contexts of context in the awareness hierarchy, as the individual reconstructs the Plan or structure of events? The answer appears to be in the affirmative. What can be called the punctuation of the algorithm coincides with the levels of knowing that have given rise to the theory of logical types. In constructing a model of the sequence, the learner moves back in reverse order through the steps in which the sequence unfolded.

In both cases, a price is paid, in both practical and theoretical terms, for ignoring the levels. At various points attention has been drawn to some of these consequences in respect of violation of the theory of logical types. We might note here some of the consequences when the levels are ignored in the case of the algorithm.

In subhuman events the levels are not ignored. Embryological development processes and instinct rituals are "soldered in" in the organism. The algorithm runs its course in accordance with the preset punctuation. However, when someone asks what would happen to a centipede if it had to decide which leg to move next, he is raising the question of the consequences of interfering with the punctuation. Punctuation determines the order in which instructions are transmitted through the hierarchy. When levels are ignored, the order is disrupted. As Koestler puts it, "Attempting to short-circuit intermediary levels of the hierarchy by focussing conscious attention on physiological processes which otherwise function automatically, usually ends in the centipede's predicament, reflected in symptoms that range from impotence and frigidity to constipation and spastic colons" (1969, p. 205). Other examples of the consequences of ignoring levels are provided by the effects on skilled movements of attending to the details of the movement. The skilled pianist who attends to what his fingers are doing will lose his high level of skill.

Such consequences of ignoring the relevance of levels applies across all control systems whether we are dealing with skills, social organizations, or interpersonal relationships. Haley (1976) has drawn attention to these consequences in his discussion of the pathological effects of cross-generational coalitions. Managing directors who know their job do not interfere on the workshop floor, and generals do not become involved in the command of battalions. In all cases what is at issue is the relevance of levels in the output hierarchy. And, as we saw, families which transgress generation lines experience pathology in behavior.

To this point, the discussion has been concerned with the relation between action and knowing, as these issues were viewed by Miller et al. nearly twenty years ago when they developed their concept of Plan to complement Boulding's concept of Image. The Plan governs action. The Image constituted the individual's structure of awareness of his universe. However, our analysis suggests that the Image metaphor is misleading and that cognition and executive action are best considered as processes which have common features though they might be said to proceed in opposite directions. Since the Plan—or the algorithm—is relatively well known and understood in this age of computers, it is not proposed to devote further attention to the output hierarchy, but to consider the input hierarchy as this has been analyzed by Bateson (1972) in his discussion of learning.

LEARNING TYPES

Bateson distinguishes five levels or types of learning:

> Zero learning is characterized by *specificity of response,* which—right or wrong—is not subject to correction.
> Learning I is *change in specificity of response* by correlation of errors of choice within a set of alternatives.
> Learning II is *change in the process of Learning I,* e.g., a corrective change in the set of alternatives from which choice is made, or it is a change in how the sequence of experience is punctuated.
> Learning III is *change in the process of Learning II,* e.g., a corrective change in the system of *sets* of alternatives from which choice is made. . . .
> Learning IV would be *change in Learning III,* but probably does not occur in any adult living organism on this earth. Evolutionary process has, however, created organisms whose ontogeny brings them to Level III. The combination of phylogenesis with ontogenesis, in fact, achieves Level IV [p. 293].

The levels which are of immediate interest are I, II, and III. Level zero refers to such learning as the fact that the drumming noise on the metal roof means that it is raining. It is characterized by information input which can be repeated without producing change in the response of the organism. Bateson lists a number of contexts in which zero learning occurs. One of these is the performance of simple mechanical devices or electronic circuits where no change occurs in the apparatus as a consequence of its activity. A point which might be noted is his comment to the effect that we should not ask whether machines can learn, but rather what level or order of learning a given machine can achieve.

Learning I. This is the type of learning which has engaged the attention of experimental psychologists to the virtual exclusion of other types of learning. It embraces such processes as habituation, classical and operant conditioning, rote learning, and extinction of learned responses. Bateson defines it as change in zero learning—that is, the organism gives a different response at time 2 from that which it gave at time 1.

He is at pains to point out that in all cases of Learning I the assumption is made that the context is the same at the two times—otherwise it would follow that all learning would be zero learning. That is, the changed behavior would be attributable to the changed context. But if the assumption of an unchanged context stands, then the case for logical typing of learning phenomena necessarily holds. That is to say, there is a choice between discarding the notion of constant (or repeated) context and with it any learning other than zero learning and retaining the notion and with it accepting "the hierarchic series—stimulus, context of stimulus, context of context of stimulus, etc." (p. 289).

He then goes on to consider how the organism determines whether the context is the same as, or different from, another context and proposes that there are context markers—signals or stimuli that serve to classify contexts. Thus in the case of a dog that has been used a number of times in a classical conditioning experiment, putting the harness on the dog may serve as a context marker. Furthermore, just as there are context markers which serve to classify contexts, so also there are markers that serve to classify contexts of contexts. Thus in the case of a play on television or on the radio, there are context-of-context markers which tell the audience that what is occurring is fiction. This is usually provided by a verbal announcement. But it sometimes happens, as occurred in the instance of the radio play "War of the Worlds," that the marker of the context of contexts is missed by members of the audience, with unforeseen consequences.

Learning II. This is learning which has variously been called "learning to learn," "set learning" (Harlow, 1949), "deutero-learning" (Bateson, 1942), and "transfer of learning." Such learning can be said to have occurred if it can be shown that experience in a learning context results in the organism's responding in a subsequent context as though both contexts had the same contingency pattern. As Bateson points out, to be adaptive such learning must be based on a valid perception of the contingency patterns. When this is the case, learning in the new context will be more rapid or involve fewer errors. Empirical evidence for such learning includes the following:

1. Hull et al. (1940, pp. 75–76) noted that, for any given subject, there is an improvement in rote learning with successive sets of material toward a maximum level of performance that varied from subject to subject.

2. Harlow (1949) presented rhesus monkeys with "problems" which they had to solve to get a food reward. He showed that if these problems were of a similar class or "set"—that is, contained similar types of task—there was a carryover of learning from one problem to the next.

3. Animals trained in classical conditioning experiments to discriminate between two stimuli (or sets of stimuli), for example, between an ellipse and a circle, are likely to show symptoms of disturbance when the difference between the two stimuli is reduced to the point where it cannot be discriminated. Since animals with no previous training, when placed in a situation where the discrimination cannot be made, do not exhibit disturbance, it would seem that the disturbed behavior results from the animals, having initially learned to treat the context as one calling for discrimination, finding it switched on them to one of random

response. Such context "switching" has disturbing effects and is incorporated in the concept of the "double bind" (Bateson et al., 1956).

Learning II is of particular interest to psychotherapists, for it is the type of learning they seek to change. Consider the description of an individual as being dependent. Such a term is not strictly applicable to the person, but rather applies to the way he interacts with his environment. An adverb and not an adjective is required to describe what is occurring. A character trait is not something in a person, but is descriptive of the way he deals with other persons or situations.

We could write the specifications for learning situations that will result in the development of a dependent pattern of interaction between an individual and his environment. This would involve ensuring that his needs were met without his having to overcome difficulties, and also ensuring that such limited initiatives as he undertook were unsuccessful. Such a combination of indulgence and experience of failure could be expected to result in the higher-level learning of dependence in which the individual controls the reinforcement contingencies by signals of helplessness.

There are dangers in the use of terms such as "dominance" or "dependence" to describe an individual's transactions. A cry for help may have the quality of command. The individual who learns to control the behavior of others by being helpless can be regarded as dominating relationships. Whether a sequence of transactions between individuals is to be described in terms of seeing the dependent person as dominant and the succoring person as submissive, or vice versa, depends upon how the sequence of exchanges between them is punctuated.

All transaction patterns between the individual and his environment that cause people to apply such trait names as "anxious," "persistent," "cowardly," "optimistic," "perfectionist," and the like, insofar as they have been acquired by learning, are the outcome of Learning II. All of these, it should be noted, refer to classes of acts and not to specific acts.

Difficulties arise in communication between professional workers in the behavioral sciences when there is failure to understand and distinguish between the levels of learning. Experimentally oriented psychologists tend to conceptualize all learning in Learning I terms, whereas psychotherapists tend to have in mind Learning II processes.

Psychotherapy requires Level II learning. This means learning to see the "facts" in a new context. It means coming to punctuate the sequence of events differently. The patient or client must replace an old Learning II with a new Learning II.

Such relearning is extraordinarily difficult. The reason why it is so difficult is that what is learned is not true or false in the sense that it can be tested objectively. To quote Bateson, "We suggest that *what* is learned in Learning II is a way of *punctuating events*. But a *way of punctuating* is not true or false. There is nothing contained in the propositions of this learning that can be tested against reality. It is like a picture seen in an ink blot; it has neither correctness nor incorrectness. It is only a *way* of seeing the ink blot" (1972, p. 300).

Bateson is making the same point as Watzlawick et al., whose position was discussed in Chapter 6. The terminology is different in that Bateson speaks in terms of punctuation while they talk about the assignment of events to classes. Once the punctuation or classification is made, it is relatively difficult to arrive at a new punctuation or classification.

The person who has acquired a fatalistic view of life will not be forced by the "facts" to change it. Whatever happens in his life can be fitted to this perspective. Equally the person who takes a "purposive" view of life—who believes that the reinforcement contingencies can be controlled by his action—will be able to accommodate any outcome to his "philosophy." If he does not achieve the outcomes he seeks, it is simply because he has not tried hard enough or not been sufficiently skillful or whatever. Moreover, the person who holds a particular outlook based on Learning II typically acts in such a way as to bring about outcomes that confirm his perspective. This is the phenomenon of the self-fulfilling hypothesis. Again to quote Bateson:

> The practitioner of magic does not unlearn his magical view of events when the magic does not work. In fact, the propositions which govern punctuation have the general characteristic of being self-validating. What we term "context" includes the subject's behavior as well as the external events. But this behavior is controlled by former Learning II and therefore it will be of such a kind as to mold the total context to fit the expected punctuation. In sum, this self-validating characteristic of the content of Learning II has the effect that such learning is almost ineradicable. It follows that Learning II acquired in infancy is likely to persist through life. Conversely, we must expect many of the important characteristics of an adult's punctuation to have their roots in early infancy [p. 301].

But change in Learning II does occur. People can, and do, change some aspects of their "assumptive systems" both in therapy and without it. Bateson suggests that this can occur both through the occurrence of Learning III—though this is probably rare—or at the level still of Learning II, which is the level at which psychotherapy typically operates. The issues involved here are somewhat complex and take us back to a consideration of change at Level I.

Change in Premises of Learning II Without Achieving Learning III. If we return to change in Learning I, it will be recalled that Learning II is defined as change in Learning I. However, not all change in Learning I need qualify as Learning II.

Consider what is called reversal learning. In such experiments the animal is trained to discriminate between two stimuli (e.g., between a square and a circle). When this has been learned to criterion, the reinforcement contingencies are reversed. If the square originally meant food and the circle no reward, then in the reversal the circle means food and the square means no reward. When this reversed meaning has been acquired to criterion—that is, the animal consistently chooses the circle—the reinforcement contingencies are again reversed so that the initial situation is reestablished. This reversal procedure continues.

Learning II would be said to occur in such an experiment if the animal in the later reversals reached criterion in fewer trials than in the earlier reversals.

However, it is apparent that the animal can learn to reverse its premises as to which stimulus means food at a stage when Learning II is extremely rudimentary if it exists at all. Hence, applying the same sort of logic in the case of change in premises of Learning II, it would seem that such change may be achieved without necessitating Learning III. This would appear to be what happens in psychotherapy or in "spontaneous" occurrences outside the therapy situation. Bateson notes that to achieve such changes in Level II premises, the therapist might fruitfully engage in one or more of the following maneuvers:

> (a) to achieve a confrontation between the premises of the patient and those of the therapist—who is carefully trained not to fall into the trap of validating the old premises;
> (b) to get the patient to act, either in the therapy room or outside, in ways which will confront his own premises;
> (c) to demonstrate contradiction among the premises which currently control the patient's behavior;
> (d) to induce in the patient some *exaggeration or caricature* (e.g., in dream or hypnosis) of experience based on his old premises [p. 302].

As Bateson goes on to point out, the therapist must ensure that the patient not find loopholes which enable him to slip through the contradictions to his Level II premises.

Learning III. Learning at this level is rare. Whereas Learning II is a learning of the contexts of Learning I and hence the achievement of the type of learning called "insight" learning, Learning III is a learning of the contexts of Learning II and hence will "lead to a greater flexibility in the premises of acquired Learning II—a *freedom* from this bondage" (p. 304).

Such learning will result in a radical redefinition of self. At the level of Learning II we have the consistent behavior patterns—the personality or character traits. These involve set ways of classifying events and constitute "roles" in relationships. Learning III will have the effect of transcending such processes and will result in a certain loss of sense of self. In Bateson's words, "To the degree that a man achieves Learning III, and learns to perceive and act in terms of the contexts of contexts, his 'self' will take on a sort of irrelevance. The concept of 'self' will no longer function as a nodal argument in the punctuation of experience" (p. 304).

Here are some examples of what would be called Learning III:

> (a) The individual might learn to form more readily those habits the forming of which we call Learning II.
> (b) He might learn to close for himself the "loopholes" which would allow him to avoid Learning III.
> (c) He might learn to change the habits acquired by Learning II.
> (d) He might learn that he is a creature which can and does unconsciously achieve Learning II.
> (e) He might learn to limit or direct his Learning II [pp. 303–304].

Learning III, as a phenomenon at the limit of human capacity, is obviously not well understood. It would seem that incipient Learning III, as well as opening possibilities for a more serene and free existence, is likely to have a very disorganizing effect on an individual's sense of "reality," with possible pathological consequences.

Learning IV. This type of learning probably never occurs in human behavior. Bateson is reported to have included it "to keep the learning categories open-ended, and to indicate that his learning theory takes in not just human beings but the whole of nature" (May, 1977, p. 87).

It is, however, interesting to speculate on the possibility of the development of machines which would be capable of Learning IV and higher orders of learning. When we discussed Lefebvre's formal system of reflexive polynomials, we suggested that his innovation might constitute a basis for the contruction of machines capable of reflexive processes—that is, of replicating the decision processes of other machines. Since his system allows for the manipulation of reflexive processes to the nth degree, it would seem that if such machines can be constructed, it should, in principle, be possible to make models capable of higher orders of reflexion—that is, of higher orders of learning.

In an age when the question as to whether machines can learn is unanswered, it may seem bizarre to suggest the possibility that at some future date man may construct machines that will surpass him in an important aspect of learning capacity. Nevertheless, the possibility seems to deserve consideration.

Before leaving this hierarchical aspect of Bateson's contribution, it may be worth noting that further evidence, beyond the body of observations he has drawn on to support his argument for treating learning as a multilevel phenomenon, is available. The substantial body of work reported by Seligman (1975) on "learned helplessness" would seem to be most satisfactorily accommodated by a Learning II model.

BATESON'S "EPISTEMOLOGY OF CYBERNETICS"

There is a further aspect in which Bateson's contribution to our understanding of the "knowing" or awareness process deserves attention. It shares much common ground with Maruyama's discussion of reciprocal causal epistemologies.

Our primary concern in outlining the former's position has been to arrive at an alternative way of conceptualizing cognition from that offered in Boulding's metaphor of the Image. It is suggested that knowledge might be conceived of as a structure of "rules" which are developed over the course of the individual's lifetime and which "govern" communicational processes within the individual and between the individual and the environment.

It is assumed that, as compared with the more rudimentary nervous system of simpler organisms, the massive development of the human brain allows for a great extension and elaboration of communication circuits within the individual, and that this provides the basis for the development of such a structure of "rules." Our concern in this section, however, is not with hierarchical order and control, but rather with the nature of organism and environment interaction which constitutes the medium in which learning occurs.

In Bateson's epistemology, all transactions between organisms and their environments, whether the latter consist of other organisms or inanimate objects, are circular. To speak of input and output, he tells us, is to suggest linear relationships. Even when care is taken to emphasize the circularity of the causal processes, terms such as "input" and "output" suggest a control center which sifts input, makes decisions, and issues instructions. He considers such a view of mind to be erroneous and to give rise to the body-mind problem.

Organismic systems function as wholes. If an organism is interacting with the environment, the system consists of both the organism and the relevant components of the environment with which it interacts. Control is exerted by the circulation of "bits" of information around the causal loops of the system. "A 'bit' of information is definable as a difference which makes a difference. Such a difference, as it travels and undergoes successive transformation in a circuit, is an elementary idea" (1972, p. 315).

The important point to note is that no part of the system has unilateral control over any other part. The control—or mental—feature is inherent in the system as a whole. To single out any part as the governing element in the system is to distort the nature of the system. The thermostat does not exert unilateral control. It is essentially a sense organ which receives a transformation of the difference between the actual temperature and some ideal temperature. It transforms this difference into an efferent message (e.g., to switch off the power). The behavior of the thermostat is determined by the behavior of other parts of the system and by its own behavior at an earlier time.

Bateson stresses the point that the behavior of any part of the causal circuit is partially determined by its own previous behavior. The time taken for the message to get around the circuit and back to a given point is a critical factor. The fact that the behavior of any part is in some measure determined by what it did at an earlier time constitutes a sort of memory effect.

He goes on to say:

> The stability of the system (i.e., whether it will act self-correctively or oscillate or go into runaway) depends upon the relation between the operational product of all the transformations of difference around the circuit and upon this characteristic time. The "governor" [of a steam engine] has no control over these factors. Even a human governor in a social system is bound by the same limitations. He is controlled by information from the system and must adapt his own actions to its time characteristics and to the effects of his own past action.... In other words, *the mental characteristics of the system are immanent, not in some part, but in the system as a whole* [p. 316].

The answer to such questions as "Can a computer think?" or "Is the mind in the brain?" depends upon whether all the components involved in the thinking and their interaction are in the computer or in the brain. If, for instance, the computer contains a device for measuring its temperature and switching on an internal fan when it gets too hot, then we have a rudimentary mental process. But the main function of computers is not to regulate their own temperature. It is to transform input differences into output differences, and in this regard the computer is only an arc in a larger circuit which includes a human being. This larger ensemble shows mental characteristics.

"Similarly, we may say that 'mind' is immanent in those circuits of the brain which are complete within the brain. Or that mind is immanent in circuits which are complete within the system, brain *plus* body. Or, finally, that mind is immanent in the larger system—man *plus* environment" (p. 317). What this means is that the mental aspect of an event is coextensive with the network of circuits that determine that event. In the case of humans interacting with the environment, "mind" extends beyond the boundaries of the body.

Bateson makes the point that the parallelism in syntax between "I hit the billiard ball" and "Billiard ball A hit billiard ball B" is totally misleading. The hitting of the ball in the first sentence is brought about by a whole system of ball–eyes–brain–muscles–billiard cue–stroke–ball. What occurs is a transmission around a circuit of transformations of differences—differences in position of balls—differences in retina—differences in brain—differences in muscles—differences in movement of cue—differences in position of balls. But that is not how it is ordinarily described. By including the personal pronoun, a mixture of mentalism and physicalism is achieved with "mind" restricted within the individual and the ball reified. The next step is reify mind on the basis that since the "self" acted upon the cue which acted upon the ball, "the 'self' must also be a 'thing'" (p. 318).

He goes on to make the point that the confusion regarding the location of self arises from such faulty thinking. Not only is the boundary between self and not self difficult to define, but conventional thinking which locates the mind in the body makes it difficult to escape from the view of mind being transcendent. If transcendence is discarded, the obvious alternative is that the mind is immanent in the body. But this cannot be because large parts of the relevant causal circuits are outside the body. The result is to

> ... force the argument toward paradox: if mind be supposed immanent in the body, then it must be transcendent. If transcendent it must be immanent. ...
>
> Similarly, if we exclude the unconscious processes from the "self" and call them "ego-alien," then these processes take on the subjective coloring of "urges" and "forces"; and this pseudodynamic quality is then extended to the conscious "self" which attempts to "resist" the "forces" of the unconscious. The "self" thereby becomes itself an organization of seeming "forces." The popular notion which would equate "self" with consciousness thus leads into the notion that ideas are "forces" and this fallacy is in turn supported by saying that the axon carries "impulses." To find a way out of this mess is by no means easy [p. 320].

It will be clear from such comments why Bateson maintains that individuals do not make free choices, but rather that choices emerge from interaction processes. It will also help to make clear, in specific terms, how it can be that the individual is "a different person" in different interactional contexts.

Finally, if we accept that therapist and client form an interacting system, it will be apparent that neither can exert unilateral control over the other. The behavior of each is determined by the behavior of the other and by his own behavior at an earlier time.

PART IV
Implications for Psychotherapy and Behavioral Science

CHAPTER 10
The World of Communication

THIS WORK SO FAR falls into two portions. Parts I and II, which utilize data and concepts currently accessible in the literature on psychotherapy and behavior change, will be readily appreciated—though not necessarily endorsed—by those with theoretical and practical interest in interpersonal relationships. In contrast Part III, with its focus on abstract principles of communication or control processes, is calculated to appeal more to academic and philosophically oriented psychologists with a primary interest in such matters as information processing.

The appropriateness of combining these two approaches within the one text may be questioned. At least the reader who is asked to stretch his attention to take in matters he may regard as being beyond the scope of his interest may justifiably ask for an indication of the mutual relevance of the two portions.

The immediate response is that an adequate analysis of the data is not possible at the level of discussion that characterizes Parts I and II. For the most part the discussion is descriptive rather than analytical. Admittedly the attempt is made to get the psychotherapist to step outside the familiar conceptual frame of his particular "school" of therapy and to look at it in a broader perspective. Schein's model, for instance, is a perspective not only onto a wide range of strategies of psychotherapy, but also onto the induction of "personality" change in such other areas of interaction as religious conversion, political indoctrination, or professional socialization, some of which would seem to be remote from the healing enterprise. However, as Schein points out, his model is a middle-level model aimed at developing generalizations that remain in relatively close contact with the observational data and can be readily checked against them. It is essentially a way of gathering together the data and putting them into an orderly pattern.

In considering the data thus drawn together, it became apparent that some important issues could not be dealt with adequately at this level of analysis. In particular the audience-performer relationship which is an important feature of change strategies—not only in major forms of psychotherapy but also in thought reform and related areas—cannot be explicated without embarking on a more fundamental analysis.

Such a more radical approach involved an examination of the exertion of interpersonal influence or attempts at interpersonal control. This must inevitably take the discussion into the realm of control systems and communicational processes, matters that occupied us in Part III.

In effect the reader who subscribes to a particular therapeutic orientation is asked to step twice outside a conceptual framework. First he is asked to step outside the bounds of the particular structure of theory and practice with which he is familiar and within which he can function comfortably, and to look at it in terms of its place in a class of social influence strategies. Having done so he is then asked to take a further step back and to look at the nature of influence or, more precisely, at the nature of control or communication processes.

Such a demand is likely to be confusing, particularly when the argument at this second level is developed in a somewhat piecemeal fashion. It is proposed, therefore, at the cost of being repetitive, to summarize the argument for an orientation to psychotherapy based upon a consideration of fundamental principles of communication. This takes us back to a discussion of the relation between the Newtonian world, or the world of objects, and the world of communication.

The Two Worlds of Objects and Communication

The difference between these two worlds is the difference between energy and information. This difference can be illustrated by considering the difference between one billiard ball hitting another and one person hitting another. In the first case there is a direct transfer of energy. The resulting motion or behavior of the ball that is struck will depend on such factors as the direction and speed of the moving ball, the point of impact on the stationary ball and the friction between the ball and the table surface. In the second case, there is a transfer of information. The resulting behavior of the recipient of the blow will depend upon the meaning the blow has for him. Meaning is dependent on context. A blow from the hand of another has one meaning in a boxing ring, another in mortal combat, and another again in a boisterous greeting between long-parted friends.

In the transmission of information, we are dealing with a situation where the recipient has its own store of energy, which is typically large in comparison with that involved in the message. The recipient may be a living organism or a part of such an organism, and, as a consequence of our twentieth-century technology, it may also be a physical body such as a satellite in the vicinity of Jupiter, which is instructed to switch on its cameras and transmit some pictures of that planet back to earth.

Since information involves energy, there is a problem in distinguishing between the two processes. Bateson has proposed that this can be resolved by distinguishing between two realms of discourse which coexist but for which a synthesis cannot, at least at present, be achieved. These two realms are the world of objects and the world of communication.

The difference between the two realms is that the former "ascribes reality to objects and achieves its simplicity by excluding the context of the context" and indeed excluding an infinite regress of such contexts or metarelationships, while in the case of the latter it is the metarelationships that are relevant and simplicity is achieved by excluding all objects.

In other words, the only relevant events or "realities" in this world are messages, including parts of messages, relations between messages, and the like. The perception of an object (or event or relation) belongs in the communicational realm. It is a neurophysiological message and, in this world, is real. But the object, *as an object,* cannot enter into this world and hence, within it, has no relevance or reality. Conversely, a message, *as a message,* has no reality in the world of objects. There it becomes no more than light waves or neural discharges.

The world of communication is a Berkeleyan world, but in a more extreme sense than the Bishop's thesis proposes. In it, reality is denied not only to objects that are not perceived but also to objects that are perceived. In the world of communication, the chair on which one sits does not exist as an object. To quote Bateson:

> My perception of the chair is communicationally real, and that on which I sit is, for me, only an idea, a message in which I put my trust. . . .
> In this world, indeed, I, as a material object, have no relevance and, in this sense, no reality. "I," however, exist in the communicational world as an essential element in the syntax of my experience and in the experience of others, and the communications of others may damage my identity, even to the point of breaking up the organization of my experience [1972, pp. 250–251].

In the world of communication, delusions and hallucinations have relevance and in that sense are real, while the solid objects that surround us have reality only as ideas on which we rely.

The fact that there are no objects as such in the communicational world means that in this realm no boundary can be drawn between the physical individual and the environment. Thus, when we are dealing with the perception of an object or event, we are dealing with messages in multiple parts of the relevant communicational system. This system is not the physical individual but a network of pathways of messages, some of which happen to be located inside the physical individual and some outside but, as Bateson goes on to say,

> ... the characteristics of the *system* are in no way dependent upon any boundary lines which we may superpose upon the communicational map. It is not communicationally meaningful to ask whether the blind man's stick or the scientist's microscope are "parts" of the man who uses them. Both stick and microscope are important pathways of communication and, as such, are parts of the network in which we are interested; but no boundary line—e.g., halfway up the stick—can be relevant in a description of the topology of this net [1972, p. 251].

It will be clear that, in the communicational world where there are no objects, the subject-object dichotomy disappears. It is difficult to grasp, in a meaningful way, the nature of such a world, and one may tend to assume that it must be of a chaotic and undifferentiated nature in which everything is connected to everything. That it is, in reality, a structured and orderly world has been the central theme of Bateson's work. Before going on to consider the nature of this structure, we can note briefly the extent of this realm of discourse.

The Scope of the Communicational World. It will be apparent from what has been said above that the communicational world embraces those events and processes usually called "mental" or "psychic" (e.g. perceiving, thinking, learning). But it goes much farther to include physiological processes (e.g. neural and hormonal "messages"), when these are viewed not as objects but as components of a network of message transmission. On another level social organizations, whether industrial, political, or military, function by means of communication, and consequently the laws that apply to communicational phenomena have relevance for them. Bateson, who has a deep interest in genetics and evolutionary processes, sees these as essentially communicational in nature and hence as being subject to the fundamental principles of communication.

The communicational world is thus coextensive with the whole realm of living matter from the gene to the large corporation or nation-state. But it extends farther. With the development of weapons control systems and computer technology during the present century, the communicational world has come to engage increasingly the attention of mathematicians, physicists, and engineers. Indeed, it would seem that the behavioral scientists whose domain of inquiry is located centrally within the communicational world are lagging behind their fellow workers in the physical and biological sciences in appreciating the significance of developments in this realm.

The Structure of the Communicational World. The world of communication is a world of hierarchical structure or order. The theme of that hierarchy is the relation of the whole to the part or of the more comprehensive superordinate system to the subordinate systems that constitute it.

The whole-part relationship has been a live issue for many years in behavioral science, where it bas been discussed under such headings as "holistic" theory and "organismic" theory. The basic theme of such theory has been the priority to be assigned to the whole over the part in the explanation of behavior. Its advocates have included both phenomenologists and systems theorists who share common ground in their opposition to reductionism.

This is not the place to embark on a discussion of the extensive literature on holistic approaches. We may note, however, that such literature does not propose absolute wholes and parts as such, but rather a hierarchical or tiered structure in which the whole at one level is a part in a more comprehensive whole at the next higher level or, conversely, where the part at one level is the whole at the next lower level. An example of such whole-part duality in a social organization would be an infantry company, which from one perspective is a whole with its own identity and constituted by subunits, while, from another perspective, it is a subordinate part in the higher level unit of battalion or regiment. As we noted earlier, Koestler (1964, 1969) who was particularly interested in this dual aspect, has coined the term "holon" to refer to the integrated unit that can be viewed as either a whole or a part. As an indication of the range of units to which he applies the term, we may note that he lists cells, organs, organisms, words, and sentences as holons and goes on to say: "organelles and homologous organs are evolutionary holons; morphogenetic fields are ontogenetic holons; the ethologist's 'fixed-action patterns' and sub-routines of acquired skills are behavioral holons; phonemes, morphemes, words, phrases are linguistic holons; individuals, families, tribes, nations are social holons" (1969, p. 211).

The fact that the cross-section of distinguished scientists present at Koestler's address, who were drawn from a representative range of biological sciences, from linguistics, from psychiatry, from child psychology, and from social philosophy, were, in the subsequent discussion and in their own papers, in broad agreement with Koestler's position suggests that it has some substance. However, the level of analysis he attempted is limited, and if it is to be carried further, it would seem necessary to bring this assorted collection of "holons" within the framework of a single realm of discourse. Such a realm, we suggest, is provided by the world of communication. Koestler's "holonic" world is the communicational world. In that world the holonic regression can be expressed in terms of a regression of contexts.

Context. We can begin a discussion of context with some examples. A piece of tissue developing within an embryo appears to be influenced by the immediate environment in which it is taking shape. We can call that environment the context for the developing tissue. Similarly the meaning of a word in a sentence is influenced by the other words and their order in the sentence. Such words and that order are the context of the word. Or, as a further example, we can take a child growing up within a family in which there is a certain structure of roles and relationships as growing up within a particular family context.

The part played by contexts can be investigated by changing the context. When Spemann (1938) transplanted some embryonic tissues, that would have become part of the skin, to the brain area, at a critical stage of embryonic development, and those tissues became adequately functioning components of the nervous system of the adult animal, he demonstrated the potency of context for the developing tissues. Similarly, when a word is transplanted from one sentence to another and its meaning undergoes radical change, we have another example of the potency of context. It is to be noted that the change occurs where there is energy to be released. In the case of the tissues it is the tissues themselves that are affected. In the case of the word it is the neural processes of the reader.

What we are calling context is not a random assortment of messages. It has pattern or configuration. It is an integrated net of interactions, which is more than the sum of its components and is thus of a higher order than the events that constitute it. It may be said to frame these events. It is essentially another way of conceptualizing the processes for which Koestler coined the term "holon."

The whole-part relationship can also be conceptualized in terms of classes and classes of classes in infite regression. By drawing attention to the fact that a class is a totality (see Appendix), Whitehead and Russell were able to provide a logical basis for a hierarchical structure in which a class is shown to be of a different—and higher—order from its members and not to be confused with them. As noted earlier, once an item or an event has been assigned to a class, its character is defined.

A further area for which the whole-part hierarchy with its potentially infinite regression has relevance is that of perception. This has been considered at some length above in terms of reflexion. As gestalt theorists have pointed out, a perception is an organized pattern or configuration. It is of a higher or more comprehensive level than the events organized, and, of course, a perception of a perception is of a higher order still. In developing a formal system based on logic and mathematics for representing this hierarchical order, Lefebvre impresses as offering a potentially useful contribution toward the elaboration of physical control systems.

The communicational world is thus a world characterized by a hierarchical structure that is of great significance for a wide range of behavior, which includes the assignment of meaning, the functioning of organizations, embryonic development, the formation and maintenance of relationships, and learning processes. We have discussed this hierarchy in terms of the whole-part relationship, but it could also have been treated in terms of metarelationships. That is to say, a context, a class, or a perception is "about" the events encompassed. The account might therefore have taken the form of a discussion of metarelationships.

From this background, we can turn to the issues of psychopathology and psychotherapy. In view of the vast literature on the former, we will restrict this consideration to some aspects that are relevant to my argument. Of particular interest is the point made by Mowrer (1948) that the most puzzling feature of neurotic behavior is the failure of the individual to profit from experience. That is, a central problem for Mowrer is to account for the perpetuation of behavior that is not only not reinforced but punished. In considering this "neurotic paradox," we can review briefly some experimental analogs that throw some light on the matter.

Experimental Analogs of the "Neurotic Paradox". Since ethical considerations prevent the induction of neurotic behavior in human beings, the experimental work in this area has been carried out with animals— mainly with rats and dogs. We can note briefly three types of study that deal respectively with:

1. Self confirming premises
2. Learned helplessness
3. "Double-bind" analogs

These types of study are taken in the order of their severity of effect on the animal, ranging from the induction of a rigid response pattern to disorganization of behavior.

1. *Self-confirming premises.* Mowrer (1948) gives a brief account of an experiment in which a rat is placed in an alleyway from which the only escape is into a safety box at one end of the alley. The rat is always placed in the alley at the end remote from the safety box. The floor of the alleyway consists of two metal grids, each extending half the length of the alley. These grids can be electrically charged independently. In the initial stages of the experiment the rat is placed in the alley with both grids uncharged. After an interval *both* grids are charged. The rat be-

comes active and ultimately finds the safety box. Over a number of trials the interval between the placing of the rat in the alleyway and the electrification of both grids is reduced until the animal seeks refuge in the safety box as soon as it is introduced into the alley. At this point a change is made. That half of the alleyway adjacent to the safety box is kept permanently charged while that part remote from the safety box is kept permanently uncharged. In this new situation the most appropriate behavior for the rat would be to stay on the grid on which it is placed and thereby avoid all shock. However, no rat trained as above learns to do this. Each time it is placed in the alley, the animal runs out of the uncharged area, across the charged area and into the safety box. This will continue until the experimenter desists.

If we anthropomorphize the rat, we would say that such behavior is consistent with the view that the rat has come to define the situation as one in which it is engaged in a race against time to reach the safety box before the shock comes on in the alley. The fact that it invariably experiences shock in the later part of its run constitutes reinforcement or support for such a premise.

We can speculate on how such a premise might be disconfirmed and such behavior changed. The logical procedure would be to place a barrier across the alleyway at a point on the electrified grill so close to where it adjoins the uncharged grill that the rat, while being able to reach it and receive shock from it, would not have room to remain on it. In such a case we would expect the rat to run down the alley to reach the charged grid, to undergo the shock and to try to get through the barrier. When unable to get through the barrier the initial reaction would predictably be one of panic, but if there is insufficient room for it to remain on the electrified grid, the rat should quickly discover that the uncharged grid provides a safe retreat. In time it should learn to remain on that end of the alleyway even after the barrier is removed.

There are certain points to be noted about this analog.

First, it is the behavior of the rat in escaping into the safety box that produces the feedback that maintains the behavior. It is a good example of how behavior based on particular premises or assumptions can bring about outcomes that confirm such premises. That much human behavior is characterized by such effects would seem to be beyond question. In continuing to utilize in adulthood solutions that were appropriate in earlier circumstances, people provoke from others responses that maintain both their premises about human relationships and their patterns of coping behavior. Thus the child who develops an aggressive style of behavior, on the premise that it has to fight to get what it wants from an unfriendly world, is likely to arouse the antagonism of others and create a situation in which it literally has to "fight for its rights." It would be expected that such behavior would change only when it became completely ineffective, thereby precipitating a crisis for the individual with outcome that would be dependent on the circumstances.

Second, it is to be noted that in this analog the behavior is partly successful. The animal does escape the shock, though at unnecessary cost. Furthermore the rat's behavior remains goal-oriented. It continues to engage in problem-solving activity. Its behavior is not disorganized. In this respect it would seem to be comparable to much human behavior, which, though misguided, "works" up to a point and allows the individual to maintain a purposive stance toward his situation.

2. *Learned helplessness.* Seligman (1975) reports a number of studies in which dogs that had been subjected to unavoidable shock (e.g. when restrained in a Pavlovian hammock), subsequently failed to learn to avoid shock by jumping over the barrier when placed in a shuttle box. Experimentally naive animals when placed in the shuttle box—a two-sided chamber in which a dog jumping over a barrier from one side to the other side turns off or escapes shock—quickly learn to jump the barrier and to avoid the shock.

The initial behavior of the dog that had previously been given inescapable shock, when subjected to shock in the shuttle box, was similar to that of the naive animal in that "it ran around frantically for about thirty seconds" (1975, p. 22). But then it lay down and quietly whined. On subsequent trials there was apparently less of the initial frantic behavior. The "helpless" behavior continued for trial after trial without change.

Seligman describes how a "cure" was effected. He tells us:

> If the central problem in lack of response initiation is the expectation that responding will not work, cure should occur when the expectation is reversed. My colleagues and I worked for a long time without success on this problem: first, we took the barrier out of the shuttle box, so the dog could lick the safe side if he chose, but he just lay there. Then I got into the other side of the shuttle box and called to the dog, but he just lay there. We made the dogs hungry and dropped Hebrew National salami onto the safe side, but still the dog just lay there. We were trying, by all these procedures, to seduce the dog into responding during shock, and thus into seeing that its response had turned off shock. Finally, we showed one of our helpless dogs to James Geer, a behavior therapist, who said, "If I had a patient like that I would give him a swift kick to get him going." Geer was right: this therapy always works on helpless dogs and rats. What it meant to us was that we should *force* the dog to respond—over and over, if necessary—and so have it come to see that changing compartments turns off shock. To this end we put long leashes around the necks of the dogs and began to drag them back and forth across the shuttle box during the CS and shock, with the barrier removed. Getting to the other side turned off the shock.

> After from 25 to 200 draggings all dogs began to respond on their own. Once responding began, we gradually built up the barrier, and the dogs continued to escape and avoid. The recovery from helplessness was complete

and lasting, and we have replicated the procedure in about 25 dogs and as many helpless rats. The behavior during leash pulling was noteworthy. At the beginning of the procedure, we had to exert a good deal of force to pull the dog across the center of the shuttle box. Usually the whole dead weight of the dog had to be dragged; in some cases the dog resisted. Less and less force was needed as training progressed. Typically, we reached a stage in which a slight nudge of the leash would drive the dog into action. Finally, each dog initiated its own response, and thereafter never failed to escape [pp. 56–57].

Seligman and his colleagues were apparently surprised by the generalization of the learned response to unavoidable shock to the situation where the shock was avoidable. We might note, however, the relevance of context. For the animal the context would include such elements as being kept in a cage, being taken from the cage to the experimental quarters probably in a standardized procedure (e.g. being put on a leash and led by the same person along the same route and being experimented upon in the same room by the same people). Within this rather broad frame the most relevant stimulus is presumably the shock. But the shock in the hammock is not an isolated event with no connection with shock in the shuttle box. Both are part of a larger context in which a number of communicational elements are linked. For the two shock situations to elicit different responses, some differentiation must occur within the broader framework. Differentiation follows generalization. The learner progressively makes finer discriminations, and his cognitive map becomes progressively articulated. In the experiments that Seligman reports, the response of inactivity that is acquired prevents the animal from having the learning experiences that would make such discrimination possible.

It is suggested that the learned inactivity to unavoidable shock is an adaptive response. When subjected to unavoidable stress, the appropriate response would be to conserve resources and endure the stress with minimum loss of energy, organization, and control. Given the premise that the shock was unavoidable, the behavior of the dogs was biologically sound. As learned in the first part of the experiment, the premise was valid, but it ceased to be valid when the experimenter changed the game.

It is to be noted that "cure" was effected—that is, the premise was corrected—by forcing the animals to engage in behavior that confronted the premise. As described, this was a gradual process in which the outcome of each response affected the subsequent response in accordance with a reciprocal causation model.

3. "*Double-bind*" *analogs.* The "double-bind" concept was developed by Bateson et al. (1956) to account for the etiology of schizophrenia. As initially formulated it was precisely and elaborately defined. It is sufficient for us here to note that the central component of a double bind is a

switching of context on a "victim." That is, the "victim" is induced to regard the context as being of a particular kind and to commit himself to responding on that basis, only to be then put in the wrong by an outcome which indicates that the context was other then he had assumed. When practiced repeatedly by a person or group in a position of power against a dependent "victim," the effects on the latter are extremely destructive.

In their later writings, Bateson and others who have found the concept useful have come to see it as a special feature of a more general communicational process that results from the hierarchical organization that characterizes the world of communication.

The two analogs that were outlined above might be said, from an external "objective" perspective, to involve a switching of context on the animal. However, this switching does not register on the animal's behavior. It does not function as a message. It does not enter the animal's communicational world. In terms of the animal's behavior it might as well not have occurred. Indeed, such pathology as occurs resides in the failure to make adaptive changes in behavior owing to deprivation of relevant information.

In the double-bind analog we are now considering, the contextual switch does enter the animal's communicational world with disruptive consequences. We can note two sets of data.

A: In Pavlov's laboratory, dogs were trained to respond differentially to a circle and to an ellipse by having the conditioned salivation response reinforced in the case of the former but not in the case of the latter. When the animal had become efficient in making this discrimination, the shape of the ellipse was progressively changed so that it came to resemble the circle ever more closely. At the point where it was no longer possible for the dog to make the discrimination, some of the animals "broke down"—that is, their behavior became disorganized.

In this case the change in the shape of the ellipse effectively constituted a change in the context from one of problem solving to one of gambling. In the initial phase success or failure in making the "correct" response was dependent on problem-solving discriminatory behavior. Once the circle and ellipse became indistinguishable, success or failure became independent of the discriminatory behavior of the animal.

B. In Maier's (1949) laboratory, rats were trained in a Lashley jumping apparatus to discriminate between the markings on two cards. Correct choice was rewarded with food, incorrect choice was punished with a bump on the nose from an unyielding card and a fall into a safety net. Under this procedure, the rats learned, over a number of trials, to make the correct discriminatory response. When this stage was reached, reward and punishment were administered on a random basis. The effect was that the rats began to avoid jumping and, when forced to jump, developed stereotyped response patterns (e.g. a rat might always jump to the card on the left). This pattern continued even though the original nature of the task was restored. It was only with great difficulty that the animals were retrained to make correct discriminatory responses again. This was achieved by forcing the animal to respond and guiding it by hand so that it consistently experienced reward.

We can note first that as with Pavlov's dogs there is a context switch from a problem-solving task to one in which success is independent of the problem-solving efforts of the animal. Second, as with Seligman's cases of trained helplessness, the "cure" consisted in giving the animals consistent experience of positive reinforcement.

Switching of context is necessarily a disorganizing experience for the subject since the premises on which it has come to rely are disconfirmed. When, as in the studies quoted, the switch is to a context in which the outcome is independent of the subject's disriminatory behavior, the most adaptive response is to conserve resources and endure the stress with minimal disturbance.

However, context switching need not take this particular form. It may merely be from one type of problem-solving situation to another type. In such a case, if the subject is unable to adjust its behavior appropriately, the result is likely to be pathological, but if it is able to restructure its premises the result may be creative.

Bateson (1972) gives an interesting account of such a creative outcome. He takes the case of a trainer who wants to demonstrate the operant conditioning of a porpoise for the public. Such a trainer would want to be able to condition a new behavior at each demonstration, but if he has only one porpoise to use for his different demonstrations, it is likely he will have difficulty in getting the animal to emit a major new behavior on each occasion. The animal must be expected to exhibit behavior that had been rewarded on the previous occasion.

Bateson gives a description of two such sets of demonstrations. The first is apparently a reconstruction of such training as it "had happened in the free natural history of the relationship between porpoise and trainer and audience." Since the process had not been carefully recorded it was replicated and careful records kept.

In broad outline, the first set of demonstrations began with the training of the porpoise to respond to a whistle as a secondary reinforcer. That is, after the whistle was blown the porpoise was fed. When this link had been established the porpoise was ready for the first demonstration. When it entered the exhibition tank it raised its head above the surface, the whistle was blown and it was fed. Then it raised its head again and was reinforced by the whistle and food. After three such demonstrations it was "sent off-stage to wait for the next performance two hours later" (1972, p. 276).

When the porpoise next came into the exhibition tank it again raised its head, but got no whistle. A new behavior was wanted. The trainer waited until it came—"a tail flap, which is a common expression of annoyance." This behavior was reinforced by whistle and food and was repeated.

In time, "the porpoise learned to deal with the context of contexts—by offering a different or *new* piece of conspicuous behavior whenever she came on stage" (1972, p. 277).

In the carefully recorded replication two points emerged:

> First, that it was necessary (in the trainer's judgment) to break the rules of the experiment many times. The experience of being in the wrong was so disturbing to the porpoise that in order to preserve the relationship between porpoise and trainer (i.e., the context of context of context) it was necessary to give many reinforcements to which the porpoise was not entitled.
>
> Second, that each of the first fourteen sessions was characterized by many futile repetitions of whatever behavior had been reinforced in the immediately previous session. Seemingly only by "accident" did the animal provide a piece of different behavior. In the time-out between the fourteenth and fifteenth sessions, the porpoise appeard to be much excited, and when she came on stage for the fifteenth session she put on an elaborate performance including eight conspicuous pieces of behavior of which four were entirely new—never before observed in this species of animal [1972, p. 277].

In other words, it was as if the switching of context by the experimenter had resulted in a higher level integration by the porpoise, which had by then "caught on" to what the game was all about. That is, it now had a grasp of the context of the context.

Bateson suggests that two points emerge from this account:

> First, that severe pain and maladjustment can be induced by putting a mammal in the wrong regarding its rules for making sense of an important relationship with another mammal.
>
> And second, that if this pathology can be warded off or resisted, the total experience may promote *creativity* [1972, p. 278].

Implications of the Analogs. The analogs are all studies of learning. From the communicational perspective, the data are in accord with the hierarchical structure that has been proposed. In each case the animal was subjected to experiences that induced the development of premises about the experimental situation, but subsequently the experimenter introduced a context swith which rendered such premises invalid. The animal, having made an appropriate adaptation in the first context, was required by the experimenter to make a new adaptation which would, in terms of our argument, involve arriving at new premises.

What we are calling premises are higher-level organizations in the communication network. They are integrations. They are not simply the sum of the processes they integrate and cannot be reduced to the latter.

They are new structures which relate the lower-order processes to each other. They are "meta" or "about" those lower-order processes.

The reality with which the animal is asked to deal is the reality the experimenter knows, but the animal can deal with that world only in terms of its own premises. Those premises need not accurately reflect the experimenter's reality. To use Korzybski's metaphor, the map is not the territory.

But the map determines the choice of route. When there is feedback that indicates a discrepancy between the map and the terrain, then steps are taken to correct the map. In this way the "cognitive maps" of human beings and other animals change. But, in the cases discussed above, such feedback was obviated. Hence a discrepancy between "map" and "terrain" continued until appropriate intervention occurred to make relevant feedback available.

The way in which the critical feedback was obviated was somewhat different in the first analog from the situation in the other two. First it is to be noted that in the case of the rat in the alley it is the context that is changed. A problem that had initially been framed within a time context was switched to one in which location was the relevant issue. Nevertheless, the context of the context remained one of problem solving. Failure on the part of the animal to "discover" the discrepancy between its "map" and the "terrain" can be attributed to the fact that the feedback was consistent with the "map"—that is, with the premise system.

In the other two cases—the "learned helplessness" and the "random reinforcement" situations—it is the context of the context that was changed. This provides a more complex and confusing situation for the learner than a simple context switch.

Seligman has argued at length, and produced supporting evidence to support his thesis, that the learned helplessness analog holds for human behavior. The appropriate training program for a child to ensure that it developed a sense of helplessness in coping with life would be to arrange that its needs were met without effort on its part, and that such attempts as it made to take the initiative in managing its life ended in failure to achieve its objectives. Such training would be expected to result in behavior that would cause others to describe the individual as dependent.

In regard to the "double-bind" analog, Bateson and others have argued that the effect of long-continued and excessive application by powerful others of this mode of relating is the development of the puzzling behavior characteristic of the schizophrenic who uses communication to deny that his communication is a communication. Such behavior, it is held, is an appropriate response for someone who has come to learn that he cannot rely on his perception of the situation without being hurt.

Of particular interst, in terms of some issues discussed in the early chapters, is Bateson's account of the training program employed with the porpoise, a program that had potential for producing pathology, but achieved creativity. In those early chapters we considered the dilemma posed for the change agent who faced the task of disconfirming the target's behavior while at the same time providing psychological support. In the porpoise training program this dilemma is a central issue.

The task for the trainer was to maintain his relationship—one of friendship and trust—with the porpoise while disconfirming its specific behaviors. The point that emerges from Bateson's account, which was not brought out in the earlier discussion, is that, as these apparently conflicting processes are not of the same order, they are not in direct opposition. The relationship constitutes the context of the context of the context of the specific events. Specific events that are inconsistent with the relationship need not disrupt it, just as a specific experience does not negate a premise with which it is inconsistent. The loving mother who spanks a disobedient child is aware that in doing so she is not destroying the relationship they share. Providing a trusting relationship is strongly and broadly based, it can survive many occurrences that are inconsistent with it and allow for corrective confrontations, which would otherwise have destructive outcomes, to produce creative effects.

The most striking data in support of this argument for a distinction between levels of communication as a relevant consideration in resolving the dilemma of simultaneously confronting and supporting another is provided by Farrelly's (Farrelly and Brandsma, 1974) intriguing procedure. It is difficult to convey to the reader unacquainted with Farrelly's approach the quality of his interaction with the client as he ridicules, burlesques, and makes fun of the latter's behavior. However, Farrelly's reply to a questioner at the end of one of his presentations of his procedure may serve to make a point:

Q. (angrily.): Do you mean to tell me that when you maliciously, viciously attack these poor patients you—
R. (interrupting.): I don't mean to tell you anything of the sort. Now, if you'll listen, I'll tell you what I *do* mean. I don't attack the patient, but I do attack his ideas. I don't ridicule him, but his assumptions and self-defeating behaviours. And I also thought I made it clear when I was talking about the use of humor in provocative therapy that the therapist is just as quick to lampoon his own role as he is to burlesque the client's ideas.

Another point should be made in this regard. It is the experience probably of most of us that we have observed a relationship between two people and wondered why Person A continued the relationship with Person B. The answer is that we either have a very skewed sampling of B's behavior in the relationship and haven't monitored all the behaviors (positive as well as negative) that B exhibits towards A; or else we are giving different valences to B's negative messages to A than A is giving. If we examine our own person relationships, a saying that we have heard not infrequently goes, "Oh, he just sounds that way, but his bark is much worse than his bite." It's one thing, in a word, to stand outside a relationship and rate it; it's another thing to live within that relationship. The former position can frequently lead to some very distorted conclusions. And, of course, the converse can be true also.

In the same way, in the provocative therapy relationship there are many positive, helpful elements that keep the client coming back, even though to an outside observer the negative aspects (the ridiculing, burlesquing, confronting, etc.) are almost immediately apparent [1974, pp. 163–164].

The fact that Farrelly's clients recognize his concern for them and his efforts on their behalf despite his consistent attack on their ideas and behavior is testimony to the complexity of communicational processes. In our view, the use of humor, at which Farrelly appears to be something of a genius, is a crucial element. As Bateson and his associates have pointed out, humor depends upon context switching—the punch line in a joke always depends upon a sharp and unexpected context switch. That is to say, humor utilizes the multilevel nature of communication.

We can reiterate the point made in Chapter 2 that humor can be regarded as an addition to Walton's repertoire of procedures whereby the power and the attitude change strategies can be integrated.

PSYCHOTHERAPY AS A RESTRUCTURING OF PREMISE SYSTEMS

The thesis that has been developed through this book is that psychotherapy is the attempt to reorganize the pattern of premises that the individual holds concerning himself and the world he inhabits. No originality is claimed for this position. For instance, Frank (1973) has proposed that therapy is concerned with changing the patient's assumptive system; Raimy (1975) has argued that the common element of the many different "schools" of psychotherapy lies in the attempt to resolve misunderstandings of the self; and Bandler and Grinder (1975) propose that the goal of therapy is to bring the client's model or map into closer accord with the territory it represents.

Our interest has been in examining the procedures whereby such reorganization is attempted. Since any such attempt is an effort to exert influence, our approach was couched in terms of influence. We argued that an examination of the literature on psychotherapy suggested the existence, either explicit or implicit, of three models each with its circle of adherents. In the light of the subsequent more theoretical discussion, we might now consider how change in the premise system is effected within each of the three models.

First it is important to note that, if we accept Bateson's formulation, there are many ways of confronting, in the hope of changing, the Learning II premises in which we are interested. In fact, it seems probable that the number of strategies is incalculable and will continue to be added to over the years. Bateson, it will be recalled, lists four classes of maneuver in which the therapist might engage for this purpose. These are broad categories, and within any one category a wide range of specific therapist behaviors are possible. Furthermore, therapists employing essentially similar overt behaviors may provide radically different rationales for the effects of their procedures.

Consider, for instance, the class of maneuvers designed "to get the patient to act, either in the therapy room or outside, in ways which will confront his own premises." Such an effect might be achieved by getting the client to role-play a part, by goading him into behaving in an atypical way, by prescribing the symptom, by giving him instructions to carry out certain acts, by inducing him to test his hypotheses, and the like.

On this basis we can now consider the models separately.

The placebo model. In the placebo model, there is a heavy emphasis on getting the client to engage in overt behavior the outcome of which will confront his premises. This is probably the most potent approach within the broad field of psychological therapy. From our discussion of experimental analogs using animals, it is clearly the most effective strategy with subhuman species. The evidence from many sources suggests that where it can be applied it is a highly effective procedure at the human level. The basic principle of such an approach is that behavioral change tends to precede attitudinal change.

The success of such a strategy can be understood in terms of Maruyama's morphogenetic epistemology in which change develops progressively through positive—or deviation-amplifying—feedback. If the individual can be induced to take even small steps that result in feedback that contradicts such premises as those of inadequacy and helplessness, then subsequent bigger steps in the same direction are likely to occur. In other words, a "virtuous" circle develops.

The problem is to get the client to take the initial steps. How is the therapist to stimulate a depressed and discouraged client into engaging in activities in which he has not previously succeeded, with sufficient zest and vigor to achieve a successful outcome? Clearly, he must present a sufficiently plausible case to persuade the client that despite past failures success is attainable. The strategy described by Fish (1973) and outlined in Chapter 4 is tailored toward this end.

Such a differentiation of stages in the formulation of the placebo model would seem to make it both more understandable and more acceptable to psychotherapists in general. It can be applied not only to such procedures as training anxious individuals to relax but also to such tactics as that of the police officer who "grounded" the delusional client. Presumably such a person has certain subjective experiences which she finds difficulty in accounting for, but which are related to feelings of vulnerability and anxiety. The more insecure she feels the more likely she is to focus on the threatening aspects of her situation with consequent deterioration in her ability to cope with it. A vicious circle is likely to develop. If she is given some sense of security, she has more chance of devoting her attention to the practical issues of daily living and becoming sufficiently absorbed in them to have an interesting and active life.

Therapists who work within a placebo model framework are typically oriented toward achieving practical results rather than formulating theory. Their aims tend to be limited to resolving the issues that cause distress for their clients. They are happy to leave the client with as much of his premise system intact as is consistent with his achieving his objectives.

The limitations of the placebo model were touched upon in Chapter 1. They stem from the problem of getting the client to engage in the behavior that would lead to relevant changes in his premise system. There are two aspects to this problem: With some clients it is by no means easy to state the sort of change that is desired, and, usually with the same clients, the necessary change may be unwelcome.

The individuals who respond most favorably to the placebo model approach are those with relatively specific problems for which they seek help. These include the various phobic conditions, feelings of inadequacy, social incompetence, and the like. The client typically knows what he wants to achieve, and the goals are relatively limited. Indeed, Fish would claim that unless such a relatively clear-cut problem can be delineated, and a goal for therapy set, then there is no problem and hence there is no basis for therapy.

However, there seem to be many clients whose problems cannot be so neatly delineated. The so-called existential neuroses characterized by a lack of purpose and meaning in life do not lend themselves to the direct approach of the placebo therapist. Other cases occur where the client has unrealistic expectations either in terms of his own ability or in terms of what he can reasonably require from others. Such clients usually have to be "brought down to earth" or "helped to face reality." It is for such clients that a resocialization model is relevant.

The resocialization model. The resocialization model has been discussed at length in earlier chapters. The comments here will be confined to some distinctive features of the strategy employed in restructuring the premise system using the highly verbal analytic approach that characterizes some of the major orientations grouped under this heading. It is true that there are placebo effects and also that any changes in the way the client communicates with others can be expected to result, via reciprocal causal effects, in further changes, but our interest is rather in such questions as how interpretations, reflections of feeling, or similar therapist interventions contribute directly to the modification of the client's premise system.

Two of the classes of maneuver listed by Bateson appear to be relevant. The first is that of confronting the patient's premises with those of the therapist while avoiding the trap of validating the old premises. Classical psychoanalysis as described by Barton and outlined in Chapter 5 constitutes a good example of this type of maneuver: The therapist restructures the patient's reality in accordance with the psychoanalytic scheme. As the strategy involved was treated in some detail, it will not be taken up here.

The second class of maneuver that characterizes the psychodynamic approach and merits our attention is the attempt to get the client to articulate his propositions about himself and his situation in clear and specific terms so that they can be checked against the observational data. This goes somewhat farther than Bateson's category of maneuvers "to demonstrate contradiction among the premises which currently control the patient's behavior." There is, however, much common ground between the two formulations.

An individual's sytem of premises constitutes his model or map of the world in which he lives and is the basis on which he responds to specific events as they occur. The map, however, is not the territory. The extent to which it is an accurate representation of the territory may vary greatly. The wider the discrepancy between map and territory, the more the individual will find himself at a loss as he tries to find his way.

The point at issue is "insight." The distinctive feature of many of the psychodynamic systems of therapy that we identify with the resocialization model has been a focusing on the development of insight. However, as was pointed out in Chapter 6, the term "insight" appears to be used ambiguously by psychotherapists. Some writers attribute insight to clients who provide explanations of how they have come to be in their present predicament that accord with the formers' own theoretical orientations. However, this is not the sense in which learning theorists, and particularly adherents of the gestalt school, use the term. For these latter, insight is the emergence of a new, more differentiated way of perceiving the situation. Insight in this sense, of necessity, involves change.

Much of the interaction between therapist and client in the lengthy verbal exchanges that take place in "psychodynamic" therapies—the various analytically oriented, Adlerian, or Rogerian approaches—is directed toward the achievement of insight on the part of the client. These are not the only therapeutic orientations that have this among their objectives, nor do dynamically oriented therapists necessarily limit their aims to this end. Nevertheless, the effort toward insight has characterized those schools of therapy that derive ultimately from Freud. Our interest here is in trying to explicate how insight can contribute to the client's well-being and how the therapist can most effectively promote it.

The most characteristic feature of animals and humans who find

difficulty in meeting the challenges of their situation is a relatively restricted preception of the alternatives open to them. Their "map" or
model lacks articulation and differentiation. This was certaintly the case
in the experimental analogs, and it also seems to apply in human situations. Bandler and Grinder (1975), in their attempt to identify the language skills of successful therapists, give us their view of the difference
between the healthy and the maladjusted person:

> Almost every human being in our culture in his life cycle has a number of
> periods of change and transition which he must negotiate. Different forms of
> psychotherapy have developed various categories for these important
> transition-crisis points. What's peculiar is that some people are able to
> negotiate these periods of change with little difficulty, experiencing these
> periods as times of intense energy and creativity. Other people, faced with
> the same challenges, experience these periods as times of dread and pain—
> periods to be endured, when their primary concern is simple survival. The
> difference between these two groups appears to us to be primarily that the
> people who respond creatively to and cope effectively with this stress are
> people who have a rich representation or model of their situation, one in
> which they perceive a wide range of options in choosing their actions. The
> other people experience themselves as having few options, none of which are
> attractive to them—the "natural loser" game. The question for us is: How is it
> possible for different human beings faced with the same world to have such
> different experiences? Our understanding is that this difference follows
> primarily from differences in the richness of their models [1975, pp. 13–14].

These authors go on to point out that people who continue to cause
themselves distress do not do so because they are "bad, crazy, or sick." In
fact, they are making the best choices open to them from the model they
have.

> The difficulty is not that they are making the wrong choice, but that they
> do not have enough choices—they don't have a richly focussed image of the
> world. The most pervasive paradox of the human condition which we see is
> that the processes which allow us to survive, grow, change, and experience joy
> are the same processes which allow us to maintain an impoverished model of
> the world—our ability to manipulate symbols, that is, to create models. So the
> processes which allow us to accomplish the most extraordinary and unique
> human acitivities are the same processes which block our further growth if
> we commit the error of mistaking the model for the reality [1975, p. 14].

Bandler and Grinder present a view of psychopathology and
psychotherapy that is in close accord with the stance taken in this book.
In a series of publications dealing with verbal, nonverbal, and group
communication processes respectively (1975, 1976, 1979), they have described in some detail how effective therapists, whom they have studied,
go about the task of helping clients to achieve greater freedom and
fulfillment. Their works are commended to the reader who wishes to

develop some practical skills for implementing the approach advocated in this book. Our immediate interest is in their discussion of verbal exchanges since these play a major part in the traditional psychodynamic orientations.

The approach they advocate bears a resemblance to that which the supervisor of a postgraduate student about to embark on the testing of a theoretical model might adopt. The student would probably begin with some vague generalizations about the realm he wanted to investigate. The supervisor would want to get the student to formulate these generalizations in clear, precise, and specific terms so that their mutual consistency and congruence with the observational data can be subjected to scrutiny.

It is noticeable that disturbed individuals are prone to use generalizations such as "nobody pays any attention to what I say" or "nothing ever seems to go right for me." They may also hold others responsible for their feelings in such statements as "my husband makes me angry." All such statements derive from the model the client has of his world. The task of the therapist is to understand clearly the nature of the model so that he can confront it. In the authors' words:

> What may at first appear to us as therapists as bizarre behavior or peculiar statements by clients will make sense to us in their models. To have a clear image of the client's model is to understand how that behavior or those statements make sense. This is equivalent to identifying the assumptions that the client is making in his model of the world. Assumptions in a model show up linquistically as presuppositions of the client's sentences. Presuppositions are what is necessarily true for the statements that the client makes to make sense (not to be true, but just to be meaningful) at all. One short-cut method for therapists to identify the portions of the client's model which are impoverished is to be able to recognize the presuppositions of the client's sentences.... Presuppositions are particularly insidious as they are not presented openly for consideration [1975, pp. 52–53].

Once the presuppositions are identified they may be challenged. As Bandler and Grinder present their case, the critical part for the therapist is in identifying the presuppositions. They invoke a linguistic meta model based on Chomsky's transformational grammar to aid them in this task and to make their procedures explicit. It is not possible here to do justice to their very thorough exposition. A brief excerpt may, however, give something of the flavor of their approach:

> The second class of special deletions can be identified by *ly* adverbs occurring in the Surface Structures the client presents. For example, the client says:
>
> (77) *Obviously, my parents dislike me.*
>   or
> (78) *My parents obviously dislike me.*

Notice that these Surface Structures can be paraphrased by the sentence
(79) *It is obvious that my parents dislike me.*

Once this form is available, the therapist can more easily identify what portion of the Deep Structure has been deleted. Specifically, in the example, the therapist asks

(80) *To whom is it obvious?*

Surface Structure adverbs which end in *ly* are often the result of deletions of the arguments of a Deep Structure process word or verb. The paraphrase test can be used by the therapist to develop his intuitions in recognizing these adverbs. The test we offer is that, when you encounter an adverb ending with *ly*, attempt to paraphrase the sentence in which it appears by:

(a) Deleting the *ly* from the Surface Structure adverb and placing it in front of the new Surface Structure you are creating.

(b) Add the phrase *it is* in front of the former adverb.

(c) Ask yourself whether this new Surface Structure means the same thing as the client's original Surface Structure.

If the new sentence is synonymous with the client's original, then the adverb is derived from a Deep Structure verb and deletion is involved. Now, by applying the principles used in recovering missing material to this new Surface Structure, the full Deep Structure representation can be recovered [1975, p. 68].

It will be clear that Bandler and Grinder seek to make the client's model fully explicit so that it can be checked for goodness of fit against the data. They maintain that this is what the most effective therapists do intuitively.

Their procedure as described in their writings is essentially inter-rogatory in nature. They first require of the client that he make clear exactly what he means by any statements he makes, and when this is established they then ask him whether his experiences accord with this more complete version. In this way they progressively challenge the client's initial formulation of his situation.

Their approach would be described as "directive" in the sense that they take considerable initiative in directing the course of the discussion. However, their procedure can be accommodated to a nondirective orientation. The competent client-centered therapist devotes his atten-tion to getting as full and complete an account of the client's model of his world as possible. His response to the client takes the form, "As I understand you, you are saying X. Have I got you correctly?" If the therapist's response is not an accurate representation of the client's meaning, the client is expected to correct him and bring him back on track. This means that the client's model is made explicit not only to the therapist but, in the process, to the client also, so that he comes to match his premises to the data.

Of course, it is not only the psychodynamically oriented therapist who insists that the client make his meaning clear and express himself in specific terms that will allow for objective verification. All competent therapists, irrespective of their theoretical persuasion, whether they are engaged in individual, group, or family therapy, do so. Our point is simply that insofar as exponents of the resocialization model are effective in helping the client to achieve a more differentiated and articulated model of his world, they open for him a wider range of choice and freedom in living.

Before closing this section on the resocialization model, the point should be made that the type of interrogatory approach—whether direct or indirect—which has been proposed is possible only within a relationship that confers authority on the therapist. One has only to try to visualize an office boy pinning down the manager and requiring that the latter make his position explicit so that it can be checked against the data, to realize the significance of power in the role of change agent.

A related issue concerns the effects of threat and anxiety. The effect of threat with consequent emotional arousal appears to be highly conducive to forceful or violent activity appropriate to emergency or dangerous situations but highly inimical to the reflexive processes that are involved in the elucidation of premise systems. These latter require a measure of security. This means that the therapist must not only occupy a position of power but also be seen in a benevolent role. In other words, his power must be legitimized.

That is, the points made in this section are complementary to those made in earlier chapters and do not reflect either conflicting or alternative perspectives.

The contextual model. Although the theoretical formulation is more elaborate, the interventive strategy of the contextual therapist has much in common with that of the placebo therapist. The emphasis is on changing the overt communicative behavior of the client rather than on changing his covert model or system of premises. Milton Erickson's statement, quoted in Chapter 1, makes clear that, for him at least, the aim is to effect a change in the client's overt behavior, which, through a process of reciprocal causation, will have a snowballing effect on the latter's subsequent activities.

These therapists rely on giving the client or clients directives or instructions to perform certain acts. If the clients follow the instructions, then new patterns of interaction between themselves and their intimates will result. The problem is to get the clients to follow the directions. Haley (1976) devotes a chapter to the issue of giving directives in which he spells out some of the difficulties that arise and how these can be handled by the therapist. His account leaves the reader in little doubt that competence in giving therapeutic directives is a highly developed skill and one that calls for a good understanding of communication principles. No doubt hypnotists who specialize in the giving of directives acquire an intuitive grasp of such principles.

The distinguishing feature of therapy within the contextual model is

the emphasis on the communicational network inhabited by the identified client, and the focus on changing the reciprocal communication
patterns within his circle of intimates. Since tbis has been discussed at
some length in Chapter 6, it will not be pursued further here.

SOME CONCLUDING COMMENTS ON PSYCHOTHERAPY

The position that has been developed through this work has been that
psychotherapy constitutes an attempt to promote differentiation in the
client's model of his world—that is, his system of premises about himself
and his situation—so that he will enjoy greater freedom, and achieve
more fulfillment, in meeting the exigencies of life.

It is argued that there are a great many strategies that can be utilized
toward this end and that similar practical strategies may be formulated
in widely differing conceptual frameworks. Consequently, at a superficial level the psychotherapy scene is one of great complexity and confusion. However, we would suggest that basically there are two broad approaches that are mutually compatible and may be combined. One is to
focus on the client's model or premise system and to make it fully explicit
so that it can be checked and corrected against the data. This is the
favored approach among psychodynamic therapists whom we have identified with the resocialization model, though it is by no means restricted
to them. The alternative approach is to induce the individual to engage
in overt communicational behavior, which will lead via reciprocal causal
processes to greater change in overt behavior and consequent change in
his premise system. This is the favored approach of therapists whom we
would group in the placebo and contextual models. It would also seem to
be relevant for tbe practice of play therapy.

At this point we would no longer wish to draw sharp lines between
the models. While the models provide a useful device for an initial attempt to structure the bewildering world of psychotherapy, and thus
constitute a starting point for an analysis of the therapeutic process, they
represent differences in emphasis rather than mutually exclusive
categories. In practice, if not in conceptualization, the different
therapies form a broad spectrum rather than a set of discontinuous
groupings, and within any particular orientation a range of behavior is
to be found not only from therapist to therapist but also from time to
time and situation to situation for any given therapist.

There are obvious difficulties facing anyone who would argue for the
superiority of a particular method of therapy. Any such claim must face
such questions as: "Superior in whose hands, for whom, in what circumstances and at what stage in the client's development?" Thus, to take only
one point, therapeutic change is a sequential process. An intervention

that would be quite inappropriate or might have negative consequences at one point in the sequence may prove strikingly effective at another point. Correct timing, or the matching of the intervention with the "state of play," would seem to be of critical importance. Kelman's concept of *Kairos* is relevant here. The fact that one form of intervention succeeded where another failed may simply be a function of timing. Therapists might be better advised to attune their interventions to the developmental phases of the change process than to commit themselves to a standardized interventive procedure.

It has not been our objective to make claims for any particular procedure. We have been more interested in indicating how different approaches may contribute to the therapeutic enterprise. However, in the light of the discussion some tentative suggestions might be made as to features of psychotherapy that would be conducive to successful outcome.

We can surmise that therapist behaviors which are likely to awaken or promote hope in the client and those characterized by surprise effects offer promise of producing the desired change. Hope is necessary if the client is to become active and engage in those behaviors that can be expected to lead to change in premises in the direction of gains in sense of competence and self-confidence. Therapies that have surprise effect are likely to gain the client's attention and alert him to the fact that patterns of thought that have become habitual for him may no longer be appropriate and require examination.

Insofar as there is substance in this argument, we can predict that not only will there be no decline in the number and variety of therapeutic technologies, but that, to the contrary, there will be an increase in both respects as therapists find new strategies and tactics for confronting the client's premises.

Before leaving the issue of psychotherapy, an important general point should be made. Therapist and client, in their interactions, can be regarded as constituting a communicational system. In such a system, as Bateson makes clear, no part can exert unilateral control over the system as a whole or over events in other parts of the system. If we accept this position, then it follows that there cannot be a perfect therapeutic strategy that will ensure the desired outcome. If there were such a strategy, the flow of influence—or causation—would be entirely from the therapist to the client. In fact, therapist and client exert influence on each other and affect each other's behavior. The strategic stance taken by the therapist, to which attention has been directed in earlier chapters, constitutes an attempt to minimize the effect of the client's behavior on the therapist and, to the extent that it is successful, strengthens the therapist's position and increases his influence vis-à-vis that of the client on the operation of the system.

Evidence from other sources supports the view that therapeutic outcome cannot be unilaterally determined. While it is certainly possible to increase the change agent's power in the system relative to that of the change target, reports based on studies of political indoctrination and coercive persuasion (Danziger, 1976, pp. 19–21) suggest that even where there is extreme disparity in power between the change agent and the change target, the latter can successfully resist change. In psychotherapy, where ethical issues impose limitations on the therapist, the balance is more even and the client's relative influence in the system correspondingly greater.

The conclusion to be drawn is that, as a significant component of the interacting system, the therapist can *influence* the functioning of the system as a whole and thus of the remaining components of the system, but he is not in a position to *control* the operation of the system.

Implications for Behavioral Science. Such contribution as this book has made has consisted in drawing together ideas from scattered sources in the behavioral sciences. A significant aspect of the present situation in the life sciences is the extent to which workers in widely different areas, with apparently little direct contact with each other, hold congruent views utilizing communicational concepts. Thus, as is clear from Lefebvre's work, phenomenologists with their humanistic orientation share common ground with systems theorists and cyberneticists who draw their inspiration from physical control systems.

As yet the mainstream of psychological theory and research does not appear to have been greatly influenced by twentieth-century developments in the world of communication. Bandura (1974) is one of the few prominent psychologists who has given expression to views in accord with such trends.

Of the two principles that have been the focus of our attention—hierarchical organization and reciprocal causation—Bandura is concerned with the latter. In attacking the unidirectional model that has characterized the traditional behaviorist position, he tells us:

> A survey of the literature on reinforcement confirms the extent to which we have become captives of a one-sided paradigm to map a bidirectional process. Environmental control is overstudied, whereas personal control has been relatively neglected. To cite but one example, there exist countless demonstrations of how behavior varies under different schedules of reinforcement, but one looks in vain for studies of how people, either individually or by collective action, succeed in fashioning reinforcement schedules to their own liking. The dearth of research on personal control is not because people exert no influence on their environment or because such efforts are without effect. Quite the contrary. Behavior is one of the more influential determinants of future contingencies. As analyses of sequential interchanges reveal, aggressive individuals actualize through their conduct a hostile environment, whereas those who display friendly responsiveness produce an

amicable social milieu within the same setting (Rausch, 1965). We are all acquainted with problem-prone individuals who, through their aversive conduct, predictably breed negative social climates wherever they go [1974, p. 866].

Bandura is particularly concerned with the question of freedom. He rejects the view "that man is but a pawn of external influence." His comments on the illogical position in which advocates of environmental determinism place themselves deserve noting:

> To contend, as environmental determinists often do, that people are controlled by external forces and then to advocate that they redesign their society by applying behavioral technology undermines the basic premise of the argument. If humans were in fact incapable of influencing their own actions, they could describe and predict environmental events but hardly exercise any intentional control over them. When it comes to advocacy of social change, however, thoroughgoing environmental determinists become ardent exponents of man's power to transform environments in pursuit of a better life [1974, p. 867].

Bandura's comments are in accord with the stance we have taken. They make clear the inadequacy of the hierarchical nonreciprocal causal epistemology as a basis for behavioral science.

It is, however, one thing to point to the inadequacy of a particular framework to comprehend the data, and quite another to provide a convincing alternative. Newtonian physics, which provided the prevailing model of science when the discipline of psychology made its bid for independence at Liepzig one hundred years ago, has a formidable record of achievement. Despite revolutionary developments within the physical sciences during the twentieth century, it is hardly surprising that behavioral scientists who have been largely insulated from those developments still adhere, implicitly if not explicitly, to the Newtonian model.

For behaviorists such as Skinner the alternative bases for the explanation of behavior have been the Newtonian paradigm on the one hand and a mentalism derived from primitive animism on the other. In view of the unacceptability of the latter position, it is hardly surprising that, as long as the alternatives are couched in such terms, there are staunch adherents of behaviorism who hold firmly—and some might say obdurately—to their position despite its demonstrated inconsistency and the weight of evidence against it. It does at least enable them to take a "scientific" stance when functioning as scientists. As Koch (1964) puts it, "it is essentially a role-playing position" (p. 6).

There have been attempts to provide more convincing alternatives than an animistic mentalism. Phenomenology with its emphasis on subjective behavior has constituted one such approach. While intuitively appealing, phenomenology does not seem, as yet, to have made a significant contribution to behavioral science. No principles of any generality have emerged from it. If we are to judge by Farson's critique (1978), humanistic psychology that is based on a phenomenological orientation does not seem to be fulfilling the hopes of its founders. Despite the efforts of its more rigorous exponents such as Merleau-Ponty (1962), phenomenology with its subjectivist stance seems to be in constant danger of drifting into an animsitic position.

A second alternative that has emerged during the twentieth century is loosely referred to as "systems thinking." Its main appeal has been to biological scientists, but it owes much to developments in the physical sciences and has had considerable impact on the behavioral or social sciences. The great appeal of systems thinking is its promise of a unified realm of discourse for science at all levels of the study of both animate and inanimate matter.

Systems thinking has proved of particular value in biological and social sciences where interaction processes have received increasing attention. Whether we consider ecological systems on a large scale or family interaction patterns, formulations in terms of systems processes have contributed significantly to an understanding of the events occurring and to effective intervention.

Bateson's contribution has been to carry systems thinking farther in his formulation of the two realms of discourse—the world of communication and the world of objects. In doing so he has offered both a new frame of reference for the study of control systems, including life processes in general and the behavioral processes which are of interest to psychologists in particular, and a way of viewing the relationship between control systems and physical matter that respects both their common ground and their distinctive differences.

His contribution has remarkably wide scope, ranging from evolutionary processes to the operation of human organizations. It integrates the phenomenological and systems approaches. Its particular appeal to us, however, is its applicability to a variety of problems in such areas as human relations and learning processes. It provides a basis for understanding the subleties of interpersonal power and influence, the importance of maintaining generation lines in organizations, and the inability of the neurotic to adjust his self-defeating behavior in the light of experience.

The communicational world is the world of Maruyama's "independent event" and "reciprocal causal" epistemologies; of Miller, Galanter and Pribram's "Plans"; of Koestler's "holons"; of Lefebvre's "reflexive polynomials"; and above all of Whitehead and Russell's "logical types." The last, as we have tried to show, is a principle of great explanatory power.

This book began with a consideration of the confusing state of psychotherapy. Much ground has been traversed in the search for order beneath the superficial chaos. Such order can be found by invoking the processes of circular causation and the hierarchial structure to which it gives rise (see Bateson, 1979, particularly pp. 106–108, for a discussion of this linkage). Cybernetics, which encompasses these processes, offers new perspectives for explanation in the life sciences. But while the impact of cybernetics in the area of technology needs no emphasis, the effects in the conceptual realm are still somewhat rudimentary. It would seem that just as overt action tends to precede attitudinal change in the realm of psychotherapy, so technological change tends to precede conceptual reorientation in the larger society. Yet if the promise of the cybernetic revolution is to unfold in the conceptual as well as in the technological realm, a radical restructuring of thinking, one that goes far beyond trying to accommodate the new ideas within an outgrown lineal epistemology, must take place.

APPENDIX

Excerpt from A. N. Whitehead and B. Russell, *Principia Mathematica*, vol. 1. London: Cambridge University Press, 1910.

"An analysis of the paradoxes to be avoided shows that they all result from a certain kind of vicious circle. The vicious circles in question arise from supposing that a collection of objects may contain members which can only be defined by means of the collection as a whole. Thus, for example, the collection of *propositions* will be supposed to contain a proposition stating that 'all propositions are either true or false.' It would seem, however, that such a statement would not be legitimate unless 'all propositions' referred to some already definite collection, which it cannot do if new propositions are created by statements about 'all propositions.' We shall, therefore, have to say that statements about 'all propositions' are meaningless. More generally, given any set of objects such that, if we suppose the set to have a total, it will contain members which presuppose this total, then such a set cannot have a total. By saying that a set has 'no total,' we mean, primarily, that no significant statement can be made about 'all its members.' Propositions, as the above illustration shows, must be a set having no total. The same is true, as we shall shortly see, of propositional functions, even when these are restricted to such as can significantly have as argument a given object *a*. In such cases, it is necessary to break up our set into smaller sets, each of which is capable of a total. This is what the theory of types aims at effecting.

"The principle which enables us to avoid illegitimate totalities may be stated as follows: 'Whatever involves *all* of a collection must not be one of the collection'; or, conversely: 'If, provided a certain collection had a total, it would have members only definable in terms of that total, then the said collection has no total.' We shall call this the 'vicious-circle principle,' because it enables us to avoid the vicious circles involved in the assumption of illegitimate totalities. Arguments which are condemned by the vicious-circle principle will be called 'vicious-circle fallacies.' Such arguments, in certain circumstances, may lead to contradictions, but it often happens that the conclusions to which they lead are in fact true, though the arguments are fallacious. Take, for example, the law of excluded middle, in the form 'all propositions are true or false.' If from this law we argue that, because the law of excluded middle is a proposition, therefore the law of excluded middle is true or false, we incur a vicious-circle fallacy. 'All propositions' must be in some way limited before it becomes a legitimate totality, and any limitation which makes it legitimate must make any statement about the totality fall outside the totality. Similarly, the imaginary sceptic, who asserts that he knows nothing, and is refuted by being asked if he knows that he knows nothing, has asserted nonsense, and has been fallaciously refuted by an argument which involves a vicious-circle fallacy. In order that the sceptic's assertion may become significant, it is necessary to place some limitation upon the things of which he is asserting his ignorance, because the things of which it is possible to be ignorant form an illegitimate totality. But as soon as a suitable limitation has been placed by him upon the collection of propositions of which he is asserting his ignorance, the proposition that he is ignorant of every member of this collection must not itself be one of the collection. Hence any significant scepticism is not open to the above form of refutation" (pp. 39–40).

REFERENCES

ANGYAL, A. (1965). *Neuroses and Treatment: A Holistic Theory.* New York: Wiley.

ASHBY, W. R. (1956). *An Introduction to Cybernetics.* London: Chapman & Hall.

BANDLER, R., AND GRINDER, J. (1975). *The Structure of Magic: A Book about Language and Therapy.* Vol. 1. Palo Alto, Calif.: Science and Behavior Books.

BANDLER, R., AND GRINDER, J. (1976). *The Structure of Magic,* Vol. II, Palo Alto, Calif.: Science and Behavior Books.

BANDLER, R. AND GRINDER, J. (1979). *Frogs into Princes: Neuro Linguistic Programming.* Moah, Utah: Real People Press.

BANDURA, A. (1974). Behavior Theory and the Models of Man. *American Psychologist, 29,* 859–869.

BARTON, A. (1974). *Three Worlds of Therapy: An Existential-Phenomenological Analysis of the Therapies of Freud, Jung and Rogers.* Palo Alto, Calif.: National Press.

BATESON, G. (1936). *Naven: A Survey of the Problems Suggested by a Composite Picture of the Culture of a New Guinea Tribe Drawn from Three Points of View.* London: Cambridge University Press.

BATESON, G. (1972). *Steps to an Ecology of Mind.* New York: Ballantine.

BATESON, G. (1979). *Mind and Nature: A Necessary Unity.* New York: Dutton.

BATESON, G., JACKSON, D. D., HALEY, J., AND WEAKLAND, J. H. (1956). Toward a Theory of Schizophrenia. *Behavioral Science, 1, 4:* 251–264.

BERGER, P. L., AND LUCKMAN, T. (1966). *The Social Construction of Reality.* New York: Doubleday.

BLAU, P. M. (1964). *Exchange and Power in Social Life*. New York: Wiley.

BOULDING, K. E. (1956). *The Image*. Ann Arbor: University of Michigan Press.

CURRAN, C. A. (1952). *Counseling in Catholic Life and Education*. New York: Macmillan.

DANZIGER, K. (1976). *Interpersonal Communication*. New York: Pergamon.

ELLIS, A. (1962). *Reason and Emotion in Psychotherapy*. New York: Lyle Stuart.

EVANS, F. J. (1974). The Placebo Response in Pain Reduction. In J. J. Bonica (ed.), *Advances in Neurology*, vol. 4, *Pain*. New York: Raven Press, 289-296.

FARRELLY, F., AND BRANDSMA, J. (1974). *Provocative Therapy*. San Francisco: Shields.

FARSON, R. (1978). The Technology of Humanism. *Journal of Humanistic Psychology, 18, 2,* 5-35.

FIEDLER, F. E. (1950). A Comparison of Therapeutic Relationships in Psychoanalytic, Nondirective, and Adlerian Therapy. *Journal of Consulting Psychology, 14, 6,* 436-445.

FISH, J. M. (1973). *Placebo Therapy*. San Francisco: Jossey-Bass.

FRANK, J. D. (1972). The Bewildering World of Psychotherapy. *Journal of Social Issues,* 1972, *28,* 27-43.

FRANK, J. D. (1973). *Persuasion and Healing: A Comparative Study of Psychotherapy.* 2nd ed. Baltimore: Johns Hopkins Press.

FRANK, J. D. (1974). Psychotherapy: The Restoration of Morale. *American Journal* Rev. ed. Baltimore: Johns Hopkins Press.

FREUD, S. (1963). *Therapy and Technique*. New York: Collier Books.

FREUD, S. (1963). *Dora: An Analysis of a Case of Hysteria*. New York: Collier Books.

GILLIS, J. S. (1974). Therapist as Manipulator. *Psychology Today,* December, 90-95.

GILLIS, J. S. (1979). *Social Influence in Psychotherapy: A Description of the Process and Some Tactical Implications.* Jonesboro, Tenn.: Pilgrimage Press.

GOFFMAN, E. (1959). *The Presentation of Self in Everyday Life*. New York: Doubleday.

GOLDSTEIN, A. P., HELLER, K., AND SECHREST, L. (1968). *Psychotherapy and the Psychology of Behavior Change*. New York: Wiley.

HALEY, J. (1963). *Strategies of Psychotherapy*. New York: Grune & Stratton.

HALEY, J. (1974). *Uncommon Therapy: The Psychiatric Techniques of Milton H. Erickson, M.D.* New York: Ballantine.

HALEY, J. (1976). *Problem Solving Therapy: New Strategies of Effective Family Therapy*. New York: Harper & Row.

Harlow, H. E. (1949). The Formation of Learning Sets. *Psychological Review, 56,* 51-65.

HART, J. T., AND TOMLINSON, T. M. (eds.)(1970). *New Directions in Client Centered Therapy*. Boston: Houghton Mifflin.

HAYEK, F. A. (1952). *The Sensory Order: An Inquiry into the Foundations of Theoretical Psychology*. London: Routledge & Kegan Paul.

HAYEK, F. A. (1969). The Primacy of the Abstract. In A. Koestler and J. R. Smithies (eds.), *Beyond Reductionism: New Perspectives in the Life Sciences*. London: Hutchinson. New York: Macmillan.

HOWARD, N. (1966). The Theory of Metagames. *General Systems, II,* 167–186. (Yearbook of the Society of General Systems Research.)

HULL, C. L., HOVLAND, C. I., ROSS, R. T., HALL, M., PERKINS, D. T., AND FITCH, F. B. (1940). *Mathematico-deductive Theory of Rote Learning*. New Haven, Conn.: Yale University Press.

JACKSON, D. D. (1957). The Question of Family Homeostasis. *Psychiatric Quarterly Supplement, 31,* 79–90.

JAMES, W. (1936). *Varieties of Religious Experience*. New York: Norton.

JANET, P. (1925). *Psychological Healing: A Historical and Clinical Study*. London: Allen & Unwin.

JANOV, A. (1970). *The Primal Scream: Primal Therapy: The Cure for Neurosis*. New York: Putnam.

KELMAN, H. (1958). Compliance, Identification and Internalization. *Journal of Conflict Resolution, 2,* 57–60.

KELMAN, H. (1969). *Kairos:* The Auspicious Moment. *American Journal of Resolution, 2,* 57–60.

KELMAN, H. (1969). Kairos: The Auspicious Moment. *American Journal of Psychoanalysis, 29,* 59–83.

KOCH, S. (1964). Psychology and Emerging Conceptions of Knowledge as Unitary. In T. W. Wann (ed.), *Behaviorism and Phenomenology: Contrasting Bases for Modern Psychology*. Chicago: University of Chicago Press, 1–45.

KOCH, S. (1971). The Image of Man Implicit in Encounter Group Theory. *Journal of Humanistic Psychology, XI, 2,* 109–128.

KOESTLER, A. (1964). *The Act of Creation*. London: Hutchinson.

KOESTLER, A. (1969). Beyond Atomism and Holism: The Concept of the Holon. In A. Koestler and J. R. Smithies (eds.), *Beyond Reductionism: New Perspectives in the Life Sciences*. New York: Macmillan, 192–232.

KOESTLER, A. AND SMITHIES, J. R. (eds.)(1969). *Beyond Reductionism: New Perspectives in the Life Sciences*. New York: Macmillan.

KOFFKA, K. (1935). *Principles of Gestalt Psychology*. London: Routledge & Kegan Paul.

Kohler, W. (1926). *The Mentality of Apes*. New York: Harcourt, Brace.

KUHN, T. S. (1962). *The Structure of Scientific Revolutions*. Chicago: University of Chicago Press.

LAING, R. D., PHILLIPSON, H., AND LEE, A. R. (1966). *Interpersonal Perception*. London: Tavistock Publishers.

LEFEBVRE, V. A. (1972). A Formal Method of Investigating Reflective Processes. *General Systems, XVII,* 181–188.

LEFEBVRE, V. A. (1977). *The Structure of Awareness: Toward a Symbolic Language of Human Reflexion*. Beverly Hills, Calif.: Sage Publications.

LEWIN, K. (1936). *Principles of Topological Psychology* (trans. by F. Heider and G. Heider). New York: McGraw-Hill.

MacDougall, W. (1915). *Body and Mind: A History and a Defense of Animism.* London: Methuen.

Maruyama, M. (1963). The Second Cybernetics: Deviation-amplifying Mutual Causal Processes. *American Scientist, 51,* 164–179.

Maruyama, M. (1968). Mutual Causality in General Systems. In J. Milsum (ed.), *Positive Feedback.* Oxford, England: Pergamon.

Maruyama, M. (1977). Heterogenistics; An Epistemological Restructuring of Biological and Social Sciences. *Acta Biotheoretica, 26,* 120–137.

Maruyama, M. (1978). Prigogine's Epistemology and Its Implications for the Social Sciences. *Current Anthropology, 19,* 2, 453–455.

May, R. (1977). Gregory Bateson and Humanistic Psychology. In J. Brockman (ed), *About Bateson.* New York: Dutton, 77–99.

May, R., Angel, E. and Ellenberger, H. F. (eds.)(1959). *Existence: A New Dimension in Psychiatry and Psychology.* New York: Basic Books.

Merleau-Ponty, M. (1962). *Phenomenology of Perception.* Trans. Colin Smith. London: Routledge & Kegan Paul; New York: Humanities Press.

Miller, G. A., Galanter, E., and Pribram, K. H. (1960). *Plans and the Structure of Behavior.* New York: Holt.

Mowrer, O. H. (1948). Learning Theory and the Neurotic Paradox. *American Journal of Orthopsychiatry, 18,* 571–610.

O'Neil, W. M. (1972). The Margaret Austin Memorial Lecture: The Study of the Person. *Australian Psychologist, 7,* 2, 72–89.

Pentony, P. (1972). The Authority of the Therapist. *Thornfield Journal, 5,* 1–25.

Polanyi, M. (1962). *Personal Knowlege.* New York: Harper & Row.

Polanyi, M. (1967). *The Tacit Dimension.* London: Routledge & Kegan Paul.

Raimy, V. (1975). *Misunderstandings of the Self.* San Francisco: Jossey-Bass.

Rausch, H. L. (1965). Interaction Sequences. *Journal of Personality and Social Psychology, 2,* 487–499.

Richardson, L. F. (1960). *Arms and Insecurity: A Mathematical Study of the Causes and Origins of War* (ed. by N. Rashevsky and E. Trucco.) Pittsburgh: Boxwood Press.

Rogers, C. R. (1942). *Counseling and Psychotherapy: Newer Concepts in Practice.* Boston: Houghton Mifflin.

Rogers, C. R. (1955). Persons or Science? A Philosophical Question. *American Psychologist, 10,* 267–278.

Rogers, C. R. (1957). The Necessary and Sufficient Conditions of Therapeutic Personality Change. *Journal of Consulting Psychology, 21,* 95–103.

Rogers, C. R. (1959). A Theory of Therapy, Personality and Interpersonal Relationships as Developed in the Client-centered Framework. In S. Koch (ed.), *Psychology: A Study of a Science,* Vol. 3, *Formulations of the Person and the Social Context.* New York: McGraw-Hill.

Rogers, C. R. (1970). *Carl Rogers on Encounter Groups.* New York: Harper & Row.

Rogers, C. R. (1977). *Carl Rogers on Personal Power.* New York: Delacorte.

Schein, E. H. (1973a). Personal Change Through Interpersonal Relationships. In W. G. Bennis, D. W. Berlew, E. H. Schein, and F. I. Steele (eds.), *Interper-*

sonal Dynamics: Essays and Readings in Human Interaction, 3rd ed. Homewood, Ill.: Dorsey, 237–267.

SCHEIN, E. H. (1973b). Brainwashing. In W. G. Bennis, D. E. Berlew, E. H. Schein, and F. I. Steele (eds.), *Interpersonal Dynamics: Essays and Readings in Human Interactions,* 3rd ed. Homewood, Ill.: Dorsey, 284–300.

SCHEIN, E. H., SCHNEIER, I., AND BARKER, C. H. (1961). *Coercive Persuasion: A Sociopsychological Analysis of the "Brainwashing" of American Civilian Prisoners of the Chinese Communists.* New York: Norton.

SELIGMAN, M. E. P. (1975). *Helplessness: On Depression, Development, and Death.* San Francisco: W. H. Freeman & Co.

SPEMANN, H. (1938). *Embryonic Development and Induction.* New Haven: Yale University Press.

SPENCER, H. (1900). *First Principles.* London: Appleton.

STRONG, S. R. (1968). Counseling: An Interpersonal Process. *Journal of Counseling Psychology, 15,* 215–224.

STRONG, S. R., AND MATTROSS, R. (1973). Change Process in Counseling and Psychiatry. *Journal of Counseling Psychology, 20,* 25–37.

SZENT-GYOERGYI, A. (1974). Drive in Living Matter. *Synthesis,* Spring, 12–24.

TORREY, E. F. (1972). What Western Psychotherapists Can Learn from Witchdoctors. *American Journal of Orthopsychiatry, 42,* 69–76.

TRUAX, C. B., AND CARKHUFF, R. R. (1967). *Toward Effective Counseling and Psychotherapy: Training and Practice.* Chicago: Aldine.

WADDINGTON, C. H. (1969). The Theory of Evolution Today. In A. Koestler and J. R. Smithies (eds.), *Beyond Reductionism: New Perspectives in the Life Sciences.* London: Hutchinson. New York: Macmillan, 357–394.

WALTON, R. E. (1965). Two Strategies of Social Change and Their Dilemmas. *Journal of Applied Behavioral Science, 1, 1,* 167–179.

WATZLAWICK, P., BEAVIN, J. R., AND JACKSON, D. D. (1967). *Pragmatics of Human Communication.* New York: Norton.

WATZLAWICK, P. WEAKLAND, J. H., AND FISCH, R. (1974). *Change: Principles of Problem Formation and Problem Resolution.* New York: Norton.

WEISS, P. A. (1969). The Living System: Determinism Stratified. In A. Koestler and J. R. Smithies (eds.), *Beyond Reductionism: New Perspectives in the Life Sciences.* New York: Macmillan, 3–55.

WENDER, P. H. (1968). Vicious and Virtuous Circles: The Role of Deviation Amplifying Feedback in the Origin and Perpetuation of Behavior. *Psychiatry, 31, 4,* 309–324.

WHITEHEAD, A. N., AND RUSSELL, B. (1910). *Principia Mathematica,* vol. 1. London: Cambridge University Press.

WOLPE, J. (1958). *Psychotherapy of Reciprocal Inhibition.* Stanford, Calif.: Stanford University Press.

YATES, A. J. (1975). *Theory and Practice in Behavior Therapy.* New York: Wiley.

Human Encounter. Film produced by Western Behavioral Sciences Institute. (A film series covering twelve sessions. Event reported occurs in twelfth session.)

Name Index

Subject Index